DOUBLE VICTORY

DOUBLE VICTORY

A Multicultural History of America in World War II

RONALD TAKAKI

LITTLE, BROWN AND COMPANY
Boston   New York   London

FIRST EDITION

Library of Congress Cataloging-in-Publication Data
Takaki, Ronald T.
Double victory : a multicultural history of America
in World War II / Ronald Takaki. — 1st ed.
p.   cm.
Includes index.
ISBN 0-316-83155-7
1. World War, 1939–1945 — United States.
2. Racism — United States. 3. United
States — Race relations. I. Title.
D769.T42   2000
940.53'73 — dc21   99-40374

10 9 8 7 6 5 4 3 2 1
Q-FG

Text designed by Steve Dyer
Printed in the United States of America

CONTENTS

Contents

DOUBLE VICTORY

1

INTRODUCTION
A Different Memory

WORLD WAR II has been a part of my memory for most of my life. On that Sunday morning of December 7, 1941, my family was living only ten miles from Pearl Harbor. Fragments of my childhood recollections remain vivid — the screams of the air raid sirens interrupting the pitter-patter lullaby of the nightly rains, the dark green window shades, the gas masks in our bedroom closets, the newsreels of the war flickering in black and white on huge theater screens, the streams of soldiers in the red-light district of Hotel Street, and my father's nearby photography studio, where young soldiers had their pictures taken before being shipped off to islands like Iwo Jima and Okinawa to fight and possibly die. Finally, over the radio came the news of the end of the war. Into the streets rushed the neighborhood kids — Japanese, Chinese, Filipino, Portuguese, Korean, and Hawaiian, all of us jumping joyously, shouting, "We won the war! We won the war!" Of course, I was too young then to ask what we had fought for and what we had won.

Looking backward as we enter a new millennium, we see World War II jutting out as the most significant event of the twentieth century. In this immense warring of nations, 100 million men bore arms and over 30 million civilians died. The Nazi-engineered Holocaust was the most massive program of "ethnic cleansing" — the extermination of 6 million Jews. The war ended with the atomic bombing of Hiroshima — an event that changed the world and may yet lead to the end of the world. Today, decades later, we still find ourselves witnessing wars of extreme ethnic nationalisms and hatreds. Borrowing William Faulkner's insightful phrase, the most terrible armed conflict of all history is "a past that is not even past."[1]

Our memory of World War II continually contours the cultural landscape of our identity as Americans — who we are and what our nation stands for. But how do we remember this "past"? History is our remembering of what happened, directly through personal recollections and indirectly through scholarship. For the study of World War II, whose stories will we retell?

The history of the war has been told through the lives of our nation's military and political leaders, or through the battlefield actions and heroism of American soldiers of European ancestry, or through the experiences of a specific minority such as African Americans or Japanese Americans.

This narrative offers a different memory. While powerful policymakers like Franklin D. Roosevelt and Harry S. Truman are studied, ordinary men *and women* from America's minority communities are given special focus. History is told from the bottom up, through the lives of everyday Americans — Joseph Kurihara as he angrily stared at the barbed-wire fence of an internment camp for Japanese Americans, Fred Smith as he joined the all-black Tuskegee squadron because he wanted to "fly and fight" for freedom, Mexican-American Alex Romandia as he enlisted with his Jewish friends in order to show that they were "more American than the Anglos," Snohomish Indian Harriet Shelton Williams as she worked on the assembly lines of Boeing Aircraft in Washington, and Jewish-American soldier Murray Shapiro as he wrote home from "somewhere in Germany" to say he was "knocking on Hitler's doorstep."[2]

Indeed, these people of multicultural America are worthy of study as subjects with names, minds, wills, and voices — what Walt Whitman called the "varied carols" of America.[3] In their autobiographies, oral histories, conversations, letters, poems, and songs, they share an eye-level view of what they experienced; in their own words, they tell us what they felt and thought. They give us a democratic history of World War II — a history of the people, for the people, and also by the people.

Moreover, in their firsthand accounts, the men and women in this study offer us a more complex understanding of what has come to be remembered as "the good war," a description Studs Terkel adopted for the title of his book on the subject. "It is a phrase," he wrote in an opening note, "that has been frequently voiced by men of this and my generation, to distinguish that war from other wars, declared and undeclared." Always alert for the contradictory and the oxymoronic, Terkel explained that he had added quotation marks around the phrase, "not as a matter of caprice or editorial comment," but simply because the adjective "good" mated to the noun "war" was "so incongruous."[4]

But the "good war" also had a different "incongruity." The fervent defense of freedom was accompanied by a hypocritical disregard for our nation's declaration that "all men are created equal." The "Arsenal of Democracy" was not democratic: defense jobs were not open to all regardless of race. The war against Nazi Germany was fought with a jim crow army. During the fight against Hitler's ideology of Aryan supremacy, ethnic enmities exploded in race riots in cities like Los Angeles and Detroit. The President who led the fight for freedom also signed Executive Order 9066 for the evacuation and internment of 120,000 Japanese Americans without due process of law. Proudly displaying the Statue of Liberty, our nation of immigrants turned away Jewish refugees fleeing Nazi terror. Founded on the "self-evident" truth of the "unalienable right" of every individual to "life," the U.S. government dropped the atomic bomb on Hiroshima, killing tens of thousands of civilians, most of them women and children.

During the "good war," criticism of this "incongruity" came from intellectuals. Pearl Buck warned in *American Unity and Asia* that Japan was trumpeting the charge that there was "no basis for hope that colored people" in Asia could expect justice from "the people who rule in the United States, namely, the white people." Buck listed the injustices: "Every lynching, every race riot, gives joy to Japan. The discriminations of the American army and navy and air forces against colored soldiers and sailors, the exclusion of colored labor in our defense industries and trade unions, all our social discriminations, are of the greatest aid to our enemy in Asia, Japan."[5] Similarly, in *The Races of Mankind,* Ruth Benedict argued that Hitler's anti-Semitism required Americans to challenge their own racism in order to "stand unashamed before the Nazis and condemn, without confusion, their doctrines of a Master Race."[6]

From the grass roots came struggles to confront the "incongruity" between our professed principles and our practiced prejudices. Campaigns against segregation in the U.S. Army broadened into an attack on the color line in society. The threatened march on Washington helped open employment opportunities in the defense industries to African Americans and other minorities. Cultural boundaries were crossed in army barracks and battlefront foxholes as well as on the assembly lines and the cafeterias of defense plants. Demanding equality in "El Norte," Mexican Americans battled the negative stereotypes driving the violence of the "zoot-suit" riot. Enlisting in the army, Japanese Americans served bravely in order to protest their unconstitutional internment. Transmitting military messages in an unbreakable code of their tribal language, Navajos demonstrated the value of our society's cultural diversity. Jewish-American criticisms of the Roosevelt administration's failure to do more for victims of Nazi genocide carried a moral message: tardiness and silence in the face of such a horrendous crisis constituted complicity. Truman's announcement of the atomic bombing of Hiroshima provoked cries of moral dismay and outrage from citizens across the country.

Demanding inclusion in the democracy they were defending, the "vast, surging, hopeful" people of America's diverse communities left the tenements of the Lower East Side, the sharecropping farms of Mississippi, the ghettos of Harlem and South Side Chicago, the Chinatowns of California and New York, the barrios of the Southwest, the reservations of Arizona and New Mexico, and the sugar plantations of Hawaii.[7] Roosevelt's war for the "Four Freedoms" — freedom of speech, freedom of worship, freedom from want, and freedom from fear — became for them what black intellectual leader W. E. B. DuBois called the "War for Racial Equality."[8]

Unlike the workers of the world onboard Herman Melville's *Pequod,* these Americans of "varied" races and ethnicities were actors in history, determined to challenge their "Ahabs," their leaders and policymakers, and make decisions to chart the destiny of their lives, communities, and nation. They insisted that America live up to its ideals and founding principles. From "below deck," they went to war not only for victory over fascism abroad but also for victory over prejudice at home.[9] In their struggle, they stirred a rising wind of diversity's discontent, unfurling a hopeful vision of America as a multicultural democracy.

2

A DECLARATION OF WAR
"Double Victory"

SHATTERING THE QUIET of a Sunday morning, the planes swooped down from the clouds, dropping bombs on the ships anchored in the calm waters of Pearl Harbor. The surprise attack was devastating. Altogether 21 ships were sunk or damaged, 164 planes destroyed, 1,178 soldiers and sailors wounded and 2,388 killed. Before Congress the next day, President Franklin D. Roosevelt gravely announced: "Yesterday, December 7, 1941 — a date which will live in infamy — the United States of America was suddenly and deliberately attacked by naval and air forces of the Empire of Japan. . . . I ask that the Congress declare that since the unprovoked and dastardly attack . . . a state of war has existed."[1] Congress immediately declared war on Japan. Three days later, Japan's allies, Germany and Italy, declared war on the United States.

Breaking News: "Everybody Was Glued to the Radio"

The sudden news announcement of the attack shocked people across America.

"One morning — I think it was a Sunday — while I was working at Palama Shoe Factory I heard, '*Pon! pon! Pon! pon!*' " recalled Seichin Nagayama. He was only a few miles from the navy base. "I was drinking coffee and I thought, 'Strange. Are they having military practice?' At the corner of Liliha and Kuakini Streets, a bomb fell in the back of a cement plant. We felt like going to see what happened, the noise was so loud. We found out that the war had started."[2]

"On December 7, 1941," said John Garcia, "oh, around 8:00 a.m., my grandmother woke me. She informed me that the Japanese were bombing Pearl Harbor. I said, 'They're just practicing.' She said, 'no, it was real and the announcer is requesting that all Pearl Harbor workers report to work.' I went out on the porch and I could see the anti-aircraft fire up in the sky. I just said, 'Oh boy.' " A pipe fitter apprentice at Pearl Harbor at the time, Garcia rushed to work. His ship, the U.S.S. *Shaw,* was on a floating dry dock. "It was in flames. I started to go down into the pipe fitter's shop to get my toolbox when another wave of Japanese planes came in. I got under a set of concrete steps at the dry dock where the battleship *Pennsylvania* was. An officer came by and asked me to go into the *Pennsylvania* and try to get the fires out. A bomb had penetrated the marine deck, and that was three decks below." Garcia knew that under that deck were ammunition and powder. "There ain't no way I'm gonna go down there. It could blow up any minute. I was young and sixteen, not stupid, not at sixty-two cents an hour." Then another officer asked Garcia to jump into the water in order to save sailors. "Some were unconscious, some were dead. So I spent the rest of the day swimming inside the harbor, along with some other Hawaiians. I brought out I don't know how many bodies and how many were alive and how many dead."[3]

On Oahu, ten-year-old Stephanie Carlson wrote a poem shortly after the attack:

Dec. 7 started like any other quiet Sunday in Hawaii.
Then things began to happen.

We heard the rumble of guns firing.
There were black airplanes in the sky.
We thought it was a drill.
The telephone rang.
My father answered it.
He was called to his destroyer because the
Japanese were attacking Pearl Harbor.
We could stand on the porch and see some of the fighting.
It looked like a Fourth of July celebration.
We saw three Japanese planes fly right over our house.
They dropped two bombs which just whistled down.
It looked like it was going to fall on you.[4]

Meanwhile, across the country, other children felt the reverberations of the bombs falling on Pearl Harbor. Nine-year-old Patty Neal was sitting with her family around the radio when the news broke. She was "chattering away," and her mother asked her to be quiet. "I kept on talking," she recalled, "and my mother, who NEVER spanked me, slapped me, and said, 'Patty, you will remember this day.' "[5]

In a small Japanese farming community in California, Mary Tsukamoto was in church. "I do remember Pearl Harbor," she said decades later, "as if it had happened this morning. It was a December Sunday, so we were getting ready for our Christmas program. We were rehearsing and having Sunday school class, and I always played the piano for the adult Issei [immigrant Japanese] service. . . . After the service started, my husband ran in. He had been home that day and heard [the announcement] on the radio. We just couldn't believe it, but he told us that Japan attacked Pearl Harbor. I remember how stunned we were. And suddenly the whole world turned dark."[6]

In San Francisco, Remo Bosia was the first one to arrive at his office at *L'Italia,* the local Italian newspaper. "The teletype was clicking away as usual, then it tolled, 'Cling!' which means a bulletin is coming in. I picked up the tape and read: 'This is the White

House, Pearl Harbor has been attacked.' I was shocked. Immediately I wrote an editorial to this effect: 'Now is the time for all Italian Americans to show their patriotism.'"[7]

In Los Angeles, while sitting in a bar, migrant farm laborer Carlos Bulosan heard the blaring newsbreak on the radio: "Japan bombs Pearl Harbor!" He rushed outside trembling and saw his brother. "It has come, Carlos!" Macario shouted. Memories of loved ones in his homeland swirled. "We had been but little boys when we left the Philippines," he thought. "And my mother! What would happen to her and my two sisters?"[8]

As Bulosan walked aimlessly down the streets of Los Angeles, a young black policeman rushed to work. "Immediately after Pearl Harbor," recalled Tom Bradley, "there was bedlam. Sirens going off, aircraft guns firing. It was panic. Here we are in the middle of the night, there was no enemy in sight, but somebody thought they saw the enemy. They were shooting at random. All policemen were ordered to their respective stations, to be ready for whatever. We were all herded into the station, awaiting orders. None came, because there was nothing. It was panic that simply overwhelmed us."[9]

That same morning in Los Angeles, several Koreans were rehearsing for a play to be presented at a program sponsored by the Society for Aid to the Korean Volunteer Corps in China. During the rehearsal, they were interrupted by the electrifying radio announcement: "The Japanese have attacked Pearl Harbor." Spontaneously, everyone on the stage exploded: "Taehan Toknip Manse!" "Long Live Korean Independence!" "No Korean, old and young alike, could control his emotions of joy," Bong-Youn Choy recalled. "Some old Korean immigrants had tears in their eyes and kept silent. Every Korean felt that the long dream for national independence would soon become a reality."[10]

Also in Los Angeles that Sunday, Socorro Díaz was at the movies when the lights were suddenly turned on. "The manager came out and announced that the Japanese had bombed Pearl Harbor, and if there were any servicemen in the audience they were to report back to their base. We didn't know where Pearl Harbor was. Somebody said it was in Hawaii, and I thought, that's far away, never realizing how much it was going to change our lives."[11]

Shortly after Raul Morin heard the breaking radio news report, he rushed to find his friends on Olvera Street in Los Angeles. As they talked about the crisis, the young men nervously tried to re-assure themselves by engaging in *vacilada,* or humor. "Ya estuvo (This is it)," one of them said. "Now we can look for the authori-ties to round up all the Mexicans and deport them to Mexico — bad security risks." Another answered: "They don't have to deport me! I'm going on my own; you're not going to catch me fighting a war for somebody else. I belong to Mexico. Soy puro mexi-cano!"[12]

Meanwhile, at a boarding school on the Navajo reservation of Ganado, Arizona, Keith Little was hunting. "We had a rabbit cooking down in the wash, and somebody went to the dorm, came back and said, 'Hey, Pearl Harbor was bombed!' One of us asked, 'Where's Pearl Harbor?' 'In Hawaii.' 'Who did it?' 'Japan.' 'Why'd they do it?' 'They hate Americans. They want to kill all Ameri-cans.' 'Us, too?' 'Yeah, us too.' Then and there, we all made a promise. We were, most of us, 15 or 16 years old, I guess. We promised each other we'd go after the Japanese instead of hunting rabbits."[13]

In Boston, Elsie Oliver was eating breakfast. "I was serving breakfast because I had guests from Camp Edwards, Massachu-setts," she recalled, "and several girls were there to meet these fel-las and we were all having breakfast together. They came up that morning, and while they were there it came over the radio of Pearl Harbor. And right away the notice came from Camp Edwards that everybody there had to report back to base for military orders."[14] Oliver would enlist and serve in an all-black battalion.

December 7 was the birthday of Timuel Black, an African Amer-ican in Michigan. "I was twenty-one in 1941 and we were cele-brating. My good friend, George, was very patriotic. He says,

'Let's have a drink: Here's to Christmas in Berlin and Easter in Tokyo.' He joined up right away."[15]

In Lawrenceville, Virginia, Rubye Seago wrote a letter to Richard Long, dated Sunday night, December 7, 1941. They had met and fallen in love three months earlier, and he was now in basic training at Camp Wheeler, Georgia.

> My Darling:
> I know you feel exactly like I do right now, I've just been listening to the radio. I've never been so blue or heartsick as I am right this minute. Oh, my darling — if it were possible I'd charter a plane — do anything — just to see you for a few minutes. . . .
> Honestly, Dick, if I don't get to see you I'm going to lose my mind. Isn't there *any* thing you can do? Cause if you don't do it now do you realize we may *never* see each other again? Of course you do — you realize how serious the situation is, even more than I. Darling, they *can't* take you . . . away — it just tears my heart out to think of it.
> Everyone in town is talking war, war, war! Everyone is sure it will be declared tomorrow. . . . I love you, Dick, more than anybody in the world. You know it already, but I want to tell you again. And I'll always love you to the end of my life.[16]

In Harlem, Myrtle Rhoden was watching a movie at Lowes Theater on 125th Street. "In the middle of the movie the lights came on and the screen went blank. And they announced, 'All military personnel report to your nearest base.' Oh, it was very dramatic. And the theater was loaded with fellas in military uniform, Marines, Navy, Army. So all these guys got up and, I mean in an instant, they kissed their dates or whoever they were with, and they were taking the stairs two at a time. Just flying!"[17]

In San Francisco Chinatown, Lonnie Quan was with her boyfriend when she heard the news. "I remember December 7th so clearly," she said forty years later. "I was living at Gum Moon Residence Club on Washington Street. It was Sunday. I didn't have a radio in the room." When her boyfriend arrived, he exclaimed: "This is it. Pearl Harbor was attacked!" The news was overwhelming: "I just couldn't believe it — it was a shock. I remember going to work in a restaurant, Cathay House, and everybody was just kinda glued to the radio."[18]

A Day of "Infamy": The Hidden History of Pearl Harbor

From Hawaii to Maine, Americans found themselves riveted to the radio that Sunday. But why was the Japanese attack on Pearl Harbor such a surprise?

Suddenly, the American people had been swept into a war they had been hoping to avoid. They still remembered their failed crusade to make the world safe for democracy during World War I. For years, Roosevelt had been struggling against the isolationist tide in order to prepare the United States for what he considered an unavoidable war against Nazi Germany. Only six months before the attack, public opinion polls showed that 79 percent of Americans expressed a desire to stay out of the war. On December 7, this strong isolationist feeling instantly disappeared. Later Roosevelt admitted to Winston Churchill that if it had not been for Pearl Harbor, he would have had "great difficulty in getting the American people into the war."[19] The President told his aide Harry Hopkins that the issue had been taken "entirely out of his hands, because the Japanese had made the decision for him." Hopkins recalled Roosevelt's great relief: "In spite of the disaster at Pearl Harbor . . . it completely solidified the American people and made the war upon Japan inevitable."[20]

However, the "disaster" was actually made "inevitable" by geopolitical interests and strategies as well as high-level decisions made not only in Tokyo but also in Washington and London.

During the 1930s, Japan's expansion toward Southeast Asia was threatening British, French, and Dutch colonial interests as well as American supplies of vital resources such as rubber, tin, bauxite, and tungsten from Thailand, Malaysia, and the East Indies. In a June 14, 1940, memorandum, the State Department's chief Far East expert Stanley Hornbeck warned: "The United States finds itself so vitally and overwhelmingly dependent on southeastern Asia that our entire foreign policy must be adjusted to that fact. . . . It is not an exaggeration to say that the United States would be compelled, for its existence as a major industrial state, to wage war against any power or powers that might threaten to sever our trade lines with this part of the world."[21]

During his confirmation hearing for appointment as secretary of the navy, Frank Knox warned in 1940: "We should not allow Japan to take the Dutch East Indies, a vital source of oil and rubber and tin. . . . We must face frankly the fact that to deny the Dutch East Indies to Japan may mean war." In a meeting with congressional leaders on the day of the attack on Pearl Harbor, Roosevelt explained the importance of this region: "We are getting a very large proportion of our supplies — rubber, tin, etc. — from that whole area of southwestern Pacific, and we are getting out over the Burma Road . . . a very large amount of very important material, such as tungsten. . . ."[22]

While Roosevelt was aware of the country's need for critical resources from Southeast Asia, he wanted to avoid war with Japan. In his November 12, 1940, report, chief of naval operations Admiral Harold Stark stated that the U.S. did not have the ships necessary to fight a two-ocean war. Thus the American strategy should be to avoid war with Japan in order to concentrate American naval resources in the Atlantic.[23]

In his negotiations with Japan, Roosevelt realized that he would have to pursue a strategy that required great finesse. On the one hand, he allowed continued trade with Japan. Referring to the oil fields in the southwest Pacific, Roosevelt told Assistant Secretary of State Sumner Welles that we were "not to shut off oil" to Japan and "thereby force her into a military expedition against the Dutch East Indies."[24]

On the other hand, Roosevelt threatened an American embargo in order to demand that Japan withdraw its troops from China as well as curtail its expansion toward French Indochina and the Dutch East Indies. Lacking its own fossil fuel resources, Japan had been importing 80 percent of its oil and 90 percent of its gasoline from the United States. Without access to this source of petroleum, Japan had only a two-year supply in stockpile.[25] On July 24, 1941, the U.S. announced it would restrict trade with Japan, and on August 1, the government revoked all licenses for oil export to Japan. However, the policy had a loophole: it permitted applications for licenses which did not include oils for aircraft. But the administration failed to state this policy clearly. This mistake, noted historian Robert Dallek, allowed federal agencies to reject all applications and establish "a de facto embargo on oil to Japan." On August 3, Roosevelt left for a meeting with Churchill on a ship in the Atlantic; the President would not realize that a full embargo was underway until early September.[26]

On September 6, the Japanese government decided to make war against the United States, Britain, and the Netherlands. According to historian Christopher Thorne, the leaders saw that they had only two "stark and simple" alternatives: "to accept growing United States dictation, backed by her control of raw materials, or to fight."[27]

Years later, in his assessment of the tense pre–Pearl Harbor negotiations, former diplomat George F. Kennan observed: "Had FDR been determined to avoid war with the Japanese if at all possible, he would have conducted American policy quite differently, particularly in the final period, than he actually did. He would not, for example, have made an issue over Japanese policy in China, where the Japanese were preparing, anyway, to undertake a partial withdrawal . . . and where this sort of American pressure was not really essential. He would not have tried to starve the Japanese navy of oil. And he would have settled down to some hard and realistic dealings with the Japanese."[28]

But Roosevelt was not the only principal policymaker making

decisions before the Japanese attack on Pearl Harbor. So was Prime Minister Winston Churchill. As early as 1936, we now know from declassified British military documents, the Royal Navy's Far East Combined Bureau in Singapore had broken the Japanese Navy Code 25, or JN-25, and had been intercepting and deciphering top-secret military messages sent from Tokyo to the Japanese navy. American military intelligence had broken only the Japanese code for diplomatic messages sent from Tokyo to Washington, and did not have the capacity to decipher JN-25 messages.

Facing the terrifying threat of Nazi Germany, wrote historians James Rusbridger and Eric Nave, the prime minister "had but one aim, and that was to bring America into the war against Germany at any price. Churchill made no secret of this to his close advisers, for he knew that without America's direct involvement Britain could not defeat the Nazis."[29]

On November 25, 1941, British intelligence in Singapore intercepted a message sent from Tokyo to a Japanese naval task force: "The Task Force will move out of Hitokappu Wan [Tankan Bay] on the morning of 26 November and advance to the stand-by position on the afternoon of 4 December and speedily complete refueling." The intelligence specialists of the Royal Navy calculated the possible targets of this task force: Pearl Harbor, which was 3,150 miles away from Tankan Bay, and Singapore, 3,394 miles. Singapore was considered a doubtful target. If the task force sailed south, it would easily be spotted by British and American air patrols and also by British merchant ships in the area. Also the refueling of the Japanese ships at sea would have been unnecessary for a surprise attack on the Malay peninsula. Their destination had to be Pearl Harbor.[30]

Churchill was in complete control of all intercepted and deciphered JN-25 messages. He did not, however, forward any of these decoded Japanese military messages to Roosevelt.[31]

At 9 P.M. on December 7 in London, Prime Minister Churchill asked his butler to bring in a small portable radio. Listening to a BBC broadcast, he heard: "Here is the news and this is Alvar Lidell reading it. President Roosevelt has just announced Japanese air attacks on American bases in the Hawaiian Islands."[32] Within minutes, Churchill placed a telephone call to the White House. "It is quite true," Roosevelt said. "They have attacked us at Pearl Harbor. We are all in the same boat now."[33]

Churchill welcomed the news of the attack on Pearl Harbor. "No American will think it wrong of me," he later wrote, "if I proclaim that to have the United States on our side was to be the greatest joy. . . . England would live. . . . How long the war would last or in what fashion it would end no man could tell, nor did I at this moment care. Once again in our long island history we would emerge . . . safe and victorious. We should not be wiped out. . . . Being saturated and satiated with emotion and sensation, I went to bed and slept the sleep of the saved and thankful."[34]

In Washington, Roosevelt had been negotiating with Japan over trade restrictions and his demands for Japanese military withdrawals from China and Southeast Asia. On November 22, U.S. intelligence intercepted a dispatch from Tokyo informing its representatives in Washington that the deadline for the successful completion of the negotiations would be the 29th, but not beyond that date. "After that," the message stated, "things are automatically going to happen." On November 24, Roosevelt told Churchill that whether Japan backed down was "really a matter of internal Japanese politics. I am not very hopeful and we must all be prepared for real trouble, possibly soon." In a meeting with his advisers the next day, the President discussed the likelihood of a surprise attack. "The question," said Roosevelt, "was how we should maneuver them into the position of firing the first shot without allowing too much danger to ourselves." The policymakers were also concerned about how they would justify a declaration of war to Congress and the American people if Japan attacked only British and Dutch colonies.[35] The meeting ended with the question: when and where would the war begin? The answer came on December 7, at Pearl Harbor.

As it turned out, the Japanese attack was a "surprise," one

planned by the military in Tokyo, but allowed to happen by Churchill in London. Stirring a passion for revenge and the cry "Remember Pearl Harbor," the sudden devastation of the Pacific fleet and the immense loss of life set in motion a racialized rage that would lead to the mass internment of Japanese Americans and later the atomic bombing of Hiroshima.

Refusing to Live "Half American"

Early that Sunday morning, Dorie Miller looked up and saw Japanese planes diving from the sky above Pearl Harbor. While his ship, the U.S.S. *West Virginia,* was being hit, Miller helped carry his wounded captain from the bridge. Then he rushed to an unmanned battle station and fired a gun at the enemy planes.[36] "When the Japanese bombers attacked my ship at Pearl Harbor," Miller said during a visit to San Francisco in December 1942, "I forgot all about the fact that I and other Negroes can be only messmen in the Navy and are not taught how to man an anti-aircraft gun. Several of the men had lost their lives — including some of the high officers — when the order came for volunteers from below to come on the upper deck and help fight the Japanese. Without knowing how I did it, it must have been God's strength and mother's blessing, I ran up . . . and I started to fire the big guns. I actually downed four Japanese bombers."[37]

Describing Miller's heroism, the *New York Times* reported that the "Negro mess attendant" had never before fired a gun.[38] Like other African Americans serving in the navy, he had been assigned to menial duties. A radical newspaper, the *Militant,* pointed out the irony embedded in Miller's story: "The Negro people for a long time have wondered what kind of war for democracy it is that must be fought by a Jim Crow navy. They have asked what is the difference between Hitler's treatment of the Jews in Germany and the treatment they receive here in a war that has been officially dedicated to the high principles of the 'four freedoms.' "[39]

Meanwhile, on the home front, a different kind of heroism

gained attention in the news media. Deciding to confront the contradiction of a jim crow army defending democracy, a cafeteria worker at the Kansas Cessna aircraft plant in Wichita sent a letter to the *Pittsburgh Courier,* published on January 31, 1942. Wrote James G. Thompson:

> Being an American of dark complexion and some 26 years, these questions flash through my mind: "Should I sacrifice my life to live half American? Will things be better for the next generation in the peace to follow? Would it be demanding too much to demand full citizenship rights in exchange for the sacrificing of my life? Is the kind of America I know worth defending? Will America be a true and pure democracy after the war? Will Colored Americans suffer still the indignities that have been heaped upon them in the past?" These and other questions need answering; I want to know, and I believe every colored American, who is thinking, wants to know. . . .
>
> The V for victory sign is being displayed prominently in all so-called democratic countries which are fighting for victory over aggression, slavery, and tyranny. If this V sign means that to those now engaged in this great conflict, then let we colored Americans adopt the double VV for a double victory. The first V for victory over our enemies from without, the second V for victory over our enemies from within. For surely those who perpetrate these ugly prejudices here are seeking to destroy our democratic form of government just as surely as the Axis forces.[40]

Two months after his letter was published, Thompson enlisted in the army.[41] Willing to die for his country, he was determined to make life better for the "next generation" by transforming America into a "true democracy." Refusing to live "half American," Thompson had issued a declaration of war for "double victory."

This powerful phrase gave voice to a democratic dream that would be widely shared across the country. The war for the "Four Freedoms" would offer opportunities for marginalized minorities to demand their rights and dignity as full Americans. Swept into the war by circumstances and policy decisions beyond their control, the people of America's protean diversity would fight on the front lines and labor on the assembly lines to defend the world's unfinished, but best hope for, democracy.

3

"BOMB THE COLOR LINE"
The War Against Jim Crow

FOR HIS DISTINGUISHED devotion to duty and great courage during the Japanese attack on Pearl Harbor, Dorie Miller was awarded the Navy Cross. The War Department sent the hero on a national tour to promote enlistments. Miller returned to the Pacific battlefront, and in December 1943 was listed as missing in action. An African-American song of World War II honored this sharecroppers' son who had given his life for his country:

> In nineteen hundred and forty-one
> Colored mess boy manned the gun
> Although he had never been trained
> Had the nerves ever seen
> God willing and mother wit
> Gon' be great Dorie Miller yet
> Grabbed a gun and took dead aim
> Japanese bombers into fiery flame
> He was aiming the Japs to fight
> Fought at the poles to make things right
> Fight on Dorie Miller I know you tried

Did your best for the side . . .
I love Dorie Miller cause he's my race.[1]

"One of the Strangest Paradoxes":
A Segregated Army Fights for Democracy

Four years before Miller's act of bravery at Pearl Harbor, Charles H. Houston of the NAACP had demanded that Franklin D. Roosevelt issue an executive order banning all racial discrimination in the armed forces.[2] But in 1940, Roosevelt signed into law the Selective Service Act, which included a provision that prohibited the intermingling of "colored and white" army personnel in the same regiments.[3] "Such a mingling [of whites and blacks] was not a part of the President's policy," stated White House aide General Edwin M. Watson, "and for practical reasons it would be impossible to put into operation. It would seem that Negroes might be inspired to take pride in the efficiency of Negro units in the Army, as representing their contribution to the armed forces."[4]

Roosevelt's refusal to integrate the armed forces provoked disbelief and anger across black America. In a telegram to the White House, A. Philip Randolph of the Brotherhood of Sleeping Car Porters declared: "We are inexpressibly shocked that a President of the United States at a time of national peril should surrender so completely to enemies of democracy who would destroy national unity by advocating segregation. Official approval by the Commander-in-Chief of the Army and Navy of such discrimination and segregation is a stab in the back of democracy."[5] The NAACP denounced the army's segregationist policy: "Declarations of war do not lessen the obligation to preserve and extend civil liberties here while the fight is being made to restore freedom from dictatorship abroad. . . . A Jim Crow army cannot fight for a free world."[6] On October 9, 1940, the *Crisis* carried the headline: "WHITE HOUSE BLESSES JIM CROW."[7]

Blacks highlighted the hypocrisy. "Democracy must wage a twofold battle — a battle on far flung foreign fields against Hitler, and a battle on the home front against Hitlerism," insisted Adam Clayton Powell, Jr., a New York City councilman. "How can white Americans expect to have a tolerant world after this war when there is racial prejudice within the ranks of those who are fighting?"[8] Black columnist George Schuyler castigated the jim crow army: "Our war is not against Hitler in Europe, but against Hitler in America. Our war is not to defend democracy, but to get a democracy we have never had."[9] In his protest against segregation in the U.S. Armed Forces, the editor of the *Chicago Defender* declared: "We are not exaggerating when we say that the American Negro is damned tired of spilling his blood for empty promises of better days. Why die for democracy for some foreign country when we don't even have it here?" In order to unite the country and win the conflict, the *Defender*'s editor demanded that America "bomb the color line."[10]

"Prove to us," blacks challenged whites, "that you are not hypocrites when you say this is a war for freedom." For African Americans, the war for freedom had to be fought in their country's own backyard. "The Army jim-crows us," complained a student. "The Navy lets us serve only as messmen. . . . Employers and labor unions shut us out. Lynchings continue. We are disfranchised . . . spat upon. What more can Hitler do than that."[11] In a letter to the NAACP, a soldier wrote: "I am a Negro soldier 22 years old. I won't fight or die in vain. If I fight, suffer or die it will be for the freedom of every black man to live equally with other races. If the life of the Negro in the United States is right as it is lived today, then I would rather be dead."[12] Scheduled to be drafted into the army, a youth declared: "Just carve on my tombstone, 'Here lies a black man killed fighting a yellow man for the protection of a white man.'"[13] In a poem published in an African-American newspaper, another young man asked:

Dear Lord, today
I go to war:

> To fight, to die,
> Tell me what for?
>
> Dear Lord, I'll fight,
> I do not fear,
> Germans or Japs;
> My fears are here.
> America![14]

The army's color line symbolized white domination in America. "Whitey owns everything," grumbled Malcolm Little, who would later rename himself Malcolm X. "He wants us to go and bleed for him? Let him fight." In 1943, Little received his induction notice. When he reported for his physical examination, he was "costumed like an actor," wearing a "wild zoot suit" and "yellow knob-toe shoes" and his hair frizzled into "a reddish bush of conk." He greeted the soldier at the desk: " 'Crazy-o, daddy-o, get me moving. I can't wait to get in that brown.' " The nurse noticed Little's strange behavior and ushered him into the office of the psychiatrist. "Suddenly, I sprang up and peeped under both doors," recalled Little, "the one I'd entered and another that was probably the closet." Then Little bent over and whispered in the psychiatrist's ear: " 'Daddy-o, now you and me, we're from up North here, so don't you tell nobody. I want to get sent down South. Organize them nigger soldiers, you dig? Steal us some guns, and kill up crackers!' " Shortly afterward, Little received a 4-F card.[15]

Unlike Little, Winfred W. Lynn of Jamaica, New York, chose to confront rather than evade the discriminatory draft law. In June 1942, after receiving his draft notice, Lynn informed his draft board that he was ready to serve in any unit of the armed forces which was not segregated by race. "Unless I am assured that I can serve in a mixed regiment and that I will not be compelled to serve in a unit undemocratically selected as a Negro group," Lynn wrote, "I will refuse to report for induction." He claimed that his induction into a segregated unit violated Section 4 of the draft act, which stated that in the selection and training of men there should be no discrimination against any person based on race.

Lynn was arrested and indicted for draft evasion. Determined to overturn the draft law, he pursued a course of complicated appeals in the courts. In its decision against Lynn, the U.S. Circuit Court of Appeals declared that the U.S. Army could segregate the races so long as blacks were accorded privileges "substantially equal" to those of whites. Lynn appealed to the highest court, and in 1944, the U.S. Supreme Court refused to hear his case. "If Congress had intended to prohibit separate white and Negro quotas and calls," the justices declared, "we believe it would have expressed such intention more definitely than by the general prohibition against discrimination appearing in Section 4."[16]

Protesting the army's jim crow policy, a soldier wrote a letter to the editor of the *Pittsburgh Courier*. He pointed out that the nation was experiencing the greatest emergency in history. "If there ever were a time that all racial prejudices and hatred should be put aside, now it is at hand, and the country should be unified in every possible respect. . . . Both White and Colored are being called up and everybody is doing his or her bit to cooperate. Negroes like the Whites are quitting their jobs to increase the military strength of this Nation, because we all think that a nation worth living in is worth fighting for." But in this struggle, "the age-old Monster of Prejudice" had raised his head high in the Army.[17]

Saturating the black press with testimonies, African-American soldiers documented the pervasiveness of this "Monster" in the U.S. Army. Recreation facilities were separate and unequal. "This camp we are at now is the worse camp we have ever been to," wrote a soldier to the *Pittsburgh Courier*. "It is Camp Berkeley, Texas near the town of Abilene. . . . There is a swimming pool here in the colored area and the colored use it on Mon. and Fri. only. They have a show where the colored go and you sit on the outside to see the picture. If it rains there isn't any picture. . . . We don't have a PX like the whites. You can get only 1 bottle of beer, 1 box of ice cream. You can't use the white PX."[18]

Camp conditions for black soldiers were degrading. In a letter to the *Baltimore Afro-American,* "A Negro Soldier" described what was happening at Camp Gordon Johnston, Florida. "The first two weeks we laid around doing nothing. . . . The third week they started us cleaning the white officers rooms, making us [make their] dirty beds and cleaning their latrine and are still doing that right at the present. We cannot go to church services on the camp. The service clubs are off limit for us because a Staff Sgt. went over with some more of our comrades to get a couple of sandwiches and were told by a civilian worker we don't serve colored, and Sir this is an Army Post. . . . Sir we sleep on sand floors with no boards or anything to bed. . . . Sir, we do not have running latrines. They have a group of colored troops who go around every morning and [pick up] the used buckets and put clean ones in. Sir, that is the way your boys who are somebody's sons are treated here in this Army, and which we are supposed to fighting for Democracy."[19]

Training programs were also segregated. In a letter to the *Pittsburgh Courier,* a soldier reported that four blacks had been sent to a tire maintenance school in Akron, Ohio, where they were told by Lieutenant Joseph J. Poggione that it was "not advisable to have both Colored and White troops attending the same classes." Euliss M. Looney, Joseph Nibitt, Walter B. Lewis, and Sammie K. Banks were forced to return to their posts in Michigan and California. "Is there nothing that can be done to right these wrongs," the writer concluded, "or to prevent such things from happening again?"[20]

The "wrongs" also included servile work assignments. Writing to the *Richmond Afro-American,* blacks in the 328th Aviation Squadron based in Pampa, Texas, protested: "We are a group of permanent K.P.'s [kitchen police]. We are allowed no other advancement whatsoever. It is true that K.P. pushers (head K.P.) are made Cpl. and Sgt. but the K.P.'s themselves are a miserable group that will be worked like slaves. We are confined to this job not because we are not fit for anything else but because we are dark. We are referred to on this post as 'that nigger squadron at the end of the field.'"[21]

Skilled blacks found themselves occupationally downgraded. "A lone soldier" wrote to the *Pittsburgh Courier:* "We are members of the 78 Aviation Sqdr, and it seems like we are not being treated fair. Most of us got trades of our own to help win this war. But instead we are servants and ditch diggers and we want better, if it ever been slavery it is now, please help us because we want better. They got us here washing dishes, working around the officers houses and waiting on them, instead of trying to win this war they got us in ditches. . . . And the sad part about it is that most of us are volunteers, but they didn't give us what we ask for, they gave us a pick."[22]

As soldiers with skills, many African Americans wanted to contribute their expertise to the war effort. Writing to the *Pittsburgh Courier,* Private Laurence W. Harris expressed his frustration: "In my civilian life I was a small tool maker. I worked for Silling and Spences Co in Hartford, Conn. Then I was doing much for the war effort, and was in hopes I could continue in the service. In the past ten months I feel as though I have been a complete failure to myself, and to the helping to win this war." In a letter to the Afro-American Newspapers, Samuel A. Connor described how black radio technicians were forced to become construction laborers. When the 2nd Cavalry Division had been placed on alert for probable shipment overseas, Connor's unit was not included in the order. "*We later learned that we were to be used as dock stevedores, unloading ships.* . . . We had visions of being the Cadre for an operations battalion because our troop is one-third radio operations and radio technicians." Instead they received an order to form a construction battalion. "In this type of battalion there isn't anyplace for radiomen," Conner complained. "To be frank, we must toss away the months, in some cases, years of training that we have had since our entrance into the army."[23]

More stressful than experiencing discrimination on army bases was facing the terrible threat of hate violence, especially in small Southern towns. While training at Tuskegee, Alabama, pilot Fred Smith of Chicago was warned by officers: "Don't go off the base or you won't come back. You'll be lynched."[24] On April 3, 1941, at Fort Benning, Georgia, the body of Private Felix Hall was found hanging from a tree, his hands bound behind his back. Denouncing the Hall murder, the *Crisis* declared: "America is marching to war for the purpose of stopping brutalities overseas, but apparently our government does not choose to stop lynching within its own borders, or even within the borders of its army camps."[25] In response to pressures from the NAACP and black newspapers, the War Department agreed to conduct an investigation of Hall's death. "There has been no report of the results of the 'Investigation,'" the *Pittsburgh Courier* complained on January 3, 1942.[26]

Later that year, Paul Parks of Indianapolis was on maneuvers in rural Louisiana as a member of the 183 Battalion of Combat Engineers. "Two of us were told by officers to go into a little town and pick up supplies," he recalled. "I got out of the truck and went into the store, and I was ordering. I started out, and the storekeeper said, 'Don't go back there!' I crowded under the porch, and I saw my comrade being dragged up and down the street until he died." Parks hid under the porch until dark and then returned to camp. There was "a big upheaval" over the killing, he said, and the military moved "us black troops out of the area immediately."[27]

In a February 13, 1943, memorandum to her supervisor, Lucien Warner of the War Information Office gave a list of incidents that had occurred in Texas:

> In Beaumont, a Negro soldier was shot last summer following an altercation on a bus.

> At Corpus Christy [*sic*] a stabbing occurred in an altercation on a bus. . . .

A Negro Sargeant [*sic*], Walter B. Springs, was killed in a Bastrop cafe by a white Military Policeman after a dispute. . . .[28]

In 1944, a black soldier was killed by a bus driver in Alexandria, Louisiana; the War Department asked the Justice Department to charge the driver with murder: "Considering the testimony of all the witnesses, and the circumstances surrounding the case, the conclusion is inescapable that there was no justification, moral or legal, for the slaying of Private Edward Green by Odell Lachnette." But the Justice Department took no action.[29]

In a "Statement to the Nation" issued in June 1943, the NAACP declared: "The continued ill treatment of Negroes in uniform, both on military reservations and in many civilian communities is disgraceful. Negroes in the uniform of the nation have been beaten, mobbed, killed and lynched." The proclamation of the "Four Freedoms," the NAACP stated, would be regarded as hypocritical by colored people around the world until President Roosevelt acted to end discrimination in the Army.[30]

In a letter addressed "Dear President Roosevelt," May 9, 1944, Private Charles F. Wilson pointed out that America's fight against fascism was "marred by one of the strangest paradoxes": fighting for "World Democracy," the U.S. Army was itself undemocratic. "Totally inadequate opportunities," wrote Wilson, were being given to "the Negro members of our Armed Forces, nearly one-tenth of the whole, to participate with 'equality,' 'regardless of race and color' in the fight for our war aims." Wilson related the contradiction to the war in Asia. "Are the Chinese to believe that we are fighting to bring them 'freedom, equality, and justice,' when they can see that in our Armed Forces we are not even practicing what we are preaching?"

In his conclusion, Private Wilson offered a concrete recommendation: Roosevelt should follow Executive Order 8802 prohibiting discrimination in the defense industries with another executive order that would outlaw discrimination in the Army. "Then and only then," Wilson wrote, would the U.S. military live up to the principles of freedom, equality, and justice for all, regardless of race.[31]

Such an executive order was never issued by Roosevelt. Thus, in the war for the "Four Freedoms," one million African Americans in the armed forces were forced to fight in a jim crow army. Equality, for them, was a "dream deferred"; but they refused to let it "dry up like a raisin in the sun" or to explode.[32] Instead, abiding while protesting, they served, hopeful their loyalty and sacrifice would make America live up to what the Declaration of Independence had proclaimed a "self-evident" truth. Enlisting in a segregated army and accepting a situation that did not represent "an ideal of democracy," explained Major Harriet M. Waddy of the Wacs, was not "a retreat from our fight" but "our contribution to its realization."[33]

Assigned to service and support duties, African Americans composed half of the Transportation Corps in Europe. They, too, landed at Omaha Beach for the D-Day invasion. Although they would not be included as heroes in Hollywood movies, black soldiers made a difference in this crucial military campaign. On the beaches of Normandy, they unloaded supplies from ships and transported them to the fighting troops. In the D-Day invasion, recalled Timuel Black, "we were really stevedores. . . . I went into Normandy with combat troops. We serviced them." Support work was especially dangerous. "The Germans aimed at our supplies," explained Black. "We were direct targets. I'd been on six-by-six trucks many nights when the Luftwaffe was strafing us, dropping those small bombs and firing those machine guns at us."

The Transportation Corps' biggest task was feeding an enormous army in movement. "We were in Belgium during the Battle of the Bulge," Black boasted. "We were at one time feeding three million soldiers: the First, the Third, the Ninth, and the British Seventh [Armies]." Without their vital support, the Allies would have been beaten back to the beaches by this fierce Nazi counterattack.

Although they were given support assignments, black soldiers in the Transportation Corps found they were sometimes needed for military duties. "We were responsible for keeping the German saboteurs from blowing up our ammunition," recalled Black. "If they had gotten us, we would have been pushed right back into the beach. The Germans had dropped young fellows who lived in places like New York and Chicago and spoke perfect English. They could talk about the Brooklyn Dodgers and the White Sox. You couldn't distinguish them from Americans. You didn't know whether the white person was an American soldier or a German saboteur." To avoid such possible confusion, the Army command ordered all white soldiers off the streets at night and assigned black soldiers to do patrol duty. "If there was a white person on the street at night," said Black, "we had orders to pick him up or shoot him. We were doing double duty. Keep the supplies moving [during the day] and patrol at night."[34]

On the home front, African Americans in the military also had to keep the supplies moving. This duty turned out to be particularly dangerous at Port Chicago, California, where black sailors worked as stevedores. On July 17, 1944, a tragic accident occurred. The sailors were loading 860,000 tons of fragmentation and incendiary bombs onto the *E. A. Bryan* and *Quinault Victory* when the ammunition suddenly exploded. In the barracks nearby, Joseph Small felt the tremendous blast. "I was laying on the top bunk on my stomach when I heard it. Then the barracks just started to disintegrate. All the windows blew out. I was picked up off the bunk and flipped over and landed on my back. But I had gripped the edge of the mattress, so it was on top of me. That prevented me from getting cut by the glass and the dunnage and the lumber and everything that fell into the barracks."[35] Equivalent to five tons of TNT, the explosion obliterated both ships and leveled most of the base. Of the three hundred and twenty sailors killed, 202 were black. "This single stunning disaster," wrote historian Robert Allen, "accounted for more than 15 percent of all black naval casualties during the war."[36] It was a tragedy waiting to happen: neither the black stevedores or their white officers had been given specialized training in munitions handling.

Ordered to return to work at a nearby ammunition depot at Vallejo on August 9, 328 black sailors refused. Admiral Carleton Wright threatened to have them arrested and executed for mutiny. "The hazards of facing a firing squad," he warned, "are far greater than the hazards of handling ammunition." Fifty of the strikers continued their resistance and were court-martialed. "An admiral called me to his office," recalled Joseph Small. "He said, 'Small, you are the leader of this bunch. If you don't return to work, I'm gonna have you shot.' Just like that. Then I did something stupid: I blew my top. I said, 'You baldheaded so-and-so, go ahead and shoot.' That branded me as a mutineer."[37] On October 24, after only a little more than an hour's deliberation, all of the strikers were found guilty of mutiny, sentenced to fifteen years in prison, and dishonorably discharged. In January 1946, the Navy released most of the men from prison. The Port Chicago case represented "one of the worst 'frameups' we have come across in a long time," observed Thurgood Marshall of the NAACP. "It was deliberately planned and staged by certain officers to discredit Negro seamen."[38] "We knew from the beginning how it was coming out," Small remarked. "Everything was rigged."[39]

While African Americans contributed significantly to the war effort in support work, they also wanted an equal opportunity to fight for their country in combat. Blacks hoped that what Lincoln called "the mystic chords of memory" stretching from battlefields and patriot graves would entitle them to dignity as full Americans after the war.[40]

Confronting the Army Air Force as a bastion of jim crow, African Americans insisted on their right to fly for their country. "They didn't want blacks to fly," recalled Fred Smith. "They said blacks were not smart enough to be pilots."[41] African Americans protested their exclusion. The editor of the *Pittsburgh Courier* asked: "How can we excuse refusal to abolish the disuniting

COLOR LINE when the life of this nation is threatened?"[42] In response to this pressure, Secretary of War Henry L. Stimson authorized the training of black aviation cadets in a segregated unit at Tuskegee Air Force Base. While welcoming the Tuskegee training program as "a step in the right direction," the *Crisis* argued that the solution still adhered to "the old Army pattern of segregation."[43]

Sent to Europe as members of the all-black 99th Pursuit Squadron and 332nd Fighter Group, the Tuskegee pilots fought the German Luftwaffe in aerial combat. For their heroic service in Sicily and Italy, two of them were awarded the Distinguished Unit Citation, the air force's highest commendation. When General Ira C. Aeker, commanding officer of the Mediterranean Air Force, inspected the 99th Pursuit Squadron on April 20, 1944, he declared: "By the magnificent showing your fliers have made since coming into this theatre, and especially in the Anzio beachhead operations, you have not only won the plaudits of the Air Force, but have earned the opportunity to apply your talents to much more advanced work than was at one time planned for you."[44]

After Italy, the pilots of the 99th Pursuit Squadron and the 332nd Fighter Group escorted bombers over France and then Berlin itself. As the protectors of white pilots flying bombers en route to enemy targets, the Tuskegee pilots earned great respect, and bombing groups began requesting them as escorts. "They all wanted us," explained Coleman Young, "because we were the only fighter group in the entire air force that did not lose a bomber to enemy action. Oh, we were much in demand."[45]

On the ground below, African-American soldiers of the 761st Tank Battalion were also in demand. "When General Patton sent for us," said E. G. McConnell, "he asked for the best tank unit in the country. Hot dog it, were we proud, proud! I was in a unit I was damn proud of, and I knew that the things we did would shape the future for my children and grandchildren. We were so proud and dedicated to the cause of progress . . . going ahead so everyone would be able to live like an American."[46]

The black tankers fought in one of the fiercest fights of World War II — the Battle of the Bulge. "They put us on flatcars in France and shipped us to Belgium, where the fighting was," recalled Johnie Stevens. "We never fell back. We never lost an inch of ground during the whole campaign. You can't find nothing in the record that says the 761st lost any of their ground."[47] During the battle, the 761st Tank Battalion joined the white paratroopers of the 17th Airborne Division. Together they attacked German forces at the French town of Tillet; after five days of close range fighting, they beat the Germans into retreat. The victory at Tillet inspired Captain Philip W. Latimer to celebrate the interracial comradery in poetry:

> Black tankers and white paratroops,
> They made a lovely sight
> Unless you were German
> And then you'd best take flight.
> Black tankers and white paratroops,
> They all were color blind.
> They went into battle
> With winning on their mind.
> Black tankers and white paratroops
> Made Patton shout with glee,
> "They fight the way I want them to.
> They're good enough for me."
> Black tankers and white paratroops
> Lie buried side by side.
> They gave their life for country,
> They gave it with pride.
> Black tankers and white paratroops,
> Our memories take us back.
> Since we've been in battle
> There is no white or black.[48]

For black America, World War II was also "her-story." The international conflict offered black women new opportunities to travel and work as well as to demonstrate their refusal to live "half American." "When I saw all the advertisement about schooling and the other benefits, and the travel which would probably be involved, I thought, This is what I want," said Gertrude La Vigne. A college graduate, Dorothy Johnson stated frankly: "I think I joined because I was bored at Spelman." A student at New York University when she enlisted, Elaine Bennett explained: "I wanted to prove to myself, and maybe the world, that we [African Americans] would give what we had back to the United States as a confirmation that we were full-fledged citizens."[49]

But wearing army uniforms did not always mean equal rights as citizens. At the bus station in Elizabethtown, Kentucky, three black Wacs experienced a brutal reminder of segregation. White policemen had told them to switch from the "white" waiting room to the overcrowded "colored" one, and then began beating them because they did not promptly respond to the order. One of the policemen barked: "Down here, when we tell niggers to move, they move."[50] While traveling on a train in the South, Charity Adams Early was waiting in line to enter the dining car. After standing for a long time, she heard the steward call: "All persons in uniform first." Dressed as a Wac, Early stepped forward, but the steward put his arm across the door and snarled: "I said all persons in uniform first." Suddenly, from behind her, a white lieutenant shouted: "Well, what in the hell do you think that is that she has on? Get your ——— arm down before I break it off for you. What in the world are we fighting this damned war for? She's giving her service, too, and can eat anywhere I can."[51]

Black Wacs served in England and France as members of the all-black 6888 Central Postal Directory Battalion. "The job of our battalion," Lucia M. Pitts wrote, "was to keep up with the addresses of our fighting men, who were constantly on the move, and see that their mail reached them. An average of 30,000 address changes had to be made every day."[52] Margaret Y. Jackson vividly recalled the frenzied work of processing the mail. "As we labored at long tables, piled high with mail," she later wrote, "we were more than objectively impressed by the stacks of letters which we sought to place in the hands of the individuals to whom they were sent. Many of these letters were from the same loved ones. . . . After weeks — even months — they finally wound up on the floor of the auditorium in the Central Postal Directory. Many of us were as pleased as the soldiers must have been when stacks of letters were distributed to them at mail call." Working together with white Wacs in the auditorium, the busy mail processors took satisfaction in seeing "mountains of mail dwindle to small hills."[53] Wherever the Wacs went in Birmingham after work, they were approached by servicemen profusely thanking them for getting their long-awaited letters and packages to them. The Wacs took pride in their motto: "No mail, no morale."[54]

Soldiers, black and white, carried valuable lessons back to America. Sailing home, Pitts crossed the Atlantic with a group of black and white Wacs; after their ship landed, they were taken together to Camp Shanks. All of them were overjoyed to be home again, reported Pitts. "They exclaimed about everything, just because it was American — houses, signs, streets, automobiles." For dinner on the first night, they had steaks. "In the evening, two of the white girls — one from Georgia, the other from Virginia — came to our rooms and said to us, 'It's been a pleasure knowing you girls. We have learned something and you have certainly demanded our respect. We're proud of you.' To the four of us, that meant a great deal. From the time we were ordered to Compiegne, we and thirty-seven white girls had been thrown closely together. Most of the white girls were from the South — Georgia, Virginia, Texas; and the First Sergeant was from Mississippi. For over a month we lived (though we slept in separate tents), bathed, ate, made formations and played together. They had undoubtedly never associated with Negroes before in their lives, and it was immensely gratifying to us to know we had given them the right impression."[55]

After he had returned home from overseas duty in 1944, a wounded black soldier also had an affirming experience. Wearing the service stripes of the Tunisian, Sicilian, and Italian campaigns, he boarded a crowded bus in Florida. Three white soldiers were sitting in the front of the bus, and one of them got up and offered his seat to the veteran. However, the bus driver instructed the black rider to move to the back of the bus. After the white soldier pointed out that there were no empty seats, the driver replied: "Niggers can't sit up front in Florida." Turning to his buddies, the white soldier asked: "Does he sit or doesn't he?" They roared: "He does!" Then the soldier told the bus driver: "Either he sits down and you drive or we'll throw you off the bus and I'll drive." The threat ended the argument.[56]

A Battle Line on the Home Front: "Freedom from Want"

At the beginning of the war, blacks were in especially dire economic straits. "The depression brought everybody down a peg or two," Langston Hughes observed. "And the Negroes had but a few pegs to fall."[57] During the decade of America's great economic crisis, the majority of blacks still lived below the Mason-Dixon Line, growing cotton as sharecroppers and tenant farmers. Their livelihoods crumpled as cotton prices dropped sharply from 18 cents per pound in 1929 to 6 cents in 1933. That year, two-thirds of the black cotton farmers broke even or went deeper into debt. Moving to Southern cities in search of work, blacks encountered angry unemployed whites, shouting: "No Jobs for Niggers Until Every White Man Has a Job!" "Niggers, back to the cotton fields — city jobs are for white folks." More than 50 percent of blacks living in Southern cities were unemployed.[58]

In Northern cities, unemployment rates among blacks also soared. The people of Harlem, reported social worker Anna Arnold Hedgeman, were faced with the reality of starvation and they turned sadly to public relief. Men, women, and children "combed the streets and searched in garbage cans for food, foraging with dogs and cats." Living in cellars and basements, thousands of people found themselves packed in "damp, ratridden dungeons," existing in "squalor not too different from that of Arkansas sharecroppers."[59] Statistics told this story of hardship and hunger. During the Great Depression, unemployment for blacks was from 30 to 60 percent greater than for whites, and blacks joined the relief rolls two times more frequently than whites.[60]

The New Deal offered little relief to African Americans. Federal programs designed to provide a safety net for people in distress forced blacks to take a backseat. The Agricultural Adjustment Administration supported white farmers and workers but shunned blacks. "The AAA was no new deal for blacks," wrote historian Harvard Sitkoff; "it was a continuation of the same old raw deal." Similarly, the National Recovery Administration failed to protect black workers from discrimination in employment and wages. Blacks denounced the N.R.A. as "Negroes Ruined Again" and "Negro Removal Act." In 1935, at a conference on "The Position of the Negro in the Present Economic Crisis," black leaders and intellectuals grimly assessed the Roosevelt administration: "The Negro worker has good reason to feel that his government has betrayed him under the New Deal."[61]

The war revived the American economy as an "arsenal for democracy." But, as it turned out, defense jobs were not democratically distributed: most of them were reserved for whites only. Seventy-five percent of the war industries refused to hire blacks, while 15 percent hired them only for menial jobs. In 1940, blacks constituted only 0.2 percent of the workers in aircraft production. Of the 6,000 employees of Vultee Aircraft in 1941, none were black. "It is not the policy of this company," the defense contractor stated, "to employ other than of the Caucasian race."[62] Only ten of the 33,000 workers of Douglas Aircraft Company were black. "While we are in complete sympathy with the Negro," the president of North American Aviation stated frankly, "it is against company policy to employ them as aircraft workers or mechanics . . . regardless of their training."[63] On the cover of its July issue, the *Crisis* featured a photograph of an airplane factory with the caption "For Whites Only." The NAACP denounced discrimination in the defense industry: "Warplanes — Negro Americans may not build them, repair them, or fly them, but they must help pay for them."[64]

Confined to the unskilled and the service occupations before the war, African Americans wanted the better and higher-paying factory jobs generated by the war. As the country began to mobilize its war economy in early 1941, branches of the NAACP organized protests against discrimination in the defense plants of Detroit, Chicago, Los Angeles, and other cities. Pickets carried signs with messages: "Let's Blitzkrieg the Color Line." "Down with Jim-Crow in National Defense." "If We Can Fight for Democracy, We Can Work for Democracy." "A Bullet Draws No Color Line But Bullet Makers Do." "Not Hitlerism But Americanism, Jobs for All."[65]

The political iron was hot. Unwilling to wait for employers to open their doors voluntarily, African Americans demanded action from the federal government. At a 1941 meeting in Chicago, a black woman called for a mass demonstration in Washington: "We ought to throw 50,000 Negroes around the White House, bring them from all over the country, in jalopies, in trains and any way they can get there, and throw them around the White House and keep them there until we can get some action from the White House."[66]

The idea of a march on Washington seized the imagination of A. Philip Randolph, president of the Brotherhood of Sleeping Car Porters. "Let the Negro masses speak," he declared. "Negroes have a stake in National Defense. It is a big stake. . . . The stake involves jobs. It involves equal employment opportunities."[67] In his "Call to the March on Washington," Randolph demanded an end to discrimination not only in the military but also in the defense industries: "Negroes, by the mobilization and coordination of their mass power, can cause PRESIDENT ROOSEVELT TO ISSUE AN EXECUTIVE ORDER ABOLISHING DISCRIMINATION IN ALL GOVERNMENT DEPARTMENTS, ARMY, NAVY, AIR CORPS AND NATIONAL DEFENSE JOBS."[68]

Randolph was determined to make Roosevelt do the right thing: translate the pronouncements of the democratic war aims abroad into practices of equality at home. "An 'all-out' thundering march on Washington," the union leader promised, "ending in a monster and huge demonstration at Lincoln's Monument will shake up white America."[69] Randolph's threat of a mass demonstration alarmed Washington officials. "What will they think in Berlin?" they anxiously asked. Blacks replied: "Oh, perhaps no more than they already think of America's racial policy."[70] The march was scheduled for July 1.

At the White House on June 18, Roosevelt met with civil rights leaders, including Randolph. Opening the discussion with small talk, the President said: "Hello, Phil. Which class were you in at Harvard?" Randolph replied: "I never went to Harvard." Roosevelt then began entertaining his guests with old political anecdotes. Impatient, Randolph respectfully interrupted: "Mr. President, time is running on. You are quite busy, I know. But what we want to talk with you about is the problem of jobs for Negroes in defense industries. Our people are being turned away at factory gates because they are colored. They can't live with this thing. Now, what are you going to do about it?"

Roosevelt offered to call up the heads of defense plants and urge them to hire blacks. "We want you to do more than that," Randolph countered. "We want something concrete, something tangible, definite, positive, and affirmative." Asked what he meant, Randolph presented his radical proposal: "Mr. President, we want you to issue an executive order making it mandatory that Negroes be permitted to work in these plants." Roosevelt said that he would not do anything unless the march was first called off. "Questions like this can't be settled with a sledge hammer." Randolph replied: "I'm sorry, Mr. President, the march cannot be called off." Then Roosevelt asked the black leader how many people would be at the march. "One hundred thousand, Mr. President."[71]

A week later, Roosevelt signed Executive Order 8802: "There shall be no discrimination in the employment of workers in defense industries or Government because of race, creed, color, or national origin . . . and it is the duty of employers and of labor organizations . . . to provide for the full and equitable participation of all workers in defense industries, without discrimination because of race, creed, color, or national origin." His order also established the Committee on Fair Employment Practices to investigate complaints of discrimination and take appropriate steps to redress valid grievances.[72]

The march was canceled. Black munitions worker Margaret Wright recalled that it was only Randolph's threat of a march on Washington that "made Roosevelt give this proclamation, because no one does anything — you never get anything — out of the goodness of people's hearts."[73]

But Roosevelt's new policy was designed for failure. In its first year of operation, the FEPC had but seven field officers and five clerical workers, with a budget of only $80,000. Even after the committee's personnel were increased, its budget totaled only $431,609, far below the funding allocated to other government departments.

Moreover, Roosevelt's FEPC had no teeth to enforce equal employment. According to a federal government report, blacks were complaining that the FEPC had "no power to penalize violators of the non-discrimination order," and that the committee's hearings were merely "a token of the government's wish to rectify the situation, rather than an actual solution of the problem."[74] In *Opportunity: Journal of Negro Life,* George E. DeMar pointed out that Roosevelt's "Executive Order was accepted as policy, but all too often not for practice, by those holding war contracts."[75] In "An Open Letter to President Roosevelt — An Editorial," the *Crisis* impatiently informed the President that in too many communities "your Executive Order 8802 was being defied and sabotaged by management and labor alike."[76]

Knowing that the government would not interfere with war production and that the FEPC had neither the power nor the will to desegregate, white laborers resisted the federal government's efforts to integrate the war industries. In 1943, for example, twenty thousand white workers rioted to protest the upgrading of black welders in the Alabama Dry Dock and Shipbuilders Company. After federal troops intervened, the FEPC agreed to allow segregation to continue in the shipyards.

Ultimately, the real pressure for employment integration came from the sheer need for labor in America's booming war industries. Almost 1 million African Americans entered the industrial labor force during the war years. At the beginning of 1942, only 3 percent of defense workers were black; by November 1944, that number had jumped to 8.3 percent. Blacks constituted 25 percent of the labor force in foundries and 12 percent in shipbuilding and steel mills.[77] They also entered employment in the auto industry. In 1943, 55,000 of the 450,000 members of Detroit's United Auto Workers were African Americans. During the war years, the wages of black families increased from 40 percent to 60 percent of that of white families.[78]

Pulled by job opportunities in the war industries, over a half million African Americans left the South. During the decade of the 1940s, the percentage of blacks living in the South declined from 77 percent to 68 percent. Following the jobs to the cities, blacks classified as urban dwellers increased from 49 percent to 62 percent. They migrated, again as they had during World War I, to the Midwestern cities like Chicago and Detroit. But this time, they also went to California, where they found war-related jobs in Los Angeles, Oakland, Richmond, and San Francisco. "I came to California in 1943," recalled Ella Johnson. "The shipyard people came to Louisiana offering $1.20 an hour to work in California. I'd work for as little as 25 cents an hour, 50 cents an hour, and thinking I was doing pretty good. Had I ever seen a ship? I imagine I had not. I didn't even know what a ship looked like. But they were hiring, so we went."[79]

As a teenager living in San Francisco at the time, Maya Angelou witnessed the movement of blacks into the Fillmore District, which had been inhabited by Japanese Americans until their evacuation and internment. "As the Japanese disappeared, soundlessly and without protest," she wrote in her autobiography, "the Ne-

groes entered with their loud jukeboxes, the just-released animosi-
ties and the relief of escape from Southern bonds. The Japanese
area became San Francisco's Harlem in a matter of months." She
offered a reflection on the sudden racial recomposition of this
community. "A person unaware of all the factors that make up
oppression might have expected sympathy or even support from
the Negro newcomers for the dislodged Japanese. Especially in
view of the fact that they (the Blacks) had themselves undergone
concentration-camp living for centuries in slavery's plantations
and later in sharecroppers' cabins. But the sensations of common
relationship were missing." The black newcomers had been recruited from the South to work in the shipyards, Angelou explained,
and were experiencing employment and housing opportunities
that had long been denied to them. Who could expect them to
share their "new and dizzying importance with concern for a race"
they had "never known to exist"?[80]

The employment opportunities in the war industries were especially "dizzying" for African-American women. The military demand for soldiers created labor shortages and opened industrial
jobs to women, including black women.[81] "When we first got into
the war," said San Francisco shipworker Lyn Childs, "the country
wasn't prepared. And as the manpower in the country was getting
pulled into the service, all of the industries were wide open. So
they decided, 'Well, we better let some of those blacks come in.'
Then after the source of men dried up, they began to let women
come in. The doors were opened."[82]

Of the 1 million African Americans who entered defense employment during the war years, 600,000 were women. Between
1940 and 1944, the percentage of black women in industry increased from 6.5 percent to 18 percent of the female workforce.
Between 1940 and 1944, their numbers in Detroit's factories had
risen sharply, from 14,451 to 46,750. In the aircraft plants of Los
Angeles, 2,000 black women were employed by North American
Aviation alone.[83] In "Negro Women on the Production Front,"
published in a 1943 issue of *Opportunity: Journal of Negro Life,*

Mary Anderson wrote: "At the same time that Negro women are contributing to the war effort in essential war and civilian jobs, they are broadening their occupational experience. . . . We must use the highest skills and the full strength of all our people, men and women, to win the war and to win the peace."[84]

For African-American women, defense work offered escape from domestic work. "We'd never had any opportunity to do that kind of work [in the defense industry]," recalled Lyn Childs. "Do you think that if you did domestic work all of your life, where you'd clean somebody's toilets and did all the cooking for some lazy characters who were sitting on top, and you finally got a chance where you can get a dignified job, you wouldn't fly through the door?"[85]

Between 1940 and 1944, the proportion of black women employed in housework declined from 60 percent to 45 percent. One of these women was Fanny Christina Hill. Moving from Tyler, Texas, to Los Angeles in 1943, she had planned to continue working as a house cleaner. "Well, I better get me a good job around here working in a hotel or motel," Hill told her sister. "No," said her sister, "you just come on out and go in the war plants and work and maybe you'll make enough money where you won't have to work in the hotels or motels." Hill took her advice and applied for a job at North American Aviation. "There was a black girl that hired with me," she recalled. "I went to work the next day, sixty cents an hour." For six weeks, Hill attended a training school where she learned to shoot and buck rivets and to drill holes. Then she was transferred to the plant. However, she discovered that workers with the right "color" were given the privileged job assignments. "They had fifteen or twenty departments, but all the Negroes went to Department 17 because there was nothing but shooting and bucking rivets. You stood on one side of the panel and your partner stood on this side, and he would shoot the rivets with a gun and you'd buck them with the bar." When Hill threatened to quit because she disliked this punishing and monotonous work, she was given a workbench assignment and then a job helping to build the tail sections of bombers. "The war made me live better, it really did," recalled Hill. "My sister always said that Hitler was the one that got us out of the white folks' kitchen."[86]

Athough the defense industries had begun to hire women, black women often had to fight to be included. After completing an auto-body training program to be a riveter, Wanita Allen found that the defense plants were hiring only white women. "I felt like I had just as much right to work as they did," she recalled, "and they had jobs and they had children and I had children." Refusing to be denied, Allen joined the United Auto Workers in challenging this discrimination. She agreed to help the union gather evidence for a lawsuit. Repeatedly, she applied for a job at the defense plant, only to be told that they "were not hiring now." After several rebuffs, Allen stood in front of the hiring office; then one day, she noticed a white woman coming out and asked her: "Oh, you were lucky too, huh, you got hired too. Maybe I'll see you in the plant, what's your name?" The woman gave her name to Allen. With this evidence showing that the company was in fact hiring white women and discriminating against black women, the UAW "won the suit and they notified all the black women to come in, so they came in droves and they hired them one by one."[87]

Even after doors were opened to black women, however, they often found themselves assigned to non-skilled jobs such as janitors and cafeteria workers. Trained as a drill-press operator by the National Youth Administration, Beatrice Marshall looked forward to working in the defense industry. "I felt like I was a champion on the drill press, and I really did like it." But when she applied for a job at the Portland, Oregon, shipyards, Marshall was told that they had no openings for drill-press operators and that she could be hired only as a painter's helper. The company actually did have jobs available in the machine shop but was not accepting black workers. Marshall hated her job as a painter's helper. "The job was in the bottom of the boat. We had to crawl on our hands and knees and carry our light on an extension cord to see because it was so dark in there. And we had a little tool, something like a spreader, where we scraped the rust off the bottom of the boat where they had to paint. We had to wear masks, there was so much rust in there until you could hardly breathe."[88] Even when placed in skilled jobs, however, black women still experienced discrimination. Westinghouse Electric Manufacturing Company, for example, hired 3,500 women, including 100 black women, to work as punch-press, drill-press, and milling-machine operators, engravers, painters, and grinders. But the black women were hired for the night shift only.[89]

Still, the new jobs in the defense industries paid what seemed like enormous wages. Employed in the Detroit auto industry, Lillian Hatcher earned double the wages she had been receiving as a cafeteria worker. "I was working not for patriotic reasons," she stated. "I was working for the money. The 97 cents a hour was the greatest salary that I had earned. Going up to $1.16 an hour — that was going to be my top rate. And I really needed that money, because my son was wearing out corduroy pants, two and three pairs a month, gym shoes and all the other things my daughters had to have, you know, clothing and shoes and all that stuff. And our house rent was the whole price of $32.50 a month and we had to save for that, in order to pay $32.50 and keep the light and gas."[90]

Working and making money in the defense industry complicated family life. Many women found that they had two shifts — one at the plant and a second at home. "When your husband came home," munitions worker Margaret White said, "he propped his feet up and got a can of beer while you fixed dinner, or even if we weren't working the same shifts you fixed dinner and left it where it would be convenient for him to get it." Wanita Allen complained that she had to "rush, rush, rush" — get dinner ready, wash clothes, iron clothes, clean the house. "By the time I got in bed it was time to get up in the morning."[91]

But the frenetic life of a defense worker was worth the trouble for many African-American women. In a 1943 article published in *Opportunity: A Journal of Negro Life,* Leotha Hackshaw described "What My Job Means to Me." "Eighteen months ago," she wrote,

"I told my friends that I was going into the war industry. Mary, a close friend, raised a horrified face and shouted, 'Lee, are you crazy? Why, that work is *killing*. You're not accustomed to the kind of thing.'" Hackshaw found a job in a company where she cemented and polished lenses for binoculars. A college graduate, Hackshaw was indeed not accustomed to such repetitious and boring work; she was also not prepared for her punishing schedule. Hackshaw had to get up at 5:30 A.M. in order to get ready for work and take her son to the babysitter. Shortly afterward, she was transferred to the night shift, working from midnight to 8 A.M. "I never realized how many different noises there are until I tried to sleep in the daytime," she said.

Hackshaw left the plant to work for Army Ordnance as an inspector of finished binoculars. "I was one of eight inspectors in the plant and the only Negro. Many of them had never worked with a Negro before. With them as with me it was a question of adjusting to each other. The company itself, I soon learned, had no Negroes in its employ with the exception of one or two porters." But labor shortages soon led to the hiring of more black women, even to assigning them to the semi-skilled assembly lines where they worked side-by-side with white women. "If anyone had expected a riot between the white girls (mostly Irish-American) and the incoming Negro girls, they must have been disappointed," recalled Hackshaw. "No interest was shown whatever."

For Hackshaw, checking the finished glasses in the ordnance plant meant more than just making money. "Often as I inspected a glass, I would visualize the use to which it would be put. The scene thus conjured up in my imagination may vary greatly from the real procedure on the field. Nonetheless, it never fails to stir me with the thrill of knowing that I am doing something worthwhile in the winning of the war." Every pair of binoculars became a symbol of liberty. "In our own time our President has raised the standard of the 'Four Freedoms.' These freedoms are not new. They have been fought for over and over again. The Negro has attained one of these and part of another. Freedom from fear and freedom from want he is fighting for now; for under them democracy can reach its fulfillment."[92]

For African Americans, men as well as women, World War II was a crossing, constituting what Robert C. Weaver of the Office of Production Management called "more industrial and occupational diversification for Negroes than had occurred in the seventy-five preceding years."[93] At the end of the war, however, the defense industry contracted, and industrial employment opportunities for African Americans suddenly disappeared. Economic reconversion hurt black workers more than white workers. From July 1945 to April 1946, unemployment rates among blacks increased more than twice as much as among whites.[94]

Unemployed, blacks found themselves joining Huddie Ledbetter ("Leadbelly") in song:

> I had a little woman, working on that national defense,
> I had a little woman, working on that national defense,
> That little woman act just like she did not have no sense.
>
> Just because she was working, making so much dough,
> Just because she was working, making so much dough,
> That woman got to say she did not love me no more.
>
> Every payday would come — her check was big as mine,
> Every payday would come — her check was big as mine,
> That woman thought that defense was gonna last all the
>   time.
>
> That defense is gone, just listen to my song,
> That defense is gone, just listen to my song,
> Since that defense is gone, that woman done lose her home.
>
> I will tell the truth and it's got to be a fact,
> I will tell the truth and it's got to be a fact,
> Since that defense is gone that woman lose her Cadillac.[95]

However, not everything was gone. The war had given African Americans a taste of the honey of equality. "A lot of blacks that were share cropping, doing menial work and stuff," said defense worker Margaret Wright, "got into the army and saw how other things were and how things could be. They decided they did not want to go back to what they were doing before. They did not want to walk behind a plow, they wouldn't get on the back of the bus anymore."[96]

African Americans would also refuse to be denied the right to "freedom from fear."

No "Freedom from Fear" in the Cities: Race Riots

As black and white workers followed the defense jobs into the cities, they often clashed violently. In 1943, at the height of industrial production for the war, urban race riots exploded across the country. The Social Science Institute at Fisk University reported that 242 racial battles had occurred that year in forty-seven cities.[97]

Detroit was the scene of the bloodiest conflict. At the beginning of the war, African Americans totaled 150,000 of this city's population of 1,600,000. Between 1940 and 1943, half a million people, including more than 50,000 blacks, moved into the city, lured by the demand for workers in the "arsenal for democracy." In an August 14, 1942, memorandum, the Office of War Information highlighted the importance of Detroit in "the Battle of Production." "It is an assembly center which dominates the nation's greatest war-industrial region and represents the culmination of the coordination of this vast industrial machine. If Detroit's part of this machine breaks down, the impact upon the regional net-work of production is tremendous."[98]

Although jobs in the defense industry were abundant, white workers were determined to continue the exclusion of blacks from the better jobs. In September 1941, 250 whites staged a sit-down strike at the Packard Motor Car Company to protest the promotion of two blacks from polishing work to assembly work. With the support of the United Auto Workers, blacks continued to be upgraded. "A new wave of protest against working with Negroes was spread by white workers at Packard Motor Car Company during the last two weeks as anti-Negro demonstrators employed a new technique in 'hate strikes,'" the *Pittsburgh Courier* reported on March 6, 1942. "The new technique calls for short stoppages while Negro workers are booed lustily by whites who ignore the pleas of foremen and union stewards to keep production rolling."[99]

On May 27, twenty thousand white workers at Packard walked off their jobs and stopped production for almost a week to protest the upgrading of three blacks.[100] Four days later, 350 white workers shut down the Dodge plant after 23 blacks had been transferred from unskilled to skilled jobs.[101] "Hate strikes" also erupted in the munitions industry. On January 23, 1942, two blacks at the Hudson Naval Ordinance Plant were transferred from the janitorial staff to jobs as machine operators. White workers promptly staged a work stoppage. Their strike was successful: after only two hours of protest, reported the Office of War Information, the black workers were sent back to "their dustpans and brooms."[102] On March 15, 1943, the Office of War Information reported that white workers resented the economic gains of blacks and believed that "the Negro must be kept in his place."[103]

Competition between whites and blacks intensified not only in the workplace but also in housing. The tremendous influx of newcomers into Detroit had created crowded living conditions. Black newcomers found themselves herded into a ghetto known as Paradise Valley. There men, women, and children found themselves "packed like sardines, in the horribly dirty one- and two-family houses and apartment buildings on Hastings and other streets in the Valley."[104] To meet the immense housing needs of the expanding workforce, the federal government constructed public housing projects. Built in a white neighborhood, the Sojourner Truth Housing Project for blacks was completed in February 1942. When black defense workers tried to move their families into the project, however, they were attacked and driven away by a thousand whites armed with clubs, knives, and rifles. Two months later, blacks were able to occupy their homes in the Sojourner Truth project, but only with the protection of 1,750 city and state police.[105]

The turmoil at the Sojourner Truth project became international news. "The Detroit housing crisis was shortwaved to the peoples of Asia by the Japs as proof of the fact that the democratic nations do not intend to extend democracy to non-white peoples," stated a federal government report marked "confidential."[106] The editors of the *Crisis* declared that Japanese radio propaganda broadcasts were using the Sojourner Truth riot as "an example to colored peoples of the Far East of the type of democracy they [could] expect from white America."[107]

By 1943, Detroit was a racial tinderbox. In early June, Walter White of the NAACP declared at a rally in Cadillac Square: "Let us drag out into the open what has been whispered throughout Detroit for months — that a race riot may break out here at any time." Then on Sunday, June 20, when sixty thousand blacks and forty thousand whites retreated from the heat to a park in the middle of the Detroit River, a scuffle broke out between a white man and a black man on the Belle Island bridge. Quickly, the fighting spread through the crowd. Rumors fanned the fiery conflict: whites had killed a black woman and her baby on the Belle Island bridge, and blacks had raped and killed a white woman on the park bridge. "By midnight," reported Earl Brown in *Harper's Magazine,* "the fight had spread north, east, south, and west, and Paradise Valley was going crazy. By three in the morning store looting was in full swing and at daybreak both black and white mobs were attacking street cars crowded with war-plant workers on their way to and from work."[108]

Detroit began to resemble a bombed city as scores of fires turned entire blocks into ashes. The hospital in the riot area was accepting injured individuals at the rate of one every other minute. "Armed with beer and pop bottles, bricks and improvised weapons of scrap iron and table legs," the black newspaper *Detroit Tribune* reported, "white mobs gathered on the edge of the Negro district and brutally beat isolated Negro citizens, overturning automobiles in which Negroes were riding and setting cars on fire. In retaliation, Negro mobs formed and stoned all whites who were caught in the ghetto. Frantically trying to keep the mobs apart, the Detroit police whipped out tommy guns and tear gas, but almost always in the direction of Negroes."[109]

This urban warfare continued until Tuesday morning when six thousand federal troops finally restored order to Detroit. By then, losses totaled $2 million in property due to looting and destruction. Hundreds of people were injured, and thirty-four killed — nine whites and twenty-five blacks.[110] "Three fourths of the Negroes killed were shot by police," editorialized the *Crisis*. "Not a single white person was shot by police. More than 90 percent of those arrested for rioting were Negroes. Yet all the pictures showed white people chasing, kicking, and beating colored people. There were many graphic and horrible pictures of the riot, but the most meaningful to the theme of this piece was the one showing a Negro being struck in the face by a white rioter as he was being escorted by *two* policemen!"[111]

As chief counsel for the NAACP, Thurgood Marshall had tried to warn Roosevelt about Detroit's powder keg of racial tensions. "In those days," he told Carl T. Rowan years later, "I would lie awake some nights worrying that Detroit and other cities that had industries that were critical to the war effort were becoming tinderboxes because whites, from the Roosevelt brain trust to the unions, wanted to keep Negroes out of the mobilization jobs. The tragedy was that Roosevelt didn't have a fucking clue as to the explosive tensions that were building up."[112]

Actually, the President had more than a clue. In a "Special Report on Negro Housing Situation in Detroit," March 5, 1942, marked "Confidential," the federal government's Office of Facts and Figures had noted the escalating racial antagonisms in Detroit. "It now appears," the report stated, "that only the direct intervention of the President can prevent not only a violent race riot in Detroit but a steadily widening fissure that will create havoc in the working force of every Northern industrial city." A clear warning was given: "Unless strong and quick action intervention by some high official, preferably the President, is not taken at once, hell is going to be let loose."[113] In a March 15, 1943, report, the Bureau of Intelligence of the Office of War Information had warned: "In Detroit, the situation is not good. Unless it is carefully handled you can have trouble there now any day, and when it bursts out it will require some harsh treatment, not in subduing the Negroes, but the whites."[114] Two days before the outbreak of violence in Detroit, Congress of Industrial Organizations president Philip Murray informed Roosevelt that the explosive situation in Detroit was "more than a problem either of mob prejudice or juvenile delinquency." Rather it was "a grave question of our relations with our allies and test of our ability to present a truly united front to the Axis."[115]

In a telegram to Roosevelt, John Sengstacke of the Negro Publishers' Association asked the President to appeal to the conscience of the nation: "We urge you to call attention of all Americans through the radio and the press to the unpatriotic activities of those who subvert the constitutional guarantee of equal opportunity for all."[116] Roosevelt felt the pressure to speak out. "Don't you think it is about time," he asked his press secretary, Steve Early, "for me to issue a statement about racial riots?"[117] In the end, however, the President decided not to make a public address on the crisis. He realized, Eleanor Roosevelt explained, that "he must not irritate the southern leaders," whose votes he needed for essential war bills.[118]

Roosevelt's silence on the Detroit crisis spoke loudly overseas. A week after the riot, the editor of the *Christian Century* stressed the international significance of the urban violence: "Some Americans may at last wake up to the way in which such racial outrages play into the hands of Japan's propagandists; they may at last see that for every person of color struck down by a white mob in this country the United States loses the confidence and comradeship of ten thousand Asiatics." The editor expressed dismay at the race hatred aimed not only at African Americans but also at Mexican Americans and Japanese Americans. "The nation is at war, according to the President, in order to make possible a world in which there shall be, for all people, freedom from fear. Freedom from fear — with mobs sweeping up and down the streets of cities, shouting 'Kill the d——n niggers!' 'Kill the d——n greasers!' 'Kill the d——n Japs!' Freedom from fear! Will not the words stick in our throats?"[119]

During the days of violence, however, there were also shouts for justice. On one occasion, three white sailors rescued a young black from a white mob. "Leave him alone!" the sailors shouted, and a rioter snarled. "What's it to you?" One of the sailors snapped: "Plenty. There was a colored guy in our outfit in the Pacific and he saved the lives of two of my buddies. Besides, you guys are stirring up here at home something we are fighting to stop."[120]

Five weeks after the bloodbath in Detroit, Harlem exploded. Conditions in this ghetto had been ready for ignition: blacks were still being excluded from many defense industry plants, 70 percent of Harlem was on relief, and people were trapped in squalid, rat-infested apartments. The match was lit on August 1. On leave from his army base in New Jersey, Robert J. Bandy was with his mother and fiancée at the Braddock Hotel in Harlem. When they returned from the movies, they found the hotel clerk and a black woman engaged in a heated argument. Called to the scene, police officer James Collins began pushing the woman to the hotel door. Bandy intervened, accusing the white officer of mistreating the woman because she was black. During the struggle that followed, Collins shot Bandy in the left shoulder.

Meanwhile, an angry crowd had assembled outside the hotel. Suddenly they were seized by a rumor that a white policeman had shot and killed a black soldier. Soon thousands of enraged people were in the streets, smashing store windows on 125th Street and looting businesses. As the rioting gathered momentum, Mayor Fiorello La Guardia rushed to Harlem; accompanied by black community leaders, he appealed to the rioters, urging them to return to their homes. La Guardia instructed city police to use only as much force as absolutely necessary and to disperse crowds as diplomatically as possible. To help calm the community, the mayor made repeated radio broadcasts to inform the people that Bandy had not, in fact, been killed.

When peace was restored, property damage to 1,450 stores totalled $5 million; 550 individuals had been arrested, 500 injured, and 6 persons killed. A child at the time, Claude Brown was in bed when he heard the screaming of the mobs in the streets and the shattering of broken windows. The next morning, he saw a scene resembling a war zone with burned-out buildings and the heavy smell of smoke. "None of the stores had any windows," he recalled, "and glass was everywhere. It seemed that all the cops in the world were on 145th Street and Eighth Avenue that day. The cops were telling everybody to move on, and everybody was talking about the riot."[121]

Assessing the devastation in an essay published in *New York PM,* Richard Wright identified the shooting of the soldier as "the spark" that set off "a spontaneous outburst of anger, stemming mainly from the economic pinch."[122] City council member Adam Clayton Powell, Jr., viewed the fury in the streets as more than an expression of economic discontent: it was "the last open revolt of the black common man against a bastard democracy," against "the whole sorrowful, disgraceful bloody record of America's treatment of one million blacks in uniform."[123]

Reports of the Detroit and Harlem riots dismayed a group of soldiers in a hospital ward in Europe. Writing to a newspaper in their home city of Detroit, they indignantly asked America: "Why are these race riots going on there in Detroit and in other cities in this land — supposedly the land of freedom, equality, and brotherhood?" The riots "make us fighters think — *what are we fighting for?*" They believed they were fighting and willing to die for the "principles that gave birth to the United States of America." In the crucible of the battlefield, they had come to understand deeply the meaning of those "self-evident" truths. "In this hospital ward, we eat, laugh, and sleep uncomplaining together." They signed their letter: "Jim Stanley, Negro; Joe Wakamatsu, Japanese; Eng Yu, Chinese; John Brennan, Irish; Paul Colosi, Italian; Don Holzheimer, German; Joe Wojiechowski, Polish; and Mike Cohen, Jewish."[124]

4

―――――❦―――――

THE ORIGINAL AMERICANS
From Battlefields to Ceremonies

Flashback at Bataan: The Long Walk

ON DECEMBER 7, 1941, Keats Begay was at Clark Field in the Philippines. He and other soldiers were getting ready for lunch when they heard the news that the Japanese had attacked Pearl Harbor. Then, as they were eating, they heard planes approaching. "Pretty soon we could see them," Begay recalled. "They were coming closer and closer. They were in rows, like groups of ducks in the sky." Then bombs began falling. "Our battery squad of about 12 soldiers was taking care of the ammunition when one of the bombs struck them. There were only cries heard. Later, when we looked, there was nothing left. All the soldiers were blown to pieces. We had to search for the body pieces."

After four days of fierce combat, the U.S. forces regrouped on the Bataan Peninsula, where they were joined by Filipino fighters. Finally, on April 9 the defenders surrendered. Of the 40,000 soldiers captured, 6,700 were Americans, 21 of them Navajos like Begay. The Japanese ordered the prisoners to march. "They did not tell us where we were going," said Begay. As the prisoners made their trek, they became thirsty but were not allowed to drink from wells along the road. "They chased one of the soldiers back when he tried to go to a well. If a soldier hesitated to cooperate with the Japanese guards, they just stabbed him with bayonets; then they left the body lying there." Begay saw "lots of dead bodies lying along the road. The bodies really stank, since it was very hot."

The brutal Bataan experience reminded Begay of what had happened to his tribe in 1863, when his people were marched by federal troops at bayonet point. "To me," he stated, "it was the same as the Long Walk, in which the poor Navajos had to march over 400 miles to Fort Sumner [the Bosque Redondo Reservation in New Mexico], and many lost their lives during that walk. Many of our elders still relate those stories to us. It was the same in the Bataan Death March. The poor soldiers had to march to the prison camp, and too many of them lost their lives."[1]

"Why Fight the White Man's War?"

Begay was already in the army when the war began. But young Indians still on the reservations now had to face the question: should they fight for the United States, even cooperate with the draft? "There may be some justice in the Indians' opposition to registration," commented a reservation official. "They feel that this country was taken away from them by white men and for that reason they should not now be required to help in case of invasion or attack." Indeed, ever since the arrival of the English colonizers at Jamestown in 1607, native peoples had been losing their lands. "We had lost our own country to foreigners," said a Navajo.[2] Now they were being asked to help defend their conquerers. "Why do you have to go [to war]," an Indian mother asked her son. "It's not your war. It's the white man's war."[3]

"Many people ask why we fight the White man's war," said Navajo Raymond Nakai, who enlisted in the marines. "Our answer is that we are proud to be American. We're proud to be

American Indians. We always stand ready when our country needs us."[4] A soldier from the Celilo Tribe expressed a similiar view: "My grandparents fought against the White man. They were defending their homes. In many respects we have been treated badly. In this land which once was ours, we are poor. Many people treat us as outcasts and inferiors. Yet our conditions have slowly been improved. The reservation schools are good. We are trained for trades and farming. The government defends our rights. We know that under Nazism we would have no rights at all. We are not Aryans and we would be used as slaves."[5]

In their declaration of war against Germany, Japan, and Italy, the Iroquois League announced: "It is the unanimous sentiment among the Indian people that the atrocities of the Axis nations are violently repulsive to all sense of righteousness of our people. This merciless slaughter of mankind upon the part of those enemies of free peoples can no longer be tolerated." The Cheyennes condemned the Axis nations as an "unholy triangle" seeking to "conquer and enslave the bodies, minds and souls of all free people."[6] The Navajo Nation declared: "We resolve that the Navajo Indians stand ready . . . to aid and defend our government and its institutions against all subversive and armed conflict and pledge our loyalty to the system which recognizes minority rights and a way of life that has placed us among the greatest people of our race."[7] In 1943, a Navajo soldier wrote to his tribal council: "I don't know anything about the white man's way. I never went outside the reservation. . . . I am proud to be in a suit like this now. It is to protect my country, my people, the head men, the chiefs of my people. . . ."[8]

A year after the attack on Pearl Harbor, the *New York Times* reported that 8,800 of the 60,000 Indian males between the ages of twenty-one and forty-four were in military uniform, a higher rate than for the general population. Indian eagerness for military service prompted the *Saturday Evening Post* to editorialize: "We would not need the Selective Service if all volunteered like Indians."[9] Many Indians, reported Indian Affairs commissioner John Collier, saw the international conflict as "more than just another war." To them, the war was a "life-and-death struggle for the survival of those things for which they [had] been unceasingly waging an uphill fight for many generations." Collier noted that a recent "rebirth of spirit, a reviving of the smoldering fires of local democracy, and a step toward economic rehabilitation" were helping Indians see "the possibilities in a world of the Four Freedoms."[10]

Praise for Indian patriotism and fighting prowess sometimes reflected stereotypical images from the frontier days. "The red soldier is tough," the *American Legion Magazine* declared. "Usually he has lived outdoors all his life, and lived by his senses; he is a natural Ranger. He takes to commando fighting with gusto. Why not? his ancestors invented it. . . . At ambushing, scouting, signaling, sniping, they're peerless. Some can smell a snake yards away and hear the faintest movement; all endure thirst and lack of food better than average." Similarly, Secretary of the Interior Harold Ickes noted how the "inherited talents of the Indian" made him "uniquely valuable — endurance, rhythm, time, coordination, sense perception, an uncanny ability to get over any sort of terrain at night, and . . . an enthusiasm for fighting."[11]

Altogether, forty-five thousand Indians served in the United States armed forces, or more than 10 percent of the Indian population. Eight hundred Indian women joined the Wacs and Waves. Constituting 20 percent of the Forty-fifth Army Infantry Division, known as the "Thunderbird," Indian soldiers fought in North Africa, Italy, and France. The casualties for this unit were extremely high — 3,747 dead, 4,403 missing, and 19,403 wounded.

There were Indians who fought with great distinction. More than thirty of them were awarded the Distinguished Flying Cross, while another seventy received the Air Medal. Despite severe wounds, Lieutenant Ernest Childers single-handedly destroyed three German machine-gun emplacements and opened the way for the advance of his battalion in Italy. In 1944, this Creek soldier was awarded the nation's highest decoration for bravery in battle — the Medal of Honor. After the attack on Pearl Harbor,

General Clarence L. Tinker was given command of the air force in Hawaii. A member of the Osage tribe, he was the first Indian to reach the rank of general in the United States Army. At the Battle of Midway, Tinker personally led the squadron of bombers that spearheaded the attack. Killed in action, he was awarded the Distinguished Service Medal for his heroism.[12]

Indians also left the reservations to work in the defense industries. "By war's end," reported historian Alison Bernstein, "40,000 persons — one half of the able-bodied men who had not entered the military and one-fifth of the women — had left Indian lands for war-related work." Indians were becoming an urban population: in 1940, less than 5 percent of the entire Native American population lived in cities; ten years later, this figure jumped to 20 percent. Trained in sheet metal and mechanics by reservation schools, Indians were applying their skills in shipyards, airplane plants, and tank factories. "The Indians are playing an important role in the agricultural and industrial production program of the war," observed Commissioner Collier. "Skilled Indian workers are to be found scattered throughout important war industries in almost every section of the country. They are doing highly technical jobs in aircraft industries on the west coast, in Kansas, and in New York state. . . . More than two thousand Navajos were employed in the construction of a large ordnance depot in New Mexico. On this particular project it was most interesting to see long-haired, fullblood Indians tying steel, operating jack hammers, doing welding, and handling some of the most difficult machine operations."[13]

Like "Rosie," Indian women became riveters. In Everett, Washington, Harriette Shelton Williams, daughter of the chief of the Snohomish Indians, went to work at Boeing Aircraft Corporation. The May 26, 1994, *Boeing News* published a picture of her dressed in her traditional clothing, with the caption: "She isn't dressed this way every day on her Boeing job, but fellow-workers say there's no mistaking the royal bearing of Princess Hiahl-tsa even when she wears a work-a-day garb."[14] Many other Indian women became janitors and office workers. Irene Stewart left the Navajo reservation to clean administrative offices in Bellemont, Arizona, and then went to Flagstaff to work in the defense industry.[15] Similarly, in 1943 Agnes R. Begay went to work for the Bellemont Corporation at the Ordnance Depot in Flagstaff. "I was selected to work in the personnel office and help people get jobs, especially Navajos who had no formal education."[16]

In the war industries, however, Indian workers often received wages lower than that of whites. At Fort Wingate, Navajos demanded the same pay for the same work. "We do not understand," the Navajo tribal council protested, "how a Navajo can be a member of the union paying dues to secure the same benefits and be forced to accept a lower pay rate."[17] The union denied the tribe's demand for equal wages, arguing that the Navajos did not pay taxes on their land and hence belonged to a special category of workers that deserved lower pay.

In the cities, Indians also experienced social discrimination. During the war, more than four thousand Indians moved to the Twin Cities; there they inhabited the first Indian ghettos. In 1944, the House Committee Investigating Indian Affairs found that Indians were being "forced to live in unwholesome surroundings or in a dirty, filthy city."[18] "I came to the Twin Cities from the reservation in 1941, the year Pearl Harbor was attacked," wrote Ignatia Broker of the Ojibway. "I went to work in a defense plant and took night classes in order to catch up on the schooling I had missed. . . . Although employment was good because of the labor demand of the huge defense plants, Indian people faced discrimination in restaurants, night clubs, retail and department stores . . . and worst of all, in housing."[19]

But Broker also saw that the urbanization of Indians during the war had created a new pan-Indian identity. The migrations to the cities had given Indians a new sense of cross-tribal "brotherhood." In the war plants, Indian workers started social groups that brought together members of different tribes such as the Ojibway, the Dakota, the Arikara, the Menominee, the Gros Ventres, the Cree, and the Oneida. These peoples had made "the trek to something new," explained Broker. "And because we, all, were isolated in this dominant society, we became an island from which a revival of the spirit began."[20]

This kind of spiritual revitalization also occurred among Navajos fighting in faraway Pacific islands.

A Secret Weapon: An Unbreakable Code

Almost 20 percent of all reservation Native Americans in the armed services came from the Navajo Nation in the Southwest.

The reasons that forty-five hundred Navajos left their reservation to fight in the war were rooted in their history. Since the seventeenth century, when they acquired sheep from the Spanish, the Navajos had been herders. After the annexation of the Southwest at the end of the Mexican-American War in 1848, they found themselves under American rule. In 1863, Kit Carson's troops destroyed Navajo orchards and sheep herds. According to one tribal account, "those who escaped were driven to the Grand Canyon and the Painted Desert, where they hid in the rocks like wild animals, but all except a few were rounded up and caught and taken away to Hwalte [Bosque Redondo]."[21]

"A majority of the Navajos," according to a member of the tribe, "didn't know the reason why they were being rounded up and different stories went around among the people." Many feared that they "would be put to death eventually." When they arrived at Bosque Redondo, they were told by the government to irrigate the land and become farmers. The general in charge of removal explained that the Navajos had to be taken away from "the haunts and hills and hiding places of their country" in order to teach them "the art of peace" and "the truths of Christianity." On their new lands, they would acquire "new habits, new ideas, new modes of life" as they ceased to be "nomads" and became "an agricultural people." In 1868, however, the government changed its policy and informed the Navajos that they were to be resettled on a reservation in their original homeland and issued sheep to replace the stock Kit Carson's forces had destroyed.[22]

Decades later, during the 1930s, Commissioner of Indian Affairs John Collier decided that many of the sheep on the Navajo reservation should be destroyed.[23] Government studies had determined that the reservation had half a million more livestock than their range could support, and that this excess had produced overgrazing and severe soil erosion. Unless the problem of erosion was controlled soon, Collier feared, the sheep-raising Navajos would experience great hardship and suffering.[24]

While Collier was concerned about Navajo survival, he was also worried about white interests. He had received reports that silt from erosion on Navajo land was filling the Colorado River and threatening to clog the Boulder Dam. Under construction during the early 1930s, the dam was designed to supply water to California's Imperial Valley and electricity to Los Angeles. The United States Geological Survey had studied the silt problem and located its origin on the Navajo reservation. Unless sheep overgrazing and hence erosion were controlled, the silt would block economic development in the Southwest.[25]

In order to protect the Boulder Dam from this problem, Collier initiated a stock reduction program on the Navajo reservation. What made the Navajos nervous was the fact that they depended on sheep for their livelihood. "Remember what I've told you," a Navajo instructed his son, "you must not lose, kill or give away young ewes, young mares and cows, because there's a million in one of those. So when anyone who comes to you and tells you to let the herd go. You mustn't let the herd go, because as soon as you do there'll be nothing left of them. The herd is money. It gives you clothing and different kinds of food. Everything comes from the sheep."[26]

But the federal agents took their sheep. One herder saw Collier's program as a "war" against the Navajos. "I sure don't understand why he wants us to be poor. They reduce all sheep. They say they only goin' to let Indians have five sheep, three goats, one cattle, and one horse." Another Navajo recalled bitterly: "A great number of the people's livestock was taken away. Although we were told that it was to restore the land, the fact remains that hunger and poverty stood with their mouths wide open to devour us."[27]

Actually, the stock reduction program was unnecessary as an erosion control program. During the 1950s, scientists would do further research on silt settlement and determine that overgrazing was not the source of the problem.[28] But the Navajos had been telling this to the New Dealers all along. They argued that erosion had been reported as early as the 1890s and was related more to drought than to overgrazing. Trying to explain this cycle of dry weather and subsequent erosion to the government experts, Navajos had pointed out that the 1930s were also years with little rain and predicted that the range would recover when the drought ended. They reminded the government bureaucrats: "We know something about that by nature because we were born here and raised here and we knew about the processes of nature on our range."[29] This wisdom was carried in a Navajo song:

> House made of dawn,
> House made of evening light,
> House made of the dark cloud . . .
> Dark cloud is at the house's door,
> The trail out of it is dark cloud,
> The zigzag lightning stands high upon it . . .
> Happily may I walk.
> Happily, with abundant showers, may I walk.
> Happily, with abundant plants, may I walk.

Grass had always returned along with the rain, Navajos knew as they searched the skies for dark clouds in the dawn and evening.[30]

By the time of Pearl Harbor, the federal government's stock reduction program had made the Navajos dependent on wage income: nearly 40 percent of their annual per capita income of $128 came from wages, mostly from temporary government employment.

Military service during World War II offered an escape from this economic hardship. "I went to war," said Wilson Keedah, "because there were no jobs on the reservation."[31] Eugene Crawford also saw the marines as a way out of squalor. "One of the recruiters tried to attract me into signing up by saying that becoming a marine would be much better than staying on the reservation," he recalled. "As a marine I could learn new skills, travel, and meet interesting people. What did it for me was the dress uniform on the poster. Crisp white hat and gloves, brass buttons against the deep blue material, boy he looked sharp! I wanted a uniform just like that."[32]

Pushed by poverty, the Navajos were also pulled into the military because they possessed something uniquely valuable to the U.S. military — their tribal language. In February 1942, Philip Johnston proposed to the marines that the Navajos be used to transmit military messages through a secure code. The son of a missionary raised on a Navajo reservation, Johnston had played with young Navajos and had become fluent in their language.[33] He explained that the Navajo was "the only tribe" in the U.S. that had not been "infested" with German students during the preceding twenty years. "These Germans, studying the various tribal dialects under the guise of art students, anthropologists, etc., have undoubtedly attained a good working knowledge of all tribal dialects except Navajo. For this reason the Navajo is the only tribe available offering complete security for the type of work under consideration."[34] Johnston's proposal was approved and quickly transformed into a program: in May the first group of Navajo code talkers was sent to San Diego for training.

The base commanding officer, Colonel James L. Underhill, gave a speech to the first class of Navajo marines. "The rest of us in the Marine Corps are Americans," he declared, "but our Americanism goes back at most no more than 300 years. Your ancestors appeared on this continent thousands of years ago — so long ago that there is no written record of them. Through your ancestors, you were Americans long before your fellow Marines were Americans. . . . I know that you will fight like true Navajos, Americans, and Marines."[35]

"The main reason for [enlisting] us Navajos was our language," explained Cozy Stanley Brown. "They liked to use our language in war to carry messages. So we were taught how to use the radio. We had to do that in a hurry. I guess that was why they forced us to complete the training in eight weeks. Then, we got together and discussed how we would do it. We decided to change the name of the airplanes, ships and the English ABC's into the Navajo language. We did the changing. For instance, we named the airplanes 'dive bombers' for ginitsoh (sparrow hawk), because the sparrow hawk is like an airplane — it charges downward at a very fast pace."[36] In their signals, many Navajo words were given military meaning: "a-ye-shi" (eggs) for bombs, "jas-chizzie" (swallow) for torpedo plane, "ne-as-jah" (owl) for observation plane, and "jay-sho" (buzzard) for bomber. The Navajo language could not be understood or mimicked by the Japanese military. Many words had sounds that could be heard only by a native speaker, and its verb forms were so complex that they had to be composed by someone who had grown up with the language. The Navajo code talkers had developed what came to be admired by the U.S. military as "the unbreakable code."[37]

The Navajos who were selected to be code talkers had to be proficient in both their tribal language and English. Minimally, they had to have a tenth-grade education. The code talker, explained Navajo Jimmy King, had "to spell 'artillery,' and then 'bivouac,' 'reconnaisance,' and then words like 'strafing' and some other military terms. . . . You had to know the English language well enough that you could spell whatever you were saying, and the terms accurately so that you can carry on your code talking efficiently and effectively."[38] Accuracy was a necessity. "There are thousands and thousands of lives involved," said King. "Let's say bombing, or strafing, shelling so many *xxx* yards from a certain point. Suppose he gets one digit wrong. Now, that digit might mean shelling, strafing, bombing of our own men."[39]

The Navajos chosen also had to have courage and a high pain threshold. As an instructor, King told his students: "And you think you love your country well enough that you would lay your life down. Supposing you were captured tonight and they had a Sumari [torture], just cutting inch by inch and making you tell what [a Navajo] word meant. And then [you] begin to bleed. The minute you saw that blood begin to run, are you gonna tell? Of course not."[40] The code talkers understood the sacrifice they might have to make. "When I was inducted into the service," said David E. Patterson, "one of the commitments I made was that I was willing to die for my country — the U.S., the Navajo Nation, and my family. My [native] language was my weapon."[41]

But embedded in the deployment of that weapon was an irony. "When I was going to boarding school," said Teddy Draper, Sr., "the U.S. government told us not to speak Navajo, but during the war, they *wanted* us to speak it!"[42] Recalling how he was not allowed to speak Navajo in his boarding school, Keith Little said he viewed his code-talking contribution as a fight for Navajo "freedom," including the cultural right to have their tribal language.[43]

The code talkers wanted to preserve their identity as a distinct people with their own culture and language, and they also wished to be accepted as Americans. However, to many fellow soldiers on the battlefields, the Navajos did not look American. "In Okinawa," Roy Notah said, "I was almost shot by soldiers on my own side, who mistook me for the enemy when I came out of a cave. One of my white buddies came out just in time to save me."[44] At Guadalcanal, Eugene Crawford was watching soldiers unloading supplies when he noticed a crate of canned orange juice and decided to help himself to some juice. "I walked over to their supply depot and started searching," he recalled, "when suddenly I felt cold, hard steel in my back and somebody growling, 'Get out of there, you damn Jap!' I tried to explain that I was with the Raider unit located down the beach, but he pushed that .45 in my back, told me to put my hands up and move out." At the command post, a lieutenant identified Crawford as "one of ours." "It still puzzles me," Crawford remarked, "that they thought I was Japanese."[45] While fighting at Palau, Jimmy King and his fellow Marines were in the "black, dark" jungle at night, feeling their way around. To identify one another, they used a password. "And I run into one fellow and he asked me for the password," he recalled. "I think it was 'lame duck' — anything that had an 'L' in it. [The Japanese had difficulty pronouncing words with "L" in them, making this letter sound like an "R."] So, I said my password, but he said, 'Say it again.' I said, 'lame duck.' He said, 'You-son-of-a-bitch.' Then he stuck a bayonet right in my back — ready to kill me." King dove into a foxhole, and found a friend, Sergeant Curtis, who shouted, "What the hell is going on?" King quickly answered: "They think I'm a Jap. They want to kill me."[46]

But the Navajo code talkers were in the Pacific because they had been chosen to fight the Japanese. They hit every beach from Guadalcanal to Okinawa. Altogether there were 420 Navajo code talkers, sending and receiving reports from the field commanders. Their secret messages carried information on enemy gun locations, movements of American troops, artillery fire, plane bombardments, and the sites of enemy entrenchments and strategic lookout points.

In February 1945, the Navajo code talkers participated in one of the most important Pacific battles — the fight for Iwo Jima. "It just seemed like the island was burning early in the morning," one of them recalled. "This shelling was coming down just like rain." Teddy Draper never forgot the fear he felt during the beach landing: "There were a lot of machine guns going along all the way around [Mount] Suribachi about 50 feet apart from the bottom to the top. Just flying shells, all over. You couldn't see. And I thought, 'I don't know if I'm going to live or not.'"[47] During the first hour of fighting, Thomas H. Begay "was scared, very scared." He vividly remembered: "Mortars and artillery were landing everywhere, but I wasn't hit."[48]

The battle focused on Mount Suribachi, a vital observation post for the Japanese defense of the island. On the third day of the battle, February 23, Paul Blatchford was pinned down by Japanese machine-gun fire. "We were flat on our backs, when we saw the flag go up on Suribachi," he said. "All the white boys started yelling, 'Hey Chief, it's all over now!' I said, 'Not here!'" Blatchford could see the American flag waving in the distance, but his unit was still under heavy enemy fire. On Suribachi itself, Navajo code talker Teddy Draper never forgot that moment of victory. "I was close to 100 feet down on the north slope when Sergeant Ray told me to send a message that Suribachi had been secured and at what time and get it down to headquarters. I didn't see the flag go up, but I passed the message when it happened."[49] The message read: "Naastsosi Thanzie Dibeh Shida Dahnesta Tkin Shush Wollachee Moasi Lin Achi." When the message was received on a ship, a Navajo translator announced that the American flag was flying over Mount Suribachi.[50]

During the first two days of the invasion, Navajo code talkers worked around the clock, sending more than eight hundred battle messages without an error. Signal officer Major Howard Conner later declared: "Without the Navajos the marines would never have taken Iwo Jima."[51]

Finally, the marines had won the battle of Iwo Jima. The fight for this island of only eight square miles was extremely bloody: nineteen thousand marines were wounded and seven thousand killed. The American dead included four Navajo code talkers — Peter Johnson, Paul Kinlahcheeny, Sam Morgan, and Willie Notah. Among the wounded was code talker James Gleason. "Jimmy and Paul Kinlahcheeny were running messages when they got hit," Mrs. Malissa Gleason said. "Machine gun fire caught both of them. Paul was hit right across the stomach, and Jimmie was shot in the left ankle. Paul's last words to Jimmie were, 'Tell my folks.' Jimmie crawled into a shell hole, and that was where he saw the flag being raised on the mountain."[52]

As Navajo and white soldiers fought together against a common enemy, many of them came to know one another. "One of my friends was in the same foxhole as I was," said Navajo soldier Sidney Bedoni. "He was a Mormon from Salt Lake City, Utah. He gave me his parents' address and a note to them if he got shot."[53] Charlie Miguel recalled how he had learned to drill and handle a rifle in a boot camp, where he found himself among whites for the first time in his life: "Every evening we drank beer, ten cents a bottle, and had nice chow. I got along all right with the white boys. I didn't know much about English, but I got along all right."[54]

The Indian "Hero" of Iwo Jima

Away from his reservation for the first time in his life, Ira Hayes also got along with his fellow white marines. A Pima of Arizona, he belonged to an agricultural people. Before the arrival of Columbus in the New World, the Pimas had developed an irrigation system to bring the water of the Gila River to their fields. But their way of life changed when the United States pursued its "manifest destiny" by declaring war on Mexico. During this conflict, the Pimas became an American ally, supplying food to the troops in the Southwest. After the war, the federal government recognized the Pimas as the "first appropriators" of Gila River water and guaranteed them an annual allocation of water from "the normal flow of the Gila." However, white settlers began to occupy lands upriver and built dams to divert the water to their farms. The lands of the Pimas became dry, and their crops failed; by 1942, economic prospects on the reservation had become grim for young men like Hayes.[55]

Only nineteen years old when Pearl Harbor was attacked, Hayes was employed as a laborer in the internment camp for Japanese Americans that had been set up on his reservation. In the fall of 1942, Hayes joined the marines. The service offered him employment and also an opportunity to fight for his country. Hayes saw himself as a Pima American. Like most members of his tribe, his parents were Presbyterians, and his family name reflected a long history of assimilation. When the cavalry took a census of western Indians in the nineteenth century, they had given the Pimas English, Scottish, and Irish names.

Hayes's letters to his parents offer a detailed personal account of his life as a marine. In a letter from the training camp in San Diego, he wrote on August 29, 1942: "Gee, this is the first time I had to write. . . . There are quite a lot of Indian boys here. I met Marvin Jones and we are in the same platoon. We are in the same tent with another Indian boy from New Mexico. . . . They gave us a Marine haircut $1\frac{1}{2}$ inches long and you should see me." He signed his letter: "From a guy who's proud he's a Marine and in his country's service."

On September 8, Hayes wrote home about his drill instructors: "One of them is always fooling with me. Asking me where is my tomahawk and bows and arrows. Then he'll start to make fun of the Indians and we'll argue. He's trying to put Marvin and the other Indian boys from Oklahoma and myself on the boxing show Saturday night. He says he's trying to prove that Indians can fight better than most white men." His fellow white marines were curious about Hayes as an Indian. On September 20, he wrote home: "The fellows are swell chums and we lay awake way into the night and they keep shooting questions at us Indians and we have to answer. They don't believe me when I tell them that I can't speak my own language but that I understand it."

In order to regain the dignity of his people, Hayes believed Indians had to make sacrifices in the war. In a letter to his parents, January 28, 1943, he wrote: "I guess you heard about the death of Richard Lewis of Sacaton, who was killed with the Marines in the South Pacific. We Pimas can be proud that he carried the fight straight to the dirty, sneaking Japs. The Indians can expect lots of casualties because there are so many of us in this war." Four months later in the Pacific, Hayes again remembered Lewis in a letter to his parents: "I'm glad you sent me the clipping about the Memorial Service in honor of Richard." He described how he had "wiped tears of pride" from his eyes when he read that Lewis was the "first Pima Indian killed in the War for the Four Freedoms." Hayes believed the sacrifice had a specific purpose: "Us Indians have so much to be thankful for, and so much to gain in this war."[56]

But the war would require terrible sacrifices on the battlefield. At Bougainville, Hayes and his fellow marines faced the ferocity of the tropical land. A marine described the "jungle" as the "practically impenetrable 'green hell' of popular imagination," varying from mangrove swamps to vine-draped forests with an overwhelming "dark stench." In the overgrown density, fighting was intense, intimate. Ed Castle vividly recounted the firefights: "They were firing from every direction. We didn't get a chance to return their fire for a while until we could observe where it was coming from. We just kept firing at the treetops. One was firing at Hayes and me. . . . I ducked down in my foxhole and hollered over to a friend of mine, Sam Taylor, to ask if he could see where he was shooting from. I gave him the direction . . . and it wasn't but a few minutes until he spotted the discharge from his rifle. Sam shot and brought him down. He was huge! He had campaign ribbons on his chest."[57]

Close-contact combat led to grisly behavior on the battlefield. Marine William Faulkner had to recover some bodies of American soldiers. "When we reached the spot where they were buried," he said, "we found the Japs had dug up the bodies and driven wooden stakes through their arms, chests, and legs, pinning them to the ground."[58] Marines also mutilated the corpses of Japanese soldiers. They sawed gold teeth from their mouths to make into chains and necklaces; they cut off heads and dried out skulls for souvenirs. "In the mutilations," biographer William Bradford Huie wrote, "Hayes recognized that some of the fiendishness came from difference. He doubted his buddies would mutilate Germans in the same fashion. To Hayes the Japs were 'dirty bastards'; to his buddies they were 'dirty yellow bastards.' Not once, in letters or conversation, did Hayes call a Jap *yellow*."[59]

In early 1944, Hayes returned home on furlough. The Pimas gathered to honor and pray for him. "I'm proud of my people," he

told them. "I'm proud I'm a Christian. I'm proud of my parents."
He promised: "When this war is over I'm going to repay all of you
for the fine things you've given me." Hayes shared a dream of a
bright future for Indian-white relations: "I think some fine things
are coming out of this war. Everybody is going to understand one
another better. White men are going to understand Indians; and
Indians will understand white men. I want to tell you I've had
some of the best white buddies anybody ever had. They have been
friendly and faithful . . . and I know I have friends in them who
would die with me."[60]

After his visit home, Hayes was shipped back to the Pacific
front, where he participated in the invasion of Iwo Jima. There
Hayes had an experience that dramatically changed his life. After
the marines had finally taken Mount Suribachi, a small group of
soldiers raised an American flag on the summit — an action pho-
tographed by Sergeant Lou Lowery. A short time later, when Joe
Rosenthal of the Associated Press climbed to the top of Suribachi,
he found a movie cameraman preparing to film a staged second
raising of the flag. Hayes had not been present when Lowery took
his photograph. However, he happened to be nearby when Rosenthal was getting ready to take a photograph of the reenactment.
Hayes was carrying a telephone line to be connected to an observation post and was asked to join the soldiers preparing to pose
for the photograph. Navajo code talker Teddy Draper recalled
what happened. "I was about 100 feet away when I saw the men
struggle with that long piece of pipe. I saw the lieutenant look
around for an extra man to help, then he yelled, 'Ira Hayes! Ira
Hayes!' Then two more of the guys jumped up to help them, and
the big flag went up. It was a sight to behold."[61]

At this second flag-raising, Rosenthal took photographs and
sent one of them on the wire news service. Unaware that the picture actually depicted a staged raising of the American flag on
Mount Suribachi, editors of newspapers and magazines across the
country published it. Instantly, Rosenthal's photograph become
the most famous news image of World War II — six marines, face-

less, their bodies bent forward beneath an American flag unfurled in victory.

When Hayes was identified as one of the flag-raisers, he suddenly became a war hero. Three of the six men in the photograph had been killed in subsequent fighting. Hayes along with Rene Gagnon and John Bradley were flown back to the United States to help lead the Seventh War Loan Drive. Hayes knew the photograph was a fraud. He had not been there for the real flag-raising, and he also tried to make another important correction: the marine at the foot of the pole, who had been officially identified as Henry Hansen, was actually Harlon Block. But Hayes was told by his commanding officer that both men were dead and that he should keep quiet about the matter.[62]

In Washington, D.C., Sergeant W. Keyes Beech was the official guardian for the bond tour. He explained to Hayes: "Chief, this is strange duty for you, and I know how you feel. You got to understand that a bond tour is show business. Show business is make-believe. You make up stories, and it's all right because it's for a good cause. And in this business you're representing the Marine Corps." Hayes asked: "What about this crock o' shit about the flag-raising?" Beech answered: "You let me and the reporters tell that story, Chief. You forget it and smile and nod your head."[63]

Following orders, Hayes went off on the bond tour, and the reporters told the story. "The tattered American flag once planted on the summit of Mount Suribachi, Iwo Jima, fluttered today from the flagstaff of the Capitol," the Associated Press reported. "With full military ceremonies, it was hoisted by the three survivors of the little group of fighting men who carried it to the top of the peak of the volcanic mountain."[64]

The bond drive began with a visit to the White House, where Hayes and his fellow heroes presented a poster of the famous flag-raising to President Harry Truman. From New York City, Hayes wrote to his family on Waldorf Hotel stationery, May 10, 1945: "I can't hardly realize I'm here in the most famous hotel in the world. . . . Tomorrow is a big day. We go to the Roxy Theater in the morning to make an appearance. Then we go to Times Square to unveil the monument of the flag-raising on Iwo Jima which is 25 feet high. And then the dinner to be held in our honor in the evening. Then we leave for Philadelphia and Boston. . . ." The experience was exhilarating for this Pima lad from an arid Arizona reservation. In Chicago, Hayes attended a dinner in his honor sponsored by the National Congress of American Indians. Assuring Indians that "good things" would come out of this war, Hayes declared: "White men are gonna understand Indians better, and it's gonna be a better world."[65]

But the tour also had irritating and disturbing moments. Reporters asked Hayes questions like: "How'd you get a name like Ira Hayes, Chief? I never heard of an Indian with a name like that."[66] Such insults angered Hayes and aggravated the distress he felt about his unearned celebrity status. He shrouded himself in silence. Asked to speak at one of the bond dinners, Hayes muttered: "I'm glad to be in your city an' I hope you buy a lot of bonds."[67] During the tour, Hayes drank heavily and became an embarrassment to the Marine Corps. General A. A. Vendegrift complained to Beech: "I understand your Indian got drunk on you last night?" Shortly afterward, Hayes was abruptly relieved of his bond-tour duty and sent back to the front. The press reported that the "brave Indian" wanted to return to military action in the Pacific.[68]

After the peace, an emptiness filled Hayes. He had hoped his people would be able to take care of themselves on their own land. But the war had made no difference in their lives: their reservation still had little water to irrigate the fields. Unemployed and depressed, Hayes drifted into alcoholic delirium and was frequently jailed for drunkenness and vagrancy. On one occasion, as a "trusty" prisoner in Phoenix, Hayes was working at the airport as a janitor. There a tourist was told that the man with the mop was the Indian hero of Iwo Jima. Upset by Hayes's degraded condition, he called Pauline Brown of the Indian Bureau and complained that Hayes should be in a veterans hospital if he had an alcohol problem. The man then offered to pay the jail fine for Hayes and give him money until the Bureau could find him a job. Brown bluntly told him: "Hayes' people have lived here three thousand years. What Hayes needs is not money but enough water to irrigate fifty acres of land. . . . While you're sunning your carcass in the Biltmore pool this afternoon, you remember that Hayes needs just about as much water a year as it takes to operate the pool."[69]

Hayes regretted his fame as the Indian "hero" of Iwo Jima: "People shoved drinks in our hands and said we were heroes. I was sick. I guess I was about to crack up, thinking of those guys who were better men than me not coming back at all. . . . On the reservation I got hundreds of letters and I got sick of hearing about the flag-raising and sometimes I wished the guy had never made the picture."[70] "I want to be out on my own," he explained sadly. "But out in Arizona the white race looks down on my own . . . and I don't stand a chance anywhere."[71]

Asked during an interview whether he had known Ira Hayes, Navajo code talker Thomas H. Begay answered: "Yeah, everybody, all the boys knew him. He was a very quiet man. He never got in trouble, didn't drink — until I guess he got back after, he said he was going back to the States for something. And when he got back over here I guess he started drinking."[72] On November 10, 1954, Hayes was honored at the dedication of the bronze Iwo Jima Monument in Arlington, Virginia. Several weeks later, on January 23, Hayes was found on a street in Bapchule: drunk, he had fallen and drowned in his own vomit.[73] An idealistic and spirited young man, Hayes had wanted not only to defend America but also to restore dignity to the Pimas as a native people. In the end, he was a casualty of the war.

Ceremony: War Heroes Return to the Reservation

After returning to the reservation, many Navajo veterans had ceremonies performed on them in order to be purified of their war experiences. George Kirk kept having dreams of enemy soldiers jumping into his foxhole; so he went to see a medicine man for a ceremony called the "Enemy Way," a symbolic slaying of the "enemy presence."[74] Coming home after his imprisonment in a Japanese POW camp for three years, Claude Hatch had a ceremony to help him heal from his traumatic battle experiences. "My father passed away shortly before I was liberated," he recalled, "but after returning home my relatives decided to have the Enemy Way ceremony for me because of all the things that had happened to me."[75] At the end of a ceremony, a medicine man told Samuel Smith: "Now my son, don't tell it no more to anybody, anywhere. That way you won't be bothered in the future."[76]

After his discharge from the marines, Dan Akee reentered high school with the support of the G.I. bill. "But I was sick at night," he told an interviewer. "I was getting nightmares all the time. Every time when I shut my eyes, I would see or hear enemy coming or I find myself yelling." The nightmares kept haunting him for over a year until Akee went "completely deaf." Finally, his father arranged a Gourd Dance. During the ceremony something "unbelievable" happened to Akee. "The first night I heard this drum, and my ear popped out and I could hear again. And from there at this Gourd Dance I gained my weight back and all this nightmare was not bad. . . . And so it was all in my mind, what I had been through. Nearly four invasions. 'Cause in my mind, I think too much about it. And that might be the reason that I was getting these nightmares. So that's the reason why I never did finish my high school. So after I got well, I just got married."[77]

Sidney Bedoni's Squaw Dance ceremony was also an act of spiritual healing, a way to put his past behind him and go on with life. "I took all my clothes off and then went into the hogan," he said. "Leave my clothes out there, my uniform. And then they have that sing for me. Get all washed up and everything. See, all that stuff that's on you, they think it's evil or something like that. They trying to chase them away. . . . That all my mind won't be overseas or anything like that. All my mind will come back to me when they have that Squaw Dance for me."[78]

Keats Begay said that he had a Squaw Dance ceremony performed on him, but he noted that there were some veterans who were still emotionally ill and were "receiving disability income."[79] Indeed, there were veterans who did not easily recover from the psychic wounds of the war.

One such veteran was described in a letter a woman had written to a marine commanding officer:

> I don't know I do rite in writin you this but no harm try. It about Big Bill ——— , can he be kept from comin home to he family, he was a fine guy till he got to be Marine, got big Head so many stripes on sleeve and decorate in front, first time come home got heap drunk, was maybe sick, cold not so bad, no want go back, next time staid over got wife take back, and made lie for him, she no like, she scared of him, all time want take car, her need live ¼ mile out of town, she work hard, he all time send for money, talk he got woman, want car is talk, last week sends from town off far, her come after him, she no money, no gas, no go, he cot ride, made hell all time, argue, argue, car, money, he hit her maby broke nose, black both eyes, kick her round, he sure bad umbra, now take car, no paid for, how he pay, she works for his two chilen and one with till school out, and he put other woman fore her for spite. Bill no not me I get this from friends, they say fraid we write, he kill them and her maby. I going away tomorrow, try not let him know where, you get these army police here, maby you say they told. Her land woman for over one year, I sure will back this up.
>
> Mrs. B———
> No like bad man buse woman.[80]

Why men like this veteran had become drunken and abusive husbands was explained by Oliver La Farge of the Association of American Indian Affairs. Writing in *Harper's Magazine* in 1947, he described how a Navajo had returned from the war only to feel he was "in a box" of poverty. The land was too dry for farming, and his welfare check was too meager. "He knew what he was going to do now," La Farge wrote. "He was going to hook a ride into town, sell his coat, buy a pint of bootleg rotgut, and get drunk. He hated what he was doing, but he could not help himself. He could not get out of the box; he could only momentarily forget it."[81]

Indeed, the problem for many despondent Navajo veterans was not simply the cultural and psychological difficulty of readjusting to reservation life after experiencing battlefield stresses. There was little economic opportunity on the reservation waiting for these military heroes. A year after the war, the New Mexico Association on Indian Affairs reported that the average male on the Navajo reservation was earning less than $100 a year. The association concluded: "The poor economic situation of the Navajo is beyond belief." The reason for this devastating suffering was revealed in a single set of statistics: the tribal population had reached sixty thousand in 1946, and the reservation lands could support only thirty-five thousand people.[82]

Although the Navajo code talkers were not victorious in their war for "freedom from want," they had won an important cultural battle: on the bloodsoaked beaches of Pacific islands, they had demonstrated the value of our society's cultural diversity. "We, the Navajo people," declared Kee Etsicitty, "were very fortunate to contribute our language as a code for our country's victory. For this I strongly recommend we teach our children the language our ancestors were blessed with at the beginning of time. It is very sacred and represents the power of life."[83]

5

A DREAM OF EL NORTE
Crossing the Tracks

"Americans All": Soldiers of "La Raza"

WHEN HE HEARD THE NEWS of the Japanese attack on Pearl Harbor, Alex Romandia was stunned. As a Mexican American, he felt righteous indignation. "Our country had been attacked," he told his brother Roberto, "and we had to defend it." Twenty-seven years old, Romandia was working in Hollywood as a stunt man and had befriended many Jewish intellectuals. Feeling rejected by the larger society, Romandia and several of his Jewish friends decided to volunteer for the army. "All of us," he said, "had to prove ourselves — to show that we were more American than the Anglos."[1]

Also living in Los Angeles, Ralph Lazo chose to register as Japanese and was taken to the Manzanar internment camp. "My Japanese-American friends at Belmont High were ordered to evacuate the West Coast," Lazo stated, "so I decided to go with them. Who can say I haven't got Japanese blood in me? Who knows what kind of blood runs in their veins?" Two years later, the authorities discovered that he was actually Mexican American. After leaving the internment camp, Lazo joined the U.S. Army.[2]

Altogether half a million Mexican Americans enlisted in the armed services — a significant proportion of this group's population of 2,690,000. They were laborers, farmers, owners of small businesses, and students; many came from the "barrios" — Mexican neighborhoods with names like "Westside" in San Antonio, "Magnolia" in Houston, "Larrimer" in Denver, "Maravilla Chiques" in Oxnard, and "East Los Angeles." Culturally they varied from English speakers to Spanish speakers, from those who were "Americanized" to those who were "Mexicanized." Many were multicultural. The "pochos" [young Mexican Americans] of California spoke little Spanish and socialized with both Anglos and Mexicans. They enjoyed Spanish songs, Latin rhythms, and Mexican mariachis as well as the latest American songs and dances.[3]

The war offered Mexican Americans a chance to claim the United States as their country and their right to equality. Urging Mexican Americans to join their Anglo compatriots in arms, the Congreso de Pueblos de Habla Española (the Spanish-Speaking Congress) declared: "We are also children of the United States. We will defend her."[4] One of the defenders, soldier Anthony Navarro, explained: "We wanted to prove that while our cultural ties were deeply rooted in Mexico, our home was here in this country."[5] The Mexican-American Movement pointed out that military service was serving as a path toward a brighter future. "It has shown those 'across the track' that we all share the same problems," declared this civil rights organization. "It has shown them what the Mexican American will do, what responsibility he will take and what leadership qualities he will demonstrate. After this struggle, the status of the Mexican American will be different."[6] A democratic discontent stirred a soldier to declare: "We too, were entitled to work, play, and to live as we pleased. Weren't *all* Americans entitled to the same opportunities?"[7]

From the barrios arose the war slogan "Americans All" and the song "Soldado Razo"(Common Soldier):

I leave as a common soldier,
I'm going to join the ranks.
I will be among the Brave boys
who leave their beloved mothers
and sweethearts in tears,
crying for their departure.
I'm leaving for the war, contented.
I'll have my rifle and gun ready.
When the shooting is over,
I will return as a Sergeant.
The only one thing I regret,
Is leaving my poor Mother alone.
Oh brunette Virgin, please take care of her.
Watch over her, she is a wonderful person.
Please take care of her till I return.
I will depart at early morn tomorrow,
right at the break of day.
And so . . . hereforth goes another Mexican
who is willing to gamble his life.
I say goodbye with this song . . .
Long live this Country of mine.[8]

One of the young men who said good-bye was César Chávez. When the war began, he was a farm laborer, forced to do stoop labor. "I would chop out a space with the short-handle hoe in the right hand while I felt with my left to pull out all but one plant as I made the next chop," recalled Chávez. "There was a rhythm, it went very fast. It's like being nailed to a cross. You have to walk twisted, as you're stooping over, facing the row, and walking perpendicular to it." In 1944, seventeen-year-old Chávez joined the navy. At boot camp in San Diego, he discovered that discrimination was a widely shared condition. "I saw this white kid fighting, because someone had called him a Polak and I found out he was Polish and hated the word Polak. He fought every time he heard it. I began to learn something, that others suffered too."[9]

Mexican Americans like Chávez left behind friends and families. "All around us," Socorro Diáz Blanchard recalled, "boys were going into the service."[10] Drafted in 1942, Nicholás Ortiz was sent to North Africa. In her first letter to Ortiz, migrant farm worker Mariá Louisa Hernández wrote: "About not seeing each other for a long time, I really don't know what to say or think. I had hopes of seeing you again soon, but I guess I will have to wait. . . . After all it is a privilege for a girl to have someone fighting for her. Darling, I do realize that it is a serious problem we've got and that is why I'm backing you."[11] Many families had several members in the armed forces. "When the Second World War started my brother, José, my brother-in-law, my cousins, and my cousins' husbands served," said Socorro Delgado. "At one time there were as many as fifteen of our immediate family who had gone to war! Every Friday Father Burns and Father Rossetti had a novena for the Sorrowful Mother. We would go and mention the names of the boys who were in the war. There was a victory candelabra with seven candles, and the candles would be lit. They lasted for a week."[12]

At home, families waited anxiously for news about husband, sons, and brothers at the battlefront. "It was very depressing when the men went off to war because it shattered our community," recalled Juanita Vásquez. "Whenever a young man was killed in action, we all felt the same pain because we all went to school together and were close friends."[13] Margaret Villanueva Lambert worked on an assembly line in a defense factory. "I remember a few times during the war," she said, "when I was working and all of a sudden there would be a loud scream followed by uncontrollable crying of a woman who had learned that her husband or son was dead. We all feared that moment when we, too, could be requested to go to the front office and find a representative of the military with an attache case tucked under his arm with a letter for the next of kin. The workers would always collect a fund for these women."[14]

Filling the pages of the Los Angeles Spanish-language newspaper *La Opinión,* articles told the story of Mexican-American military service and sacrifice. "The Navarez family has seven sons in the U.S. Armed Forces and Navy. They were sent a letter of congratulation by James Forrestal of the U.S. Navy. The family is from Los Angeles." "Four brothers are in the military: Ray, Manuel, and Ignacio have been in France, and Joe in the Pacific. Their mother, Mrs. Villalobos, lives in Los Angeles."[15]

This community newspaper also announced the enlistments of women: "Faustina Merino has been sworn in in the local recruiting station. Miss Merino graduated last year from Roosevelt High School and left her job to fulfill her desires as she expressed: 'I want to do more for victory than just buy war bonds, and to replace my cousin who died in combat.'" "Three Mexican Women Enlisted as WAVES: They are Mariá Moreno, Luisa Chávez, Herlinda Lillian Campos. They showed interest in nursing courses so it is likely that they will learn to attend to the wounded soldiers."[16]

The Spanish-language newspaper proudly published news of military awards: "Sergeant José López was awarded the highest honor in the military — the Congressional Medal of Honor — after killing 100 Germans. He is from Mission, Texas, and is referred to as a 'one-man army.'" "Sergeant Francisco Navarro of the Army Air Force is currently enjoying a well-earned rest after flying 295 missions (800 hours of flight) aboard a C-47 in India-Burma. He has earned the Distinguished Flying Cross, two Oak Leaves." "The Congressional Medal of Honor was awarded to Macario García from Camp Hood, Texas, for bravery in combat. García, a Mexican national, became a U.S. citizen. He lived in Sugarland, Texas, growing and picking cotton."[17]

Casualties were also reported in *La Opinión:* "Gustavo Romero, Sgt., was killed in action in Luzon. He has three brothers: Epifanio, Marines, Enrique, Navy, and Jess, Army, who is in Germany." "Raymundo Cervantes died in combat in Iwo Jima. He graduated from Fremont High School and was the oldest of six." "Roberto Rincon died at Okinawa. PFC Rincon had been honorably discharged, but he re-enlisted after the attack on Pearl Harbor."[18]

In an autobiographical statement written in 1994, José D. Carrasco gave an eye-level account of the war. After the D-Day Invasion, he had joined the U.S. forces in Normandy, where he experienced his first day of combat. "I remember it was very dark and raining," he said. "We attacked, we had to cross some open space and the earth was muddy everywhere we took a step. Our feet would go down in the mud." When enemy artillery fire began exploding around him, Carrasco fell face down. Shrapnel hit a 60 mm mortar he was carrying. "If it hadn't been for the mortar, it would have hit me on the right side of my head. So I believe that the mortar saved me."

Then, in December came the Battle of the Bulge. Carrasco vividly described the fighting at Bastogne. "The trees were covered with snow. Visibility was poor. I somehow noticed an enemy machine gun, three enemy soldiers were ready and waiting for us to go by. They were camouflaged very good." Carrasco surprised the would-be ambushers from behind and captured them. "We were still in the Battle of the Bulge and one day, it was getting late so it was getting dark and another soldier and I saw about four or five enemy soldiers going into a broken down house, and my friend said, 'Let's go and get them!' I said, 'Let's wait until tomorrow morning. They are looking for a place to spend the night, just like us.' So we waited until the next morning and went slowly to the place where they were. When we got there, much to our surprise they were sitting down. They froze to death during the night."

While guarding captured German soldiers, Carrasco and his fellow soldiers were having a conversation in Spanish. A German officer approached them and gave them a snappy salute. "He spoke to us in Spanish! Boy, were we surprised. I guess he was surprised to hear us speaking in Spanish too!" The POW explained that he had spent time in Central America; Carrasco said the war was over. "So we saluted and said our good-byes."[19]

Like Carrasco, Raul Morín was also on the European battlefront. He had enlisted in March 1944 when the draft reached into the older age bracket for recruits and reclassified married men. Although Morín had a wife and three small children, he welcomed the call to arms. "Most of us," he wrote in his autobiography, "were more than glad to be given the opportunity to serve in the war. It did not matter whether we were looked upon as Mexicans; the war soon made us all *genuine* Americans, eligible and available immediately to fight and to defend our country, the United States of America."

At Camp Roberts, where he did basic training, Morín found army buddies of "la raza" — mixed-race Latinos of Indian, Spanish, and African ancestries. They were from the Los Angeles barrios of Maravilla, Flats, Dog Town, Boyle Heights, Vernon, and Watts. "Every evening," Morín wrote in his autobiography, "after getting back to camp from the long hikes and hard field problems, you could always see them jostling around. Young *'pachuquitos'* [Mexican-American teenagers dressed in flashy clothes], who often bragged of being veterans of the *Pachuco-Zoot-Suit war* [the 1943 Los Angeles race riot], would be wrestling, fighting, cursing, and yelling."

Camp Roberts also gave them a chance to make friends with Anglos. Mexican Americans "ganged around together," Morín recalled, "and in addition, we had picked up a lot of *'gabacho'* (Anglo) buddies. For instance there was Tony Despagne, born and raised in Texas, who could understand *chicano* [working-class Mexican Spanish] talk better than English . . . Leonard Muschinsky, a young Polish kid . . . and Robert Smargeanian, an Armenian, who got indoctrinated with *pachuco-ism* in East Los Angeles." They got "a bang out of hanging around with the Mexican-American *plebe* [ordinary people]."

After basic training, Morín boarded a ship bound for Europe. "Now here I was on my way over, and with the possibility of never returning," he wrote. "What if I were killed? . . . What would happen to my wife, my three children? My mother? . . . All the horrible thoughts imaginable would grip me, and before I could find the answers, other thoughts would begin to swirl in. I remembered about us, the Mexican Americans . . . how the Anglo had pushed and held back our people in the Southwest. . . . Why fight for

America when you have not been treated as an American?" But he was overwhelmed by feelings he had for his American homeland, the country of his birth. "All we wanted," he decided, "was a chance to prove how loyal and American we were."

Assigned to Company I of the Third Battalion, Morín had his first combat experience at Forêt de Parroy in France. His unit had been ordered to charge German positions in the woods. In notes written on the battlefield, Morín recorded his fear: "Things are happening too fast for me. . . . I'm just a green replacement and I feel inadequate. . . . Smoke shells explode near the woods, and the whole area is clouded with smoke." Morín and his fellow soldiers attacked. "We go down the hill into a gully and the Jerries open up, they throw everything at us . . . murderous artillery, machine guns. . . ." Morín jumped into a trench. "As I turn to my right, I am startled and surprised, all of a sudden, I see him — my first dead German! how frightening and grotesque he looks! And I can't keep my eyes off him. His eyes are wide open. He has a bullet hole in his left temple where the blood still trickles out. His face is turning blue, his mouth is wide open. He is still standing behind his machine gun."

In his field notes, Morín described the death of another soldier — an Italian American from San Francisco. At a small village close to the German border on December 14, his platoon head, Lieutenant Marty Bachiero, was preparing to lead an assault. "Behind a tree," wrote Morín, "I am surprised to find Lt. Bachi with a very frightened look on his face. 'What's the matter, Bachi? You're not scared?' I only meant it as a joke, but he has taken it as an insult. He comes out from behind, stands erect and orders, with a twist of anger in his voice, 'Let's go!'" At a small creek, Morín and Bachi knelt behind a fence. "Lt. Bachi starts to rise to get a better view. 'Bachi!' I yell, 'Stay down!' Too late." Bachi was hit, his body falling on Morín. "He has been hit right above and between his eyes. The top of his head is torn off, his brains spill out. There is still a quiver in his membrane."

Crossing into Germany shortly afterward, Morín was almost

killed. In a night assault, he suddenly stumbled onto a German foxhole and heard a voice, *"Achtung! Wer is dort!"* He jumped back quickly, but a flare went up and bullets were flying everywhere around him. Hit in both legs, he lay in the snow. The medic treating him, said: "Well, Morín, you got your million dollar wound!"

With casts on both legs, Morín was sent to De Witt General hospital near Auburn, California. "Among the patients there from Los Angeles I met 'Memo' Terrazas, who was slowly recovering from a brain injury, partially paralyzed, and loss of speech. I also met Frank Carrillo, and Florencio Rodríguez, both veterans of the North African campaign; Vincent Gonzáles, Ernie Ochoa, Larry Vásquez, George Yorba. . . . There must have been over one thousand Mexican Americans in that hospital."[20]

Indeed, Mexican-American soldiers had given their lives and limbs for their country. Expressing gratitude, California Congressman Jerry Voorhis pointed out the debt America owed to the people of the barrio: "As I read the casualty lists from my state, I find anywhere from one-fourth to one-third of those names are names such as Gonzáles or Sánchez, names indicating that the very lifeblood of our citizens of Latin-American descent in the uniform of the armed forces of the United States is being poured out to win victory in the war. We ought not to forget that. We ought to resolve that in the future every single one of these citizens shall have the fullest and freest opportunity which this country is capable of giving him, to advance to such positions of influence and eminence as their own personal capacities make possible."[21]

An Army of Workers: The Bracero and Rosa the Riveter

Mexican Americans also served on the home front, in a country many of them still regarded as "occupied Mexico." Once a part of Mexico, the Southwest had been annexed at the end of the Mexican-American War. During the early twentieth century, large numbers of immigrants crossed the border into a country they affectionately called "El Norte." A song conveyed their dreams:

If only you could see how nice
the United States is;
that is why the Mexicans
are crazy about it.

Your watch is on its chain
and your scarf-pin in your tie
and your pockets always filled
with plenty of silver.[22]

In California, a Mexican recounted the immigration fever that
had swept through entire villages. People wrote to friends and relatives back home: "Come! come! come over it is good here." The
news set off a chain reaction that brought "others and others." In
this way, just one person had led to the migration of twenty-eight
families from his village. A land of promise in the north was beck-
oning. "Since I was very small I had the idea of going out to know
the world, to go about a lot in every direction," Jésus Garza recalled. "As I had heard a lot about the United States it was my
dream to come here."[23]

Mexicans were pulled here by the labor needs of agriculture. In
California, farmers turned increasingly to Mexican labor as immigration laws excluded Chinese and Japanese laborers. By the 1920s,
at least three-fourths of California's 200,000 farm laborers were
Mexicans.[24] Between 1900 and 1930, the Mexican population in
the Southwest grew from 375,000 to 1,160,000.

Although farmers were eager to employ Mexican laborers, they
did not intend them to stay permanently. "While the Mexicans are
not easily assimilated," an immigration commission stated, "this is
not of very great importance as long as most of them return to
their native land after a short time." The strategy was to bring
Mexicans here so long as their labor was needed and then return
them to Mexico when the demand diminished.[25]

The Great Depression drastically reduced the need for labor. Already on the edge of survival, Mexicans were pushed into jobless-

ness and deepening poverty. Rendered superfluous as laborers and blamed for white unemployment, they became the targets of repatriation programs. "If we were rid of the aliens who have entered this country illegally since 1931," a Los Angeles county supervisor declared, "our present unemployment problem would shrink to the proportions of a relatively unimportant flat spot in business."[26] By the tens of thousands, Mexicans were placed in box cars and shipped across the border. Many of them had been born in the United States. The Los Angeles Chamber of Commerce estimated that 60 percent of the "repatriated" children were American citizens "without very much hope of ever coming back into the United States."[27] Altogether about 400,000 Mexicans were "repatriated."

Forced to leave El Norte, Mexicans crossed the border, with a bitter song on their lips:

> And so I take my leave,
> may you be happy.
> Here ends the song,
> but the depression goes on forever.[28]

However, employers viewed repatriation as a temporary program; the border existed only when Mexican labor was not needed. "The Los Angeles industrialists," observed Carey McWilliams, "confidently predict that the Mexican can be lured back, whenever we need him."[29]

The border disappeared again when the war began. To meet new demands for agricultural production, the federal government initiated the "bracero" program (from the Spanish word "brazos," or arms).[30] Recruited in Mexico, these guest laborers would work here under contract and then be returned at the end of their term. Their labor agreement specified several conditions:

> Discrimination against braceros is forbidden.
>
> They shall be guaranteed transportation, food, hospitalization and repatriation.

They shall not be used to displace other workers nor to lower wages.

Braceros will be allowed to form associations and elect a leader to represent them.[31]

On September 29, 1942, the first 1,500 braceros were brought to California by train. During the war years, the federal government spent $100 million on this labor importation program and recruited workers by the thousands: 4,000 in 1942, 52,000 in 1943, 62,000 in 1944, and 120,000 a year later. By 1947, 200,000 of them had worked in the U.S.[32]

Agriculture was a "war industry": it contributed a vital military need — food. The braceros worked in twenty-one states, where in 1944 alone they harvested crops worth $432 million.[33] "They're all right, good workers," a Washington farmer commented. "I only hope I can get them again." Other farmers agreed: "These Mexicans are as good as any help I ever had." "We wouldn't trade one of these Mexicans for ten of the kind of help we have had on this job before."[34]

In their oral histories and in their songs, the braceros told stories of what life was like in El Norte. They understood the importance of their work in the fight against fascism:

> If this war carries on
> We're all damned!
> We'll have to punch
> Hirohito out. . . .
>
> We'll have to give our help
> To the United States.
> If we do that, no doubt
> We'll never be beaten.
>
> Long live the stars and stripes
> And also the tricolor flag

And the eagle with its claws
Shall tear apart the traitor.[35]

But what spurred the migrant farm workers even more than patriotism was poverty in Mexico:

Braceros cross and cross
During summer and spring. . . .
I go and come, come and go
Looking for bread for my children. . . .
Braceros cross and cross.[36]

El Norte offered them opportunities to earn money:

From Morelia I came as a bracero,
To earn dollars was my illusion.
I bought shoes, I bought a sombrero,
And even put on new pants.

However, reality shattered this illusion. "I remember the first time
I went to the United States of America," said the spoken part of a
song. "'I did not go on a pleasure trip there, I went to pick cotton!'
I wrote my mother, 'Mom, I have a new *saco*.' And my mother
went around town making a big fuss, telling everybody, 'My son is
well-dressed. He has a new *saco!*' Heck, a new cotton-picking
sack!"[37]

Paid low wages, the laborers were sometimes cheated by their
employers. "Many times, we worked twelve hours a day," a
bracero protested, "but we never got paid for more than eight."
Another worker said: "The boss I worked for . . . robbed us of our
pay, because he used crooked scales for weighing the cotton we
picked. I came up here to try to support my family, but I have had
a hard time with what I make."[38]

Exploited as "arms," the migrant workers were forced to do
stoop labor with short-handle hoes:

And now I find myself
Breathless,
I'm a shoemaker by profession
But here they say I'm a camel
And I work just with a shovel and a hoe.

"We come here like *animales rentados* (rented animals), not like men," complained a farm laborer.[39]

They work us like slaves
They treat us like dogs.
All we need is for them to ride us
And to put the bridle on us.[40]

"We are not animals," declared a bracero. "We are human beings who have suffered much to come to the United States and work. . . . I think we should not come to the U.S. where we are treated badly, abused, and looked down upon."[41]

The migrant farm laborers lived in squalid and dangerous labor camps. "The only thing that the owner of the ranch provided was a tent," said Gonzálo B. García. "And everybody brought their own utensils, own food. We'd have to go out and scrounge around for an old oil can and cut a hole in it and make a stove."[42] These kerosene stoves were fire hazards. "Our barracks burned down, destroying all our clothes and money we had saved," a bracero said. "We were never paid back for what we lost."[43] The pesticides and unsafe drinking water frequently made workers ill. "There was much diarrhea in the camp because of bad food," a worker reported.[44]

During the weekends, the braceros often went into the nearby towns, only to be turned away from restaurants and other businesses. Sometimes they were attacked by young white men. In a letter to Mrs. Roosevelt, a woman protested incidents of racialized rowdiness in Idaho. She wanted the President to do "something about the Nazi minded element, by that I mean the people who are persecuting these boys [braceros]." Such behavior was "pure sabotage," argued the writer, because it jeopardized Idaho's labor supply. "So long as these boys are here, helping on the home front (and they are doing a good job of it), it seems to me that they should enjoy the same rights and privileges as a United States citizen, and so long as they are not drunk and disorderly they should be able to go in any place that a white man can go, and be waited on in a like manner. Does not our Constitution demand liberty and justice for all?"[45]

This was the question the braceros themselves were also asking. In May 1944, migrant farm workers in Idaho struck for higher wages. The growers forced them to return to work by threatening to jail them for breaking their contracts. However, strikes continued to erupt and spread to Washington as well as Oregon. As the producers of food for "Las Democracies," the braceros were demanding justice for all regardless of race.[46]

Already living in the U.S. when Pearl Harbor was attacked, Mexican Americans were also struggling for equality. Initially, they found themselves excluded from the defense industries. In an August 18, 1942, report marked "Confidential," the Office of War Information reported: "The airplane industry of Southern California has been consistent in asserting that it does not discriminate, but payrolls show almost no Mexicans employed. One plant personnel man stated that his company would employ them if they were not 'too racial' — 'too dark.' American-born girls of Mexican ancestry in San Diego have taken training courses, have come out at the top of their class, only to find that employers have passed them up to take less competent white girls."[47]

However, the rapidly inclining demand for labor in the defense industries forced employers to turn to Mexican labor. In 1941, the number of Mexicans employed in the Los Angeles shipyards was zero; by 1944, it had jumped to 17,000. Employment opportunities for them expanded throughout the defense industries — steel, armaments, and aircraft. However, they found themselves relegated to the low-wage jobs. At San Antonio's Kelly Field, where

10,000 of the 35,000 employees were Mexicans, none of them held a position above that of laborer or mechanic's helper.

Mexican Americans turned to the Fair Employment Practices Committee to help them fight discrimination. But federal authorities in Washington frustrated the FEPC's efforts. In a memo, June 20, 1942, Undersecretary of State Sumner Welles advised President Roosevelt that the State Department was "strongly opposed" to the public hearings that the FEPC was planning to hold in the Southwest. Welles explained that he was concerned that America's enemies would exploit public disclosures of discrimination. "Axis agents and others seeking to discredit this country in Mexico and the other American republics," Welles wrote, "have been and are making effective use of racial discrimination in this country." He then warned: "It would be most unfortunate, if through the record of public hearings conducted by an agency of this Government, we should afford them further material which because of its official character could be used even more effectively against us." Referring to Welles's memo, Roosevelt instructed aide Marvin McIntyre on June 23: "Take this letter up today with [FEPC Chairman Malcolm] MacLean and tell him really for international reasons public hearings should be stopped. And tell Sumner Welles that you are doing so and that he also may do it." Subsequently, the hearings were canceled.[48]

Roosevelt undermined the work of the FEPC further when he transferred this committee to the War Manpower Commission. Critics charged that the motive for this bureaucratic relocation was to appease "white Southern political pressure" by maintaining "discrimination as usual." When A. Philip Randolph learned about this administrative reorganization, he angrily asserted that the White House was pursuing a policy that was completely "emasculating" the usefulness of the committee. The reduction of the FEPC into "a small Federal bureau without power," FEPC Chairman MacLean noted, was bound to make minorities feel that "the Boss [had] deserted them."[49]

However, wartime labor shortages were opening doors to

skilled jobs. *La Opinión* carried advertisements in Spanish: "Martin Ship Service Company needs Mexican Workers for repair and maintenance work. You don't need to speak English. We have Mexican supervisors. You only need a birth certificate. You don't need to be a U.S. citizen." "No Experience Necessary: We need men, 16–50 years old, for war production industries. We speak Spanish. Come by between 10 and 4 p.m."[50] On January 23, 1944, *La Opinión* reported that twelve thousand Mexicans were employed by Douglas Aircraft in southern California.[51]

Many of these new workers were women. On April 2, 1942, *La Opinión* announced: "Roosevelt High School will open an aviation class for national defense, especially for women, on Tuesday and Thursday nights. This class will teach mounting, perforation, etc., as is taught by the various aircraft production companies."[52]

For the first time in their lives, Mexican-American women were no longer forced to be farm laborers, maids, and garment workers. "Prior to the war," recalled Natalie Martínez Sterling, "the only jobs available to young Mexican women were non-skilled types of occupations such as making cardboard boxes and sewing clothes. The war allowed us job opportunities as sales clerks and defense workers. The government was actually training us with job skills that would help us after the war."[53] Felicia Ruiz welcomed the chance to work in the defense industry. "During the depression," she said, "the only jobs available to young Mexican American women were limited primarily to sewing and laundry work, hotel maids, and as domestics. These jobs were both physically demanding and paid very little. When the war broke out, defense jobs were all of a sudden open to us because of the labor shortage with the men off to war. Many of us left these menial jobs into highly skilled occupations with good to excellent pay with overtime."[54]

During the tremendous employment expansion, thousands of Mexican-American women became riveters. One of them was Margarita Salazar. In 1942, she was twenty-five years old, working in Molly's Beauty Shop, where customers were telling fantastic stories about women assembling airplanes. "I quit Molly's and went to work for defense," Salazar recalled. "I could make more money. I could see that I wasn't going to make that much money working as an operator and the money was in defense. Everybody would talk about the overtime and how much money it was. And it was exciting. Being involved in that era you figured you were doing something for your country — and at the same time making money." She applied for a job at a Lockheed assembly plant and was hired immediately. An Italian worker taught Salazar how to drill: "Jeanette broke me in," she said.[55]

On the assembly lines of aircraft production, women were required to wear factory clothes. "Many of our mothers and aunts who worked in the defense plants never really adjusted to wearing what they considered to be men's clothing," said a worker. "Here were women who had worn only dresses all their lives, and were now required to wear pants and shirts."[56]

Sexual harassment was a problem in the factories. "Male workers told us that we should be home taking care of our children and that defense work was not for women," recalled one woman. "We often complained to our male supervisors regarding our problems with some of the men but nothing was ever done. Sometimes when we were working, one of the men would come by and grab us in a sexual way which made us very angry concerning this ugly treatment of women in the plant. Many women didn't formally complain, however, in fear of possibly losing their jobs."[57]

Working on the assembly lines, Mexican-American women learned not only how to rivet but also how to get along with workers of other races. "Aircraft work generally required a team of two women for riveting — one person working outside the plane and the other person inside," recalled Carmen Caudillo. "At one particular plant, there were many white women from Missouri who refused to have anything to do with the Black workers. One supervisor decided to pair several Black and Mexican women together. At first, there was some prejudice on both sides, but as time passed, we became good friends both in and out of the plant."

Women of different ethnicities also became friends in the factory cafeterias. "There were other Mexican women," said Margarita Salazar, "but I don't recall too many colored girls, not in our little section. But when we'd go to lunch, I'd see a lot of them. We all blended in — men, women, Mexican, Italian."[58] At another plant, Antonia Molina also had affirming experiences. "I remember one day when some new Black workers came to our factory. From the start, some white workers absolutely refused to even say hello. The next day, some of us Mexican women invited the Black women over to our table for lunch. We did so because we knew what it was like to be discriminated against. By the end of the week, several white workers also joined us for lunch. We soon realized that we had to set aside our differences in order to win the war."[59]

Working in the defense industry was particularly difficult for mothers. "I knew women who hated coming to work because of the daily pain of leaving their children at someone's house as they worked in the factory," said Esther Beard. "They couldn't wait for the war to be over so they could return to a normal family life."[60] Daily schedules became frenetic. Assigned to the night shift at an assembly plant, Esperanza Montoya Padilla had a punishing schedule: "I used to drill and buck — make holes for rivets on the planes. I'd [then] come home and clean the house and wash and take care of the kids and fix everything up, and then do the laundry. I went from one job to the other."[61]

Married women often found that their husbands did not like their working. When Beatrice Morales Clifton was told that the aircraft factories in Pasadena were hiring women, she decided to apply. "So I took the forms and when I got home and told my husband, oh! he hit the roof. He was one of those men that didn't believe the wife ever working; they want to be the supporter. I said, 'Well, I've made up my mind. I'm going to work regardless of whether you like it or not.'" Clifton went to work as a riveter for Lockheed. She found the work challenging but also exhausting, returning home each day very tired. "My husband, he didn't have much to say, 'cause he didn't approve from the beginning. As time went on, his attitude changed a little, but I don't think he ever really, really got used to the idea of me working." Having a paying job was important to her. "I was just a mother of four kids, that's all. But I felt proud of myself and felt good being that I had never done anything like that. I felt good that I could do something, and being that it was war, I felt that I was doing my part."[62]

Work in the war industries was a transforming experience. "I wasn't doing very well in high school," wrote Socorro Díaz Blanchard in her autobiography. "Seems like I had lost interest." In April 1943, she became a shipping clerk at Shelly Air Force Base, where she learned that the job offered certain privileges. "There was a PX in the base for the civilian employees. I could buy cigarettes which were very scarce. I was very popular on our block because everybody knew I could get cigarettes." She also had enough money to buy a car. "I wasn't eighteen yet so it had to be in my dad's name. I paid for it myself. It was a 1938 Dodge, four-door, creamy white. To me it was a Cadillac."[63]

For Mexican-American women, the car symbolized self-reliance. "Through earning our own wages," Carmen Chávez said, "we had a taste of independence we hadn't known before the war. The women of my neighborhood had changed as much as the men who went to war. We developed a feeling of self-confidence and a sense of worth." Alicia Mendeola Shelit experienced a similar feeling. With her earnings as a worker at Douglas Aircraft, this single parent purchased her first home. Shelit was proud that she was bringing "the money in to feed [her] kids, like a man."[64]

For Mexican Americans in the defense industry, the war represented a convergence of patriotism and personal growth. "We didn't understand the international politics that led to the war," said a woman who had worked in a factory. "We did know, however, that the Japanese had cowardly bombed Pearl Harbor and had killed hundreds of young American boys — boys who were my brothers' ages. The Japanese had attacked our country. I say our country because I was born here. My generation went proudly to war because this country, despite the discrimination, had provided my family with a better life than my relatives had in Mexico."[65] A better life meant a different one. "All of us were definitely changed by the four years of defense work," observed Victoria Morales. "Prior to the war, we were young women with few social and job skills. But the war altered these conditions very quickly. By the end of the war, we had been transformed into young, mature women with new job skills, self-confidence, and a sense of worth as a result of our wartime contributions."[66]

The "Poison Gas" of Nazi Doctrine in California

During the war, however, this sense of worth was assaulted when "ugly prejudices" stirred fear and hatred against Mexican-American teenagers. Viewed as outrageously dressed juvenile delinquents and gang members, they found themselves swept into the storm of the Sleepy Lagoon murder and the zoot-suit riot of 1943.

In *The Labyrinth of Solitude,* published in 1950, Octavio Paz offered an explanation for the behavior and dress of these alienated barrio youths. What distinguished them from other teenagers, he wrote, was their "furtive, restless air." Their sensibilities were like a "pendulum," swinging violently back and forth. Their "lack of a spirit" had given "birth to a type known as the *pachuco*." Belonging to a gang, the pachuco was an "instinctive" rebel: he displayed a "grotesque dandyism and anarchic behavior," a demonstration of his determination to remain "different." According to Paz, the pachuco was hiding insecurities beneath the flashy attire of the "zoot suit" with its exaggerated draped pants and ostentatious presentation.[67]

Actually, Paz's portrayal of the pachuco was a stereotype: it fit his thesis of the Mexican "solitude" enmeshed in a "labyrinth." Teaching at the University of California during the 1940s, Emory S. Bogardus studied the Mexican-American youth of Los Angeles and urged caution in generalizing about them. "Not all zoot suiters are members of gangs, only a small percentage," he wrote in 1943. "Not all gangsters are Mexican-Americans, only a small fraction. . . . Out of about 36,000 youth of Mexican parentage in the County of Los Angeles who are of school age. . . no one has seriously claimed that more than from 750 to 1,000 are involved in 'gangs' of various types."[68]

Mexican-American teenagers themselves also thought that the presence of zoot suiters and gang members was exaggerated. "We actually started seeing the drape pants around that time," Margarita Salazar McSweyn recalled, "but we didn't approve of it and we didn't dress that way. I've got pictures galore of my brothers and none of them have anything like that." The zoot suiters, she added, were gang members and dropouts. "We kept away from them and they never tried to go to our dances and to our parties. We figured it's an exaggerated style of dress that's going to come and go away."[69]

Moreover, pachucos were not "instinctive" rebels: their defiance was forged within an economic and cultural crucible that denied Mexican-American youth educational and employment opportunities. They belonged to impoverished families: in 1941, the median income of Mexicans in Los Angeles was only $792 a year, far below the $1,312 that the government recommended as a minimum for a family of five.[70] Mexican Americans were forced to attend inferior segregated schools. Section 8003 of the California Education Code stated: "The governing board of any school district may establish separate schools for Indian children . . . and for children of Chinese, Japanese, or Mongolian parentage."[71] Mexican-American students were considered part Indian. With little education, these young people were then relegated to dead-end jobs.

In a report on "Spanish-Americans in the Southwest and the War Effort," dated August 18, 1942, and classified "confidential," the Office of War Information bluntly described the harsh conditions of discrimination and poverty: "These people do not live, they exist. Malnutrition, sickness and disease are prevalent among them. Their housing, both in and out of cities, is the worst in the nation. . . . Their younger generation is confronted with insurmountable obstacles in education. . . . The schools they attend are frequently segregated and generally inferior, their curricula and programs are unequipped to cope with their needs. . . . The culture of the cities for them has been the slum, which has taken a heavy toll in personal disorganization, juvenile delinquency and crime."[72]

The problems identified in this government report had already begun to tear apart society in Los Angeles. In the slum of the East Side barrio, on August 2, 1942, the body of José Diáz was found at a local swimming hole known as the "Sleepy Lagoon." In her autobiography, Socorro Diáz Blanchard recalled the moment she learned about her brother's death: "A gang of pachucos had tried to crash a baptismal party at our neighbor's house. They were told to leave, that it was a private party. Joe and his friends were at the party. The pachucos returned with all their gang and crashed the party, destroying everything in sight, beating up two women. Everybody ran, but they caught up with my brother Joe and beat him to death. . . . Joe was supposed to have reported to the Army on the following morning."[73]

After receiving reports that members of the 38th Street gang had been in the vicinity of Sleepy Lagoon, the police arrested twenty-two gang members on the charge of conspiracy to commit murder. At the trial, Los Angeles police captain Edward Duran Ayres presented testimony saturated with stereotypes. "While Anglos fought with the fists," he stated, "Mexicans generally preferred to kill, or at least let blood."[74] This propensity for violence, he insisted, could be traced to the predominance of "Indian blood" in their racial composition, for Indians had "utter disregard for the value of life."[75]

The chief probation officer of Los Angeles County condemned Mexican-American gang members as disloyal to the country. "Those who are unemployed should be at work," he told the press. "Those who are employed and engage in this sort of activities (social disturbances) are no better. In this time of war they are all saboteurs because we need to conserve every dollar and every man for the war effort and not waste our time upon kid gangsters. If these kids want to fight so much, why don't they join the armed forces? Why waste their energy fighting each other when the very life of the nation is at stake?"[76] Judge Edward R. Brand gave the trial a patriotic framework. "In times like these," he declared, "the behavior of some few members of the fine Mexican-American colony is a disgrace to America, and he who shames America in wartime is a traitor to the democracy that shelters him."[77]

Three of the defendants were found guilty of first-degree murder and sentenced to prison at San Quentin. Nine were found guilty of second-degree murder, five were convicted for lesser offenses, and five were acquitted. But all of them had already been convicted in the press. For its story on the "Sleepy Lagoon" murder, the *Los Angeles Times* blazed the front-page headline: "Jury Delves into Boy Gang Terror Wave."[78] Repeatedly the *Times* gave descriptions of pachucos with their defiant dress and demeanor.

One of the supporters of the convicted young men was Anthony Quinn. As a child, he had traveled to El Norte with his mother on a coal car of a train. When they arrived in Juarez at night, they were tired, hungry, and dirty from the coal. A stranger let them stay in her home and fed them a breakfast of eggs. Years later, a woman came to Quinn's mother, asking for his help. "She remembered our name, and tracked my accomplishments. Her grandson, a boy named Levas, was one of the twenty-two kids charged with first-degree murder in a famous Los Angeles gang killing. . . . I was under contract to 20th Century–Fox at the time, and my mother looked to me for help. 'Mama,' I said, 'what the hell do you want me to do?' 'The eggs, Tony,' she said. 'Remember the eggs.' I remembered the eggs, so I agreed to raise money for the boy's defense."[79]

During the trial, the Los Angeles police arrested hundreds of young Mexicans, singling out those dressed in zoot suits. One of them, Alfred Barela, protested this police harassment. In a letter to Judge Arthur S. Guerin, May 21, 1943, he wrote:

> Ever since I can remember I've been pushed around and called names because I'm a Mexican. I was born in this

country. Like you said I have the same rights and privileges of other Americans. . . .

Pretty soon I guess I'll be in the army and I'll be glad to go. But I want to be treated like everybody else. We're tired of being pushed around. We're tired of being told we can't go to this show or that dance hall because we're Mexican or that we better not be seen on the beach front, or that we can't wear draped pants or have our hair cut the way we want to. . . . I don't want any more trouble and I don't want anyone saying my people are in disgrace. My people work hard, fight hard in the army and navy of the United States. They're good Americans and they should have justice.[80]

Reflecting on the pachuco gangs in the *New Republic,* January 18, 1943, Carey McWilliams explained that juvenile delinquency among barrio youth was rooted in poverty and racism. "It takes a war apparently to reveal the 'sore spots' in our society," he wrote. "For at least twenty-five years, social investigators have repeatedly warned the County of Los Angeles about the thoroughly disadvantaged position of its large resident Mexican population; but the community saw fit to ignore these warnings until with the war, it became impossible to pretend that no problem existed." McWilliams refused to blame the victims. "It is no secret," he argued, "that this second generation group has faced discrimination in the schools, in the community generally, and that, like most second generation groups (particularly when a degree of color difference exists), these youngsters show evidence of social and cultural maladjustment." In his conclusion, McWilliams cautioned: "For the time being, the issue has simmered down, but it has by no means died out."[81]

Six months later, on June 3, 1943, after some fights between young Mexican Americans and servicemen in downtown Los Angeles, hundreds of soldiers and sailors went on a rampage. Riding in taxis, they chased young Mexicans dressed in zoot suits, condemning their victims as draft dodgers. In their hunt for zoot suiters, mobs of sailors invaded movie theaters — the Orpheum, the Rialto, Loews, the Roxy. Cruising up and down the aisles, they shouted for pachucos to stand up and then stripped them naked on the stage. At one theater, the rioters found two young men dressed in zoot suits watching a movie; they dragged them to the front of the theater, stripped them, and then, as a final insult, urinated on their zoot suits.[82] On the streets, the attacks were indiscriminate. All young Mexican Americans, in zoot suits or not, became targets of mob violence; blacks and Filipinos were also victims of this fury.

"It was like the sailors and Marines were taking over the whole city," a Mexican-American teenager recalled angrily. "They had bottles and belts, clubs and iron pipes in their hands. They were waving them over their heads. . . . Some sailors near us called, 'Come on you pachucos, you yellow bastards, we'll get you, all of you.' The crowd laughed and moved, pushing every way and everybody. Then we heard a roar and somebody yelled, 'They got 'em, they got 'em. They got those goddamned zoot suiters."[83] Hospitalized with a broken jaw, a twelve-year-old boy protested: "So our guys wear tight bottoms on their pants and those bums wear wide bottoms. Who the hell they fighting, Japs or us?"[84] A young Mexican American named Mingo angrily exclaimed: "Hell, man, this is a street in Germany tonight. This isn't Los Angeles." "They're going in the houses looking everywhere for us guys," teenager Freddie said. "They beat up old Jésus Santiago when they saw him sitting on his porch cause they said maybe he was the father of a zoot suiter. They knocked him out cold, him with Felix [his son] in the South Pacific."[85]

During this melee, the police merely watched, refusing to intervene; then they arrested young Mexican Americans for "vagrancy" and "rioting."[86] A police captain praised the aggressive sailors for teaching those "gaming dandies" a moral lesson by "unfrocking" the "garish" costumes that had become "a hallmark of juvenile delinquency."[87]

The news media also cheered on the sailors. The front-page

headline story of the June 7 *Los Angeles Times* announced: ZOOT SUITERS LEARN LESSON IN FIGHTS WITH SERVICEMEN.[88] Imagery of the war infused press reports of the assaults and beatings. "Sailors made it a landing party, sought out the zoot suiters in their hangouts, and then proceeded with mopping up operations," a newspaper reported. The *Los Angeles Examiner* described the sailors' attack as a "blitz," and the *Herald Examiner* informed readers that the "Zoot Forces" were "QUIET ON EASTERN FRONT." The *Daily News* declared: "They [zoot suiters] are the type of exuberant youth that Hitler found useful. He gave them brown shirts and guns and made their violence legal."[89]

News of the Los Angeles riot rippled across the Pacific: the Japanese media gleefully reported the violence as another example of racism in America. On June 11, the United Press reported: "Radio Tokyo yesterday seized upon the Los Angeles disorders."[90] That very day, military authorities ended the rioting by placing the downtown section and the barrio off-limits to servicemen.

The City Council blamed the young men dressed in zoot suits for the rioting and passed a resolution: "Now, therefore, be it resolved, that the City Council by Resolution find that the wearing of Zoot Suits constitutes a public nuisance and does hereby instruct the City Attorney to prepare an ordinance declaring same a nuisance and prohibit the wearing of Zoot Suits . . . within the city limits of Los Angeles."[91]

At a grand jury inquiry held shortly after the riot, young men insisted on their right to wear a zoot suit. One of them was John B. Thomas, a young black who appeared in court wearing "a bright green zoot suit." Exhibiting his Army enlistment papers, Thomas asserted he was entitled to wear this outfit until he donned the military khaki, which he was scheduled to do that very day. "I'm not a gangster," he said. "I just like this style." Similarly, awaiting a call after enlisting in the U.S. Marines, Raymond Serma told the grand jury: "I'm not a bad guy; I'm not a rowdy. I like this style, which is easier to dance in."[92]

At a press conference on June 16, Eleanor Roosevelt expressed concern about the growing race problem. "For a long time, I've worried about the attitude toward Mexicans in California, and the States along the border."[93] Three days later, C.I.O. leader Philip Murray appealed to President Roosevelt to use his personal influence to remedy the "extremely dangerous situation" in Los Angeles. Denouncing the "lynch spirit" of the military mobs, Murray wrote in a letter to the White House: "I urge you to order the War and Navy Departments to undertake an educational campaign among the armed forces . . . to eradicate the misconceptions and prejudices that contributed to these attacks on their fellow-citizens."[94]

The zoot-suit riot was more than a border problem, however, and the solution to the "lynch spirit" required more than education to eradicate stereotypes. Castigating the rioting sailors as the "spearheads of the hooliganism," the *Chicago Defender* traced the source of the hate crimes to the "Jim Crow policies" of the U.S. Army.[95] In an article published in the *Crisis,* Chester B. Hines related the zoot-suit riot to the Detroit race riot. "What could make the white people more happy," he asked, "than to see their uniformed sons slapping up some dark-skinned people? It proved beyond all doubt the bravery of white servicemen, their gallantry. Los Angeles was at last being made safe for white people — to do as they damned well pleased."[96]

For Mexican Americans and concerned citizens, the "Sleepy Lagoon" murder trial and the zoot-suit riot underscored the need to fight for "double victory." A Spanish-language newspaper in Los Angeles, *El Espectador,* denounced the racism of the police and the mainstream media as similar to Nazism:

> Not all of the police can be blamed for the sadistic methods employed by some members of the force in the manhandling of offenders; but we can expect very little understanding from the men in the law enforcement ranks, when the heads of the department make such reports as the one presented by a Captain of the Los Angeles County

Sheriff's department to the Grand Jury in regards to the Sleepy Lagoon murder case. In that report it was charged that "all Mexicans are inherently vicious." And there is the assertion of the Lieutenant of the Hollywood police force that said: "A Mexican is always a good suspect." The metropolitan press and radio must also bear the brunt of the responsibility for our ten days of terror [the zoot-suit riot]. Both have raved very much like the loud-mouth Goebbels in directing his diatribes against the Semites.[97]

On October 4, 1944, the District Court of Appeals found that the trial judge in the Sleepy Lagoon case was biased against the defendants and overturned the convictions. Leading the appeal struggle was a defense committee whose membership included Bert Corona, Rita Hayworth, Anthony Quinn, Orson Welles, Henry Fonda, and Carey McWilliams. "It wasn't only seventeen boys who were on trial," the committee declared. "It was the whole of the Mexican people, and their children and grandchildren." In their conclusion, they issued a call to arms against the ideology of white superiority on the home front: "Nazi logic guided the judge and jury and dictated the verdict and sentence. We are at war not only with the armies of the Axis powers, but with the poison gas of their doctrine, with the 'biological basis' of Hitler and with his theories of race supremacy."[98]

6

DIVERSITY AND ITS DISCONTENTS
Who Is an American?

How the Chinese Became "Friends"

TWO WEEKS after the attack on Pearl Harbor, *Time* magazine explained how to distinguish the Chinese "friend" from the Japanese "enemy":

> HOW TO TELL YOUR FRIENDS FROM THE JAPS: Virtually all Japanese are short. Japanese are likely to be stockier and broader-hipped than short Chinese. Japanese are seldom fat; they often dry up and grow lean as they age. Although both have the typical epicanthic fold of the upper eyelid, Japanese eyes are usually set closer together. The Chinese expression is likely to be more placid, kindly, open; the Japanese more positive, dogmatic, arrogant. Japanese are hesitant, nervous in conversation, laugh loudly at the wrong time. Japanese walk stiffly erect, hard heeled. Chinese, more relaxed, have an easy gait, sometimes shuffle.

Two photographs — one of a Japanese, another of a Chinese — were used as illustrations. Previously maligned as the "heathen Chinee," "mice-eaters," and "Chinks," the Chinese were now "friends" and allies engaged in a heroic common effort against the "Japs."[1]

The Chinese had been in America for a long time. They had begun arriving in America during the 1849 Gold Rush to California; by 1930, 400,000 of them had sailed east across the Pacific, carrying a dream of America. Immigrant Lee Chew described what had happened to him. As a sixteen-year-old he saw the triumphant return of a Chinese migrant from the "country of the American wizards." With the money he had earned overseas, the migrant invited his fellow villagers to "a grand party where they were served a hundred roasted pigs, along with chickens, ducks, geese, and an abundance of dainties." Inspired, Chew left for the land the Chinese called "gold mountain."[2]

In America, Chinese immigrants helped build the transcontinental railroad; they also worked in the factories of San Francisco as well as the agricultural valleys of California. But the Chinese experienced harsh discrimination. The 1790 Naturalization Act denied them the right to become citizens: this law provided that in order to be eligible for naturalized citizenship the applicant had to be "white."[3] The 1882 Chinese Exclusion Act severely restricted immigration from China. Competing for jobs, white workers forced the Chinese to retreat to Chinatowns, where they worked in small businesses like restaurants and laundries.

One of these immigrants was Andrew Kan. "When I first came," he told an interviewer in 1924, forty-four years after his arrival, "Chinese treated worse than dog. Oh, it was terrible, terrible. At that time all Chinese have queue and dress same as in China. The hoodlums, roughnecks and young boys pull your queue, slap your face, throw all kind of old vegetables and rotten eggs at you." Although Kan could not become a citizen, he knew he was deserving. "Since I have lived and made money in this country," Kan declared, "I should be able to become an American citizen."[4]

After the Japanese attack on Pearl Harbor, Chinese Americans realized that they were still viewed as foreigners, and they also re-membered that the Chinese had been called "Japs" in the early twentieth century.[5] In Chinatown during the early weeks of the war, shopkeepers displayed signs declaring, "This is a Chinese shop," and people wore buttons saying: "I am Chinese." Recalling the fear in the community, Nelly Wong wrote:

> When World War II was declared
> on the morning radio,
> we glued our ears, widened our eyes.
> Our bodies shivered. . . .
> Shortly our Japanese neighbors vanished
> and my parents continued to whisper:
> We are Chinese, we are Chinese.
> We wore black arm bands,
> put up a sign
> in bold letters.[6]

During the 1930s, Chinese Americans had anxiously watched Japan systematically unveil its plan for the control of China. On September 18, 1931, the Japanese army attacked Mukden, then marched into Manchuria. Five months later, Japan violently seized Shanghai. As they witnessed the brutal acts of Japanese imperial-ism, Chinese Americans felt a deep concern for the homeland of their parents. In Chinese school, they listened to the principal give speeches about how Chiang Kai-shek should do more to resist the Japanese. "If you were Chinese-American, you certainly felt the fate of China was important," recounted James Low. "I remember the teachers would always complain, 'China is weak, and look at the treatment we get here.'"[7]

By "treatment," Low was referring to the discrimination that young Chinese Americans were experiencing. They wanted to break away from the immigrant status of their parents, and hoped that education would open doors of employment in the profes-sions and skilled occupations. But they discovered that their education mattered little. "Even if you had an education, there was no other work than in a laundry or restaurant," complained David Chin, himself the owner of a laundry in New York. Two Chinese engineers wrote to fifty engineering companies applying for positions in their field and received only negative responses. Similarly Peter Soohoo graduated from the University of Southern California with a degree in electrical engineering in 1923; two years later he told a Stanford University researcher: "I have tried to get into the engineering field but thus far have not been able to do so." After failing to find a job as an engineer, a Chinese graduate of the Massachusetts Institute of Technology became a waiter in a Chinese restaurant. Young Chinese Americans wondered whether they had a future outside of Chinatown. The Great Depression made the employment picture even bleaker. "With thousands of . . . blue-eyed collegians at his elbows, looking for a job, with thousands of similar tinted fellows working for a raise, ready to take his place the moment he slips," asked a Chinese youth, "is there a chance for a person with a yellow skin?"[8]

Lamenting this employment discrimination, the San Francisco Chinese newspaper *Chung Sai Yat Po* advised American-born Chinese to "return" to China. "In the fields of agriculture and aviation, China is much lacking in Western knowledge. Unlimited opportunities are ahead. . . . Indeed, your future lies with China, not with America." Compared to America, China seemed to be a society where they would not have to worry about being rejected for a job because they were Chinese. Stanford University student Louise Leung told an interviewer: "The Chinese who are trained in the schools here do not expect to remain in the United States, but they are looking toward China for the future." Chinese college graduates had the education and qualifications — "everything but the color" for professional employment in America.[9]

"We were all immigrants in those days, no matter where we were born," recalled Victor Wong bitterly. "Between the Chinese and the English education, we had no idea where we belonged. Even to this day, if I wanted to say, 'I'm going to China,' I would never say it that way; I would say 'go back to China.' Because I was taught from the time I was born that this was not my country, that I would have to go to China to make my living as an adult."[10]

The entry of the United States into the war suddenly gave Chinese Americans a chance to make this their country. They passionately joined the war effort to save China and also to win equality for themselves at home. In Chinatowns across the country, patriotism exploded. In "A Memo to Mr. Hitler, Hirohito & Co.," the *Chinese Press* of San Francisco warned:

> Have you heard the bad news? America is out to get you. America has a grim, but enthusiastic bombing party started, and you're the target in the parlor game.
>
> San Francisco Chinatown, U.S.A., is joining the party. Chinatown will have fun blasting you to hell. Chinatown is proud to be a part of Freedom's legion in freeing all the decent people of the world from your spectacle.
>
> Chinatown's part of the party will cost $500,000. Admission price to the fun is purchase of a U.S. War Bond. We're all going to buy a War Bond for Victory.
>
> P. S. More bad news. Everyone in Chinatown is going to this party. We're NOT missing this one.[11]

In New York Chinatown, excited crowds cheered wildly when the first draft numbers drawn were for Chinese Americans. Chinese boys, too young for the armed services, tried to enlist by giving the authorities their "Chinese age," usually a year older than the age indicated on their birth certificates.[12]

Emily Lee Shek became the first Chinese woman to join the Wacs. "She tried to join up right in the beginning [of the war]," the *Chinese Press* reported in September 1942, "but the 105-pound weight minimum barred her. When the requirement was dropped five pounds, she drank two gallons of water and lived on a special Chinese diet, and made it — yes, with one pound to spare."[13]

Altogether 13,499 Chinese served in the U.S. Armed Forces —

22 percent of all Chinese adult males. "To men of my generation," explained Charlie Leong of San Francisco Chinatown, "World War II was the most important historic event of our times. For the first time we felt we could make it in American society." The war had given them the opportunity to get out of Chinatown, don army uniforms, and be sent overseas where they felt they were part of the great patriotic United States war machine out to do battle with the enemy. Harold Liu of New York Chinatown recalled: "In the 1940s for the first time Chinese were accepted by Americans as being friends because at that time, Chinese and Americans were fighting against the Japanese and the Germans and the Nazis. Therefore, all of a sudden, we became part of an American dream. We had heroes with Chiang Kai-shek and Madame Chiang Kai-shek and so on. It was just a whole different era and in the community we began to feel very good about ourselves."[14] Kamin Chin explained: "My family had been here for over 100 years. I can't change the shape of my eyes. But I am an American. I was fighting discrimination."[15]

Chinese Americans also served on the home front. Confined for decades to low-wage jobs, Chinese workers suddenly found new employment opportunities, especially in the defense industries, where labor shortages were acute. Waiters left the restaurants and rushed to the higher-paying industrial jobs. In 1942 four restaurants in New York Chinatown had to shut down because of a lack of waiters, and the proprietor of Li Po, a restaurant in Los Angeles, remarked: "I was just ready for another venture. But I can't now. No men to run it." In Los Angeles, three hundred Chinese laundry workers closed their shops to work on the construction of the ship *China Victory*. "At Douglas, home of the A-20 attack planes and dive bombers," the *Chinese Press* reported in 1943, "there are approximately 100 Chinese working at its three plants — Santa Monica, Long Beach, and El Segundo." Chinese workers constituted 15 percent of the shipyard workforce in the San Francisco Bay Area in 1943. They also found employment in the Seattle-Tacoma Shipbuilding Corporation, the shipyards of

Delaware and Mississippi, and the airplane factories on Long Island.[16]

One of these new defense industry workers was Arthur Wong. After arriving in New York Chinatown in 1930 at the age of seventeen, he found himself confined to the ethnic economy: "I worked five and a half days in the laundry and worked the whole weekend in the restaurant. And then came the war, and defense work opened up; and some of my friends went to work in a defense plant, and they recommended that I should apply for defense work. So I went to work for Curtiss-Wright, making airplanes. I started out as an assembler, as a riveter."[17]

The war also opened employment opportunities for Chinese women. After graduating from college, Jade Snow Wong found that she could not find suitable employment because she was Chinese. Then the war industries began to demand workers. "By this time the trek to the shipyards was well underway," wrote Wong. "The patriotic fever to build as many ships as possible, together with boom wages, combined to attract people from all types of occupations," and Wong was hired as a typist-clerk in a shipyard in Marin County. Several hundred "alert young Chinese-American girls," the *Chinese Press* reported in 1942, "have gone to the defense industries as office workers." The paper proudly presented a partial roster of these workers in the Bay Area, including Fannie Yee, Rosalind Woo, and Jessie Wong of Bethlehem Steel, and Anita Chew, Mildred Lew, and Evelyn Lee of Mare Island's Navy Yard. "They're part of the millions who stand behind the man behind the gun." A year later, in an article on "Women in the War," the *Chinese Press* informed its readers about Alice Yick, the Boston Navy Yard's only Chinese woman mechanical trainee, who could run light lathes, grinders, shapers, planers, and other machine tools. "Helen Young, Lucy Young, and Hilda Lee," the paper continued, "were the first Chinese women aircraft workers in California. They help build B-24 bombers in San Diego."[18]

Writing for *Survey Graphic* in 1942, sociologist Rose Hum Lee reported the integration of previously marginalized Chinese workers into the economic mainstream: "They have gone into the army and navy, into shipbuilding and aircraft plants. Even the girls are getting jobs." But while the Chinese were participating in the war effort as Americans, Lee noted critically, they were still denied full citizenship in terms of immigration and naturalized citizenship. "Surely racial discrimination should not be directed against those who are America's Allies in the Far East and are helping her in every way to win the war." Lee brought the war home. "To be fighting for freedom and democracy in the Far East, at the cost of seven million lives in five years of hard, long, bitter warfare, and to be denied equal opportunity in the greatest of democracies, seems the height of irony." The contradiction was too evident to be ignored and too embarrassing to the United States to be allowed to continue.[19]

The war for democracy abroad required reform at home. In 1942, the California League of Women Voters of San Francisco launched an educational campaign to remove racial discrimination from the immigration laws. A year later, Congress began considering a bill to repeal the Chinese exclusion law and also to allow a quota for Chinese immigration. During her tour of the country, Madame Chiang Kai-shek promoted the repeal legislation. At a dinner party on May 15, she told several key congressmen that rescinding the Chinese exclusion laws would boost Chinese morale and buttress her country's war effort. Chinese-American lobbying activities in support of the bill were widespread and intense. In a letter to Mrs. Franklin Roosevelt, Mrs. Theodora Chan Wang of the Chinese Women's Association of New York explained that Chinese Americans wanted an immigration quota so that they would be accorded the privileges enjoyed by "our companions in ideology and arms." The Chinese Consolidated Benevolent Association of New York condemned the exclusion law as a violation of the fundamental principles of equality and friendly cooperation between China and the United States. At a conference in San Antonio in September 1943, Chinese Americans called the exclusion legislation "the stumbling block between China and America," and urged their American friends to "repeal it right now, not to wait till the war was over."[20]

Responding to the pressure, President Roosevelt supported the repeal. "China is our ally," Roosevelt wrote on October 11, 1943. "For many long years she stood alone in the fight against aggression. Today we fight at her side. She has continued her gallant struggle against very great odds." Aware that the legislation was essential to the war effort in Asia, the President urged Congress to "be big enough" to acknowledge an error of the past: "By the repeal of the Chinese exclusion law, we can correct a historic mistake and silence the distorted Japanese propaganda."[21]

Japan had been appealing to Asia to unite in a race war against white America. Its propaganda had been condemning the United States for its discriminatory laws and for the segregation of the Chinese in ghettos, where they had been relegated to "the most menial of occupations, despised and mistreated and at best patronizingly tolerated with a contemptuous humor." Tokyo broadcasts claimed that the Chinese in the United States suffered from "a campaign of venomous vilification of the character of the Chinese people." "Far from waging this war to liberate the oppressed peoples of the world," Tokyo argued on the air waves, "the Anglo-American leaders are trying to restore the obsolete system of imperialism." In June 1943, when the House committee delayed action on the repeal bill, the Japanese radio in Manila editorialized: "Agitation in the U.S. for the repeal of the Chinese Exclusion Act met an early death due to the opposition of anti-Asiatic congressmen, which bears out the fact it was never meant to be sincere, that it was only a gesture, empty words."[22]

This Japanese propaganda alarmed U.S. policymakers. A retired navy officer told a congressional committee holding hearings on the repeal bill that the Chinese exclusion law was worth "twenty divisions" to the Japanese army. Supporters of repeal argued: "It is time for us to realize that if nations cannot be gracious to each other, cannot respect each other's race, all talk of democracy is in vain." They also expressed fear that the war could turn into a racial conflict. "The Japanese have been carrying on a propaganda campaign seeking to align the entire oriental world behind Japanese leadership, seeking to set the oriental world against the occidental world," one congressman warned. "They have called it a campaign of Asia for Asiatics." "Suppose the Chinese do capitulate and join Japan," another congressman echoed, "then all Asia is apt to go with her. Then you will have a race struggle in which we are hopelessly outnumbered that will last, not for 1 year or 5 years, but throughout generations to come." The Chinese exclusion law had to be repealed, he argued, for the "salvation of the white race" depended on continued Chinese friendship and military cooperation. China, a Chicago newspaper declared, was America's "white hope" in the East.[23]

In order to help win the war in Asia, Congress repealed the exclusion act and provided an annual quota of 105 Chinese immigrants and their right to naturalized citizenship.

Back to Bataan: Filipino Fighters from America

Filipino Americans also viewed the war from a trans-Pacific perspective — America and the homeland they had left behind. After the U.S. annexation of the Philippines in 1898, Filipinos began arriving to work in the cane fields of Hawaii, the farms of California, and the canneries of Alaska. By 1930, 140,000 Filipinos had made the crossing to America.

The newcomers believed it would be easy to earn and save money in America. "My sole ambition was to save enough money to pay back the mortage on my land," explained one of them. "In the Philippines a man is considered independent and is looked upon with respect by his neighbors if he possesses land." As he said farewell to his brother in the Philippines, a Filipino laborer promised: "I will come back and buy that house. I will buy it and build a high cement wall around it. I will come back with lots of money and put on a new roof. Wait and see!"[24]

On the West Coast, however, Filipinos experienced labor exploitation, mob violence, and segregation. On the doors of hotels and other businesses, they often read signs declaring, Positively No Filipinos Allowed. They also could not become citizens. In 1934, the Supreme Court had declared: "'White persons' within the meaning of the statute [the 1790 Naturalization Law] are members of the Caucasian race, as Caucasian is defined in the understanding of the mass of men. The term excludes the Chinese, the Japanese, the Hindus, the American Indians and the Filipinos."[25]

"I have been four years in America," a Filipino immigrant in California sadly remarked, "and I am still a stranger. It is not because I want to be. I have tried to be as 'American' as possible. I live like an American, eat like an American, and dress the same, and yet everywhere I find Americans who remind me of the fact that I am a stranger."[26] In 1934, Congress established the Philippines as a commonwealth and prohibited Filipino immigration.

However, the war would offer new opportunities for Filipinos to become Americans. The heroic resistance of Filipino fighters at Bataan was widely recognized. "The gallant United States and Philippine forces in Bataan peninsula surrendered today after enduring the tortures of hell," reported correspondent Frank Hewlett. "They were beaten, but it was a fight that ought to make every American bow his head in tribute. . . . The Americans fought for everything they loved, as did the Filipinos, WITH THEIR FIERCE LOVE OF LIBERTY." In her tribute to the brave men of Bataan, Eleanor Roosevelt highlighted the interracial brotherhood forged on the bloodstained battlefield: "Fighting in Bataan has been an excellent example of what happens when two different races respect each other. Men of different races and backgrounds have fought side by side and praised each other's heroism and courage." Writer and California farm worker Carlos Bulosan conveyed in poetry the meaning of Bataan for Filipino Americans:

Bataan has fallen.
With heads bloody but unbowed, we yielded to the
    enemy. . . .

We have stood up uncomplaining.
Beseiged on land and blockaded by sea,
We have done all that human endurance could bear. . . .
Our defeat is our victory.[27]

At Bataan, thousands of Filipinos had fought beside American soldiers, and stories of their courage forced whites to revise their attitudes toward Filipinos in the United States. "No longer on the streetcar do I feel myself in the presence of my enemies," recalled Manuel Buaken. "We Filipinos are the same — it is Americans that have changed in their recognition of us." A Filipino working in a Pullman car was pleasantly surprised by the abrupt change in the attitudes of white travelers. "I am very much embarrassed," he remarked. "They treat me as if I have just arrived from Bataan."[28]

Anxious to defend their homeland, Filipino Americans rushed to the recruiting offices. They were refused, however, for Filipinos were classified as "nationals" and hence ineligible for service in the U.S. Armed Forces. Responding to their protests, President Roosevelt promptly changed the draft law to include Filipinos, and on February 19, 1942, Secretary of War Henry Stimson announced the organization of the First Filipino Infantry Regiment: "This new unit is formed in recognition of the intense loyalty and patriotism of those Filipinos who are now residing in the United States. It provides for them a means of serving in the armed forces of the United States, and the eventual opportunity of fighting on the soil of their homeland."[29]

Filipinos enthusiastically responded to the call to arms. In California alone sixteen thousand — 40 percent of the state's Filipino population — registered for the first draft. Filipino soldiers had, Doroteo Vite explained in 1942, "a personal reason to be training to fight the invaders. My home and my family and all the things that were dear to me as a boy are there in the path of the Japanese war machine."[30]

For Filipinos, service in the U.S. Army was also viewed as a path

Symbol of "double victory" in the *Pittsburgh Courier*, February 7, 1942. "Let we colored Americans adopt the double VV for a double victory," wrote James G. Thompson in a letter to the editor. "The first V for victory over our enemies from without, the second V for victory over our enemies from within."

(LEFT) Children in Hawaii wearing gas masks. Fragments of my childhood memory remain vivid—the gas masks in our bedroom closet.
(U.S. Army Museum, Hawaii)

(RIGHT) The V for Victory sign on V-J Day in Honolulu. The children jumped joyously in the streets, shouting, "We won the war! We won the war!" But what had we fought for and what had we won?
(U.S. Army Museum, Hawaii)

Dorie Miller, a hero of Pearl Harbor. The "Negro mess attendant" had never before fired a gun. (U. S. Navy photo)

Tank troops getting ready for battle, 1944. (National Archives)

Tuskegee pilots in Italy. They wanted to "fly and fight" for freedom.
(Office of War Information, National Archives)

Wacs sort mail in France. For black America, World War II was also
"her-story." *(U.S. Army photo)*

Picketers outside a defense plant, demanding jobs. *(Photo by Robert Shurlock. Schomburg Center for Research in Black Culture)*

Janitors at the North American aircraft factory, in V formation. Within the war industry, blacks were assigned to the menial, low-wage jobs. *(Office of War Information, National Archives)*

Dock workers in Mobile, Alabama, 1943. The war for "double victory" helped to integrate employment in the war industries. *(National Archives)*

Women welders at the Todd Erie Basin dry dock in Pennsylvania.
(Library of Congress)

No "freedom from fear" during the race riot in Detroit. Police protect a bloodied victim from the angry mob. *(Schomburg Center for Research in Black Culture)*

A Cherokee mother on a North Carolina reservation buys a war bond from an Indian postmaster. *(UPI/Bettmann Newsphotos/Acme Photo)*

Navajo code talkers
in the Pacific war.
(U.S. Marine Corps photo)

(LEFT) Marine Ira Hayes in his parachute outfit. "Us Indians have so much
. . . to gain in this war." *(U.S. Marine Corps photo)*

(RIGHT) Marine Guy Louis Gabaldon, a Japanese-speaking Mexican-
American humanitarian war hero. *(U.S. Marine Corps photo)*

Braceros on their way to the fields to harvest food for the war effort.
(Library of Congress)

Women workers polish the transparent noses of A-20 attack planes at the
Douglas Aircraft factory in Long Beach, California. On January 23, 1944,
La Opinión reported that 12,000 Mexicans were employed at this plant.
Many of them were women. *(Franklin D. Roosevelt Library, Hyde Park, New York)*

Mexican-American railroad workers during World War II. *(Library of Congress)*

Young Mexican-Americans attacked and stripped of their clothes by white sailors during the "zoot-suit" riot in Los Angeles, 1943. *(Wide World Photos)*

Rose Ong, a seamstress in San Francisco, with photographs of her six sons serving in the U.S. military. *(National Archives)*

(LEFT) Mrs. Emily Lee Shek became the first Chinese-American woman to join the Wacs. She is pictured with Eleanor Roosevelt. *(U.S. Army photo)*

(RIGHT) Waiters in Chinatown became welders in the defense industry. *(National Archives)*

Filipino-American soldiers in the Pacific. The war gave Filipinos a chance to show themselves to America as "soldiers of democracy," as "men, not houseboys." *(U.S. Army photo)*

(LEFT) A Japanese-American veteran wears his uniform and decorations to protest his unconstitutional evacuation from the West Coast. Like Joseph Kurihara, he had served in the U.S. Armed Forces during World War I. *(National Archives)*

(RIGHT) A Japanese-American grandmother and her grandchildren on their way to an internment camp. Each family was registered and given tags with their numbers to be attached to their baggage and hung from their coat lapels. *(National Archives)*

The internment camp for Japanese-Americans at Heart Mountain, Wyoming. The barracks were surrounded by barbed-wire fences with guard towers. *(National Archives)*

Japanese-American soldiers with German prisoners of war in Italy. *(U.S. Army photo)*

The desperate passengers of the SS *St. Louis* at the dock in Havana, May 27–June 2, 1939. *(AP/Wide World Photos)*

A poster appealing for money to help rescue Jewish refugees, by the Hebrew Sheltering and Immigrant Aid Society of Boston.

African-American soldiers confront the horror of Buchenwald, April 11, 1945. *(U.S. Holocaust Museum, Washington, D.C.)*

A Nisei soldier with liberated Jewish prisoners at the Dachau death camp. *(Photograph by Sus Ito. Courtesy of the Japanese-American Resource Center and Rudy Tokiwa)*

President Harry Truman, Secretary of State James Byrnes, and Admiral William Leahy. As chairman of the Joint Chiefs of Staff, Leahy believed that there was no military necessity for the dropping of the atomic bomb on Hiroshima. *(U.S. Army photo)*

Hiroshima near point zero, after the atomic attack. After the destruction of Nagasaki, Truman confided to Henry Wallace that "the thought of wiping out another 100,000 people was too horrible," and that he did not like the idea of killing "all those kids." *(National Archives)*

President Harry Truman and the 100/442nd Regimental Combat Team at the White House, 1946. "You fought for the free nations of the world," Truman told the Japanese-American soldiers. "You fought not only the enemy, you fought prejudice — and you won. Keep up that fight . . . continue to win — make this great Republic stand for what the Constitution says it stands for: 'the welfare of all the people, all the time.'"
(U.S. Army photo)

to acceptance in America. Their very wearing of a uniform was a political statement. "In a few months I will be wearing Uncle Sam's olive-drab army uniform," said a Filipino. "I am looking forward to that day, not with misgiving but with a boyish anticipation of doing something which up to now I have never been allowed to do — serving as an equal with American boys." The war, noted the wife of a soldier, gave Filipinos the chance to show themselves to America as "soldiers of democracy," as "men, not houseboys." One of these soldiers explained: "In all the years I was here before the United States went into the war, I felt that I did not belong here. I was a stranger among a people who did not understand and had no good reason to understand me and my people. . . . In other words, it was a pretty difficult business to be a Filipino in the United States in the years preceding Pearl Harbor."[31]

But in many places being Filipino was still "a difficult business." Stationed at Camp Beale, soldiers of the First Filipino Infantry found they were unwelcome in nearby Marysville, California. Dressed proudly in their U.S. Army uniforms, several Filipino soldiers went into the town during their first weekend pass to have a good dinner and see the sights. They entered a restaurant and sat down, but no one came to serve them. After waiting for half an hour, one of them got up and asked for service, and was told: "We don't serve Filipinos here." Filipino soldiers were turned away from theaters or were forced to sit in a segregated section, and their visiting wives were refused accommodations at the hotels. Concerned about the discriminatory treatment his men were receiving, Colonel Robert H. Offley met with the Marysville Chamber of Commerce. "There," as Private First Class Manuel Buaken put it, "he laid down the law of cooperation with the army — or else. Then the merchants and the restaurant proprietors and the movie houses changed their tune." Though the Filipinos were served in restaurants, the "soul of enjoyment" was gone for Buaken and his brothers. They felt that in their hearts those people were hating and ridiculing the Filipinos, laughing at their brown skins.[32]

But the war opened doors for Filipinos. Aliens who served in the U.S. Armed Forces were allowed to become citizens. On February 20, 1943, at Camp Beale, twelve hundred Filipino soldiers stood proudly in V formation as citizenship was conferred on them. During the ceremony, the commanding officer declared: "Officers who returned from Bataan have said there are no finer soldiers in the world than the Filipinos who fought and starved and died there shoulder to shoulder with our troops. I can well believe it as I look at the men before me. On those faces is quiet determination and a consciousness of training and discipline with a definite end in view. I congratulate them on their soldierly appearance and on their approaching citizenship." In the concluding speech, a judge welcomed the Filipinos: "Citizenship came to us who were born here as a heritage — it will come to you as a privilege. We have every faith you will become and remain loyal, devoted citizens of the United States."[33]

A year after the war ended, Congress extended citizenship to Filipino immigrants and permitted an annual token entry of 100 Filipino immigrants. Assessing the impact of the war on the status of Filipinos in 1946, sociologist R. T. Feria reported that employment opportunities had expanded for Filipinos as they entered the shipyards of Wilmington and San Pedro and the plants of Lockheed, Douglas, and Vultee. "The majority became wielders, technicians, assembly or office workers, and a few became engineers." Most important, Feria observed, the war had forced Filipinos to make a decision — "to go home and help in the reconstruction of their homeland" or "to spend the rest of their days in America." Granted citizenship and feeling a sense of greater acceptance, thousands of Filipinos chose to make America their permanent home. But would whites forget the bravery of Filipinos at Bataan when the economic prosperity of the war slackened, Feria wondered, and would they invoke another "interminable era of dishwashing and asparagus cutting"?[34]

Korean Americans: A War to Free Their Homeland

Like the Filipinos, Korean Americans also had a homeland to liberate. "Korea for Victory with America," they shouted. The *Korean National Herald-Pacific Weekly* declared that "every Korean born" was "an enemy born for Japan."[35]

Koreans had been in America for nearly four decades. Between 1903 and 1907, seven thousand Koreans arrived in Hawaii and California. "My parents were very poor," said a Korean woman. "One year, a heavy rain came, a flood; the crops all washed down. Oh, it was a very hard time. . . . Under the Japanese, no freedom. Not even free talking." She had heard stories about the islands. "Hawaii's a free place, everybody living well. Hawaii had freedom, so if you like talk, you can talk; you like work, you can work. . . . Then I could get to America! That land of freedom with streets paved of gold!"[36]

However, reality in America punctured this inflated dream. Like the Japanese, Koreans were not allowed to become naturalized citizens. The question of Korean eligibility for citizenship was tested in the courts after World War I by Easurk Emsen Charr. Drafted into the U.S. Army in 1918, he petitioned for citizenship in a federal district court in 1921, arguing that his military service entitled him to naturalized citizenship. However, the court declared that Koreans were "admittedly of the Mongol family" and hence were not eligible for naturalized citizenship.[37]

Excluded from citizenship in America, Korean immigrants found themselves cut off from their home country in 1910 when Japan annexed Korea. The immigrants dedicated themselves to patriotic organizations struggling against Japanese colonialism. "I was earning money then," recalled one woman, "and decided that I wanted to become a member of the Korean Nationalist Association, pay dues to support the Korean newspaper, and also to contribute to the patriotic fund. I gave one-tenth of my pay — which was optional for women, but I felt so good to be able to do so."[38] Grieving over the loss of his homeland, a Korean immigrant urged his compatriots in America to organize their lives around nationalistic resistance against Japan: "Now our business should be for all Koreans and our activity should be based on the welfare of our mother country. Thus we are not sojourners, but political wanderers, and we are not laborers but righteous army soldiers."[39]

Although Koreans were fiercely anti-Japanese, they were often mistaken for Japanese. "When World War Two broke out," Jean Park remembered, "we were still living in Reedley." Her immigrant Korean father decided to move the family to southern California. When Park and her family arrived at their new home, they found whites staring at them and shouting, "Japs go home!" "They were ready to stone us with rocks and descend on us because they had that evil look in their eyes."[40]

Government policies also failed to distinguish Koreans from the Japanese. In 1940, the Alien Registration Act had classified Korean immigrants as subjects of Japan; after the United States declared war against Japan, the government identified Koreans as "enemy aliens." In February 1942, the *Korean National Herald–Pacific Weekly* insisted the government reclassify them as Koreans. "The Korean is an enemy of Japan," the editorial declared, underscoring the torturous irony of the situation. "Since December 7, the Korean here is between the devil and the deep sea for the reason that the United States considers him a subject of Japan, which the Korean resents as an injustice to his true status. . . . What is the status of a Korean in the United States? Is he an enemy alien? Has any Korean ever been in Japanese espionage or in subversive activities against the land where he makes his home and rears his children as true Americans?"[41]

In Hawaii, Korean immigrants employed on defense projects in the islands experienced an even more painful insult: they were classified as Japanese. "For years we've been fighting the Japanese and now they tell us that we're Japs," Koreans snapped angrily. "It's an insult!" Placed in a restricted category, these Koreans had to wear badges with black borders. "Why in the hell do they pull a trick like this on us," a Korean worker asked, "when we hate the Japanese more than anyone else in the world?" After their protests, they were allowed to have printed on their badges: "I am Korean."[42]

Korean immigrants were anxious to help win the war against Japan. Many of them posssessed an invaluable weapon which the U.S. military needed — knowledge of the Japanese language, which they had been forced to learn in Korea under Japanese control. Korean immigrants were employed as Japanese language teachers and translators of secret Japanese military documents; they also served as propaganda broadcasters in the Pacific front and agents for underground activities in Japanese-occupied areas of Asia. An instructor in oriental languages at the University of California at Berkeley, Bong-Youn Choy recalled his energetic effort during the war: "I delivered lectures on Korean and Japanese politics to the Office of War Information for three months. In addition, I was asked to teach Japanese to the special Army Training Program classes." Commissioned as Navy interpreters, Yi Jong-gun and Pak Yong-hak were sent to the Solomon Islands and participated in the Guadalcanal campaign.[43]

In Los Angeles, 109 Koreans — one-fifth of the city's Korean population — joined the California National Guard. Ranging in age from eighteen to sixty-five, they were organized into a Korean unit called the Tiger Brigade or "Manghokun." They drilled regularly on Saturday and Sunday afternoons for three to four hours in Exposition Park, preparing to defend California against an enemy invasion. Congratulating them, an army official declared: "I myself have learned the real meaning of patriotism during my participation in this Tiger Brigade, and I cannot find adequate words to describe your contribution in winning this war." Meanwhile, elderly Korean women served in the Red Cross, and old men volunteered as emergency fire wardens. Koreans everywhere bought defense bonds: between 1942 and 1943, they reportedly purchased more than $239,000 worth of them — an immense sum for a population of only ten thousand. At the celebration of the Korean National Flag Day on August 29, 1943, the Los Angeles mayor raised the Korean flag to honor the uniformed men of the Tiger Brigade as they marched past City Hall.[44]

A year later, Hawaii territorial delegate Joseph R. Farrington introduced in Congress a bill for Korean immigration and naturalization. Farrington's bill did not pass, but Koreans had gained greater acceptance and also helped to defeat Japan and free their homeland.[45]

India: Passage to America

Like Korean immigrants, immigrants from India also saw the war as an opportunity to win acceptance in America. They had begun arriving in the U.S. at the beginning of the century, and by 1920, they numbered 6,400, most of them working in California as farmers and agricultural laborers.

When asked why he had left India, Deal Singh Madhas told an interviewer: "To make money and then return to the Punjab [northern India] and farm for myself instead of on the ancestral property." To pay for their transportation to San Francisco, many Punjabis mortgaged some of their land. Even if they had to become debtors to get to America, they thought the promise of getting ahead was worth the sacrifice. Paid only ten or fifteen cents a day in India, they were told they could earn two dollars in America. An immigrant later recalled how California seemed "enchanted."[46]

The majority of the immigrants were Sikhs. Wearing their traditional headdress, the newcomers from India were described as "the tide of turbans." "Always the turban remains," a witness wrote, "the badge and symbol of their native land, their native customs and religion. Whether repairing tracks on the long stretches of the Northern Pacific railways, feeding logs into the screaming rotary saws of the lumber-mills, picking fruit in the luxuriant orchards or sunny hillsides of California, the twisted turban shows white or brilliant . . . an exotic thing in the western landscape." Their strikingly unusual dress and dark skin provoked taunts and verbal abuse from whites. "I used to go to Marysville every Saturday," recounted a Sikh. "One day a drunk *ghora* (white man) came out of a bar and motioned to me saying, 'Come here, slave!' I said I was no slave man. He told me that his race ruled India and America, too. All we were slaves. He came close to me and I hit him and got away fast."[47]

In an article on "The Hindu, the Newest Immigration Problem," *Survey* magazine editorialized in 1910: "The civic and social question concerns the ability of the nation to assimilate this class of Hindus and their probable effect on the communities where they settle. Their habits, their intense caste feeling, their lack of home life — no women being among them — and their effect upon standards of labor and wages, all combine to raise a serious question as to whether the doors should be kept open or closed against this strange, new stream." Seven years later, Congress prohibited the entry of Asian-Indian laborers.[48]

However, the question of the political status of Asian Indians already in the United States remained. The federal law of 1790 had reserved naturalized citizenship for "whites" only, providing the basis for excluding Chinese, Japanese, and Korean immigrants from citizenship. But Asian Indians were Caucasian. Would they be entitled to naturalized citizenship? In the 1923 *Bhagat Singh Thind* case, the Supreme Court ruled that Asian Indians were ineligible for naturalization. Arguing that the definition of race had to be based on the "understanding of the common man," the Court held that the term "white person" meant an immigrant from northern and western Europe. "It may be true," the Court declared, "that the blond Scandinavian and the brown Hindu have a common ancestor in the dim reaches of antiquity, but the average man knows perfectly well that there are unmistakable and profound differences between them today." Thus Asian Indians, while they were "Caucasian," were not "white." The intention of the Founding Fathers was to "confer the privilege of citizenship upon that class of persons" they knew as "white."[49]

Asian Indians denounced this discrimination. In 1940, Khairata Ram Samras petitioned a federal court to overturn the *Thind* decision. "Discrimination against Hindus in respect to naturalization," Samras argued, "is not only capricious and untenable but in violation of constitutional provisions."[50] A year later, the issue of citizenship for Asian Indians was swept into the vortex of World War II. In August 1941, President Roosevelt and Prime Minister Winston Churchill issued the Atlantic Charter, a broad statement of principles including the right of peoples to choose their own form of government. Asian Indians saw the Charter as an opportunity to press for their rights in the United States. The India Welfare League and the India League of America demanded both independence for India and naturalized citizenship for Asian Indians in the United States.

The war forced American policymakers to recognize the strategic military location of India. Japan could exploit Indian disaffection with British rule, create political chaos in the Asian subcontinent, and drive its military machinery across India. Here was indeed a grim military prospect — the unification of Japanese and German armed forces in the Middle East.

In March 1944, Congress considered a bill that would provide a small immigration quota from India and naturalization rights. A leading supporter of the proposed legislation, Emmanuel Celler of New York, argued that oppressed people throughout the world looked to the United States for justice and equality, and that "our breaking down of immigration and naturalization barriers" would "dull the edge of Jap propaganda."[51]

Four months later, in his support for this legislation, S. Chandrasekar, a lecturer at the University of Pennsylvania, highlighted the need to combat Nazi ideology by repudiating racism at home:

> Today, more than ever, the United States is vitally interested in attitudes of Asiatic peoples toward this country. Hitler's justification of Nazi oppression in Europe is supposedly based on the right of the mythically superior Nordic to superimpose his *Kultur* on the other so-called inferior peoples of Europe. If the United States is success-

fully to combat such dangerous ideas, it can ill afford to practice racial discrimination in its relations with Asiatic countries. The immigration policy of this country now excludes nearly a quarter of the human race. America cannot afford to say that she wants the people of India to fight on her side and at the same time maintain that she will not have them among her immigrant groups.

Clearly, the United States could not have it both ways: it could not oppose the racist ideology of Nazism and also "practice" racial discrimination. America had to put its "principle of equality" into its laws and policies, Chandrasekhar concluded, in order to reaffirm the faith of the millions in India looking to America for "justice and fair play."[52] Two years later, Congress permitted India to have a small immigration quota and granted the right of naturalized citizenship to Asian-Indian immigrants.

Germans and Italians: "Just Like Everybody Else"

Shortly after the Japanese attack on Pearl Harbor, the FBI visited the home of William Hohensee of Munith, Michigan. "Because I was born in Germany," he recalled, "the FBI questioned me at great length regarding my German activities that took place in various German Clubs and establishments in Detroit. From January 1942, until my induction into the Army in 1943, they harassed me periodically with their constant questioning. They were even instrumental in me losing my job as a Teamster employee in the trucking industry. Much to their dismay, I was unable to enlighten them on any German activities simply because I was never involved in anything."[53]

But Hohensee and his fellow German Americans did not experience a repeat of the backlash that had occurred during World War I. In 1917–1918, federal authorities excluded German aliens from sensitive military areas such as wharves and railroad depots, and interned several thousand of them for minor violations of this order. Numerous states disenfranchised German aliens; half of the states prohibited instruction in German. In many communities, Bach and Beethoven were banned, and German books were burned.[54]

But such extreme anti-German reactions did not happen during World War II. The army ordered a curfew for German aliens on the West Coast, and the FBI detained three thousand German aliens suspected as security threats. Several German-American Bund leaders were indicted for sedition. However, German Americans were not subjected to mass exclusion or detention. To have done so would have been a logistical nightmare. By 1940, there were 5 million German Americans, including 1,237,000 immigrants. They represented considerable voting power and were important economically as businessmen and workers in the northeast and midwest. Assimilated into mainstream society, Germans were regarded as Americans, especially since they included individuals with names like Lou Gehrig and Dwight D. Eisenhower.

At first, Italian aliens on the West Coast were suspected of disloyalty. Between 1900 and 1920, 3 million Italians had landed at Ellis Island. About half of them were sojourners with plans to make money and then return to their villages. "Most Italians remain in the United States from two to five years," reported Victor Von Borosini in "Home-Going Italians," published in a 1912 issue of *Survey*.[55] In 1924, responding to nativist backlashes, Congress passed the National Origins Act, instituting an annual quota for immigration based on 2 percent of the foreign-born population of each nationality residing in the United States in 1890. In that marker year, before the great influx from Italy, foreign-born Italians numbered only about 300,000; thus the quota for Italy was less than 6,000 a year.

Cut off from their country of origin, Italian immigrants and their children continued to be targets of prejudice in Protestant America. Often they experienced ugly stereotyping. "You don't call . . . an Italian a white man?" a construction boss was asked. "No, sir," he replied, "an Italian is a Dago." Italians were said to be criminally inclined and violent. "The knife with which he cuts his bread," a prison authority commented, "he also uses to lop off another 'dago's' finger or ear. . . . He is quite as familiar with the sight of human blood as with the sight of the food he eats." Italian workers also found themselves restricted in employment opportunities. The Bricklayers Union of New York, for example, successfully pressured the city to exclude unnaturalized Italians from working on the construction of the subways.[56]

After America entered World War II, unnaturalized Italians suddenly found themselves suspected of disloyalty. On the West Coast in February 1942, the army placed a curfew on ten thousand "enemy" Italian aliens and excluded them from restricted zones on the waterfront areas for reasons of "military necessity." "Italians who were not citizens," recalled Alfonso Zirpoli, "were ordered to move out of the area north of Beach Street [in San Francisco]. One Italian came to see me; his son had been killed at Pearl Harbor. He wanted to know what he should do — should he move?"[57]

In San Francisco, Italian fishermen were required to stay away from their boats. "I'll never forget Mr. Maniscalco," recalled Alessandro Baccari, Jr. "He was a fisherman, the most respected at the wharf. I went to grammar school with his son, John. One day, I was visiting their house and he greeted me by saying, 'Alessandro, I can no longer go aboard my boat at the wharf.' Italian aliens were compelled to remain fourteen blocks away from the waterfront. He couldn't comprehend. With tears in his eyes, he told me, 'I'm gonna break the law. My boat is my life.' He would sneak out to see his boat and the waterfront."[58]

In his angry denunciation of the "enemy alien" classification, Frank Buccellato described the ordeal of his mother-in-law. Although her husband was an American citizen, she was not. The army ordered her to move fifteen miles from Pittsburgh, California, a militarily sensitive area. Protesting the order, Buccellato went to the draft board and told them: "This doesn't seem right. My family and my wife's family each have two boys in the service, fighting for the United States of America. We're American citizens;

we're all born here in this country. So what do we care about Italy. . . . ? This is our country, right here. Why would . . . my mother-in-law want to sabotage this country?"[59]

In the end, however, only 85 Italian aliens were detained as security threats, and a proposed evacuation of "enemy" Italian aliens was ruled out. The congressional committee headed by John H. Tolan decided that "evacuation policies instituted for German and Italian aliens on the west coast [would] have direct nationwide import because there are many thousands of these aliens in other parts of the country. . . . Any such proposal is out of the question if we intend to win this war."[60] Interning Italian Americans was also out of the question in a country where one of the most famous baseball players was Joe DiMaggio and the mayor of New York was Fiorello La Guardia. In May 1942, the waterfront restriction on Italian aliens was rescinded, and on October 12, 1942, Attorney General Francis Biddle announced that Italian aliens would no longer be classified as "enemies."[61] Told he was no longer an "enemy," an Italian immigrant snapped scornfully: "I am an American again, huh?"[62]

In "Americans in Concentration Camps," published in the *Crisis* in September 1942, Harry Paxton Howard compared the experiences of three American groups — German, Italian, and Japanese. The 120,000 Japanese on the West Coast were evacuated and imprisoned in concentration camps; 40,000 of them, born in Japan, were classified as "enemy aliens." "If they were 'white,' the great majority of them would not be aliens at all." Although most of them had been in America for more than thirty years, they had not been allowed to become citizens because they were "Asiatic." In contrast, over a million German and Italian immigrants entered this country at the same time as the Japanese immigrants and were allowed to become naturalized citizens because they were "white."

On the East Coast, Howard pointed out, the military danger was from Germany and Italy. Enemy submarines had been destroying American shipping, and had even landed agents, some of whom had been apprehended. "But the American government,"

Howard wrote, "has not taken any such high-handed action against Germans and Italians — and their American-born descendants — on the east coast, as has been taken against Japanese and their American-born descendants on the west coast. Germans and Italians are 'white.'"

To illustrate his point, Howard referred to the "New York at War" parade of June 13. Up Fifth Avenue, Mayor Fiorello La Guardia had led a spectacular procession of American and Allied forces and delegations of loyal German Americans and Italian Americans. "There was one omission in the parade," wrote Howard. "Americans of Japanese ancestry were not permitted to take part." Their absence was noticed by four members of the American Civil Liberties Union. Florina Lasker, Reverend John Paul Jones, Mary Dreier, and Guy Emery Shipler sent an indignant protest to the mayor: "We learn with amazement that the committee in charge of the patriotic parade in support of the United Nations on Saturday has refused to permit loyal Japanese-Americans to march, although permitting German-Americans and Italian-Americans to participate. Such discrimination on purely racial grounds is a shocking violation of our democratic professions."

In his conclusion, Howard offered a lesson for black America. "What has happened to these Americans [of Japanese ancestry] in recent months is of direct concern for the American Negro. For the barbarous treatment of these Americans is the result of the color line."[63]

The significance of the color line was revealed in a remark made by the California attorney general. In his recommendation that the military restrictions against Italian aliens be lifted, Earl Warren told the Tolan committee that it would be "disruptive of national unity" to expel Italian aliens, for they were "just like everybody else."[64]

But, in Warren's view, the Japanese in California whether aliens or citizens by birth were not "just like everybody else." In an interview, Peter Mangiapane and his mother, Nancy, recalled what had happened to Italians and Japanese in California. As Italians, "we were in the same position as the Japanese," he said. She added: "The only difference was they put them into camps. They lost more than we did." Also noting the difference in the ways the government handled the Italians and the Japanese, Benito Vanni recalled that the Japanese were treated "rotten." "Right around the corner from me was a Japanese laundry, and the owner was a good friend of mine. When you went through the front of the laundry, if you had to judge a book by its cover, you'd say, 'What a dump.' But when you went past the laundry into the living quarters you had to take your shoes off. I was there when they picked him up and his whole family. He was crying. I was crying, 'cause I lost a pretty good friend."[65]

Vanni's friend had been taken away, along with the other Japanese Americans on the West Coast, and forced to spend "years of infamy" imprisoned in internment camps.[66]

7

⛬

REMEMBERING PEARL HARBOR
From Internment to Hiroshima

UNLIKE THE Germans, Italians, and other Asian groups, Japanese Americans were classified as "enemies." Beginning in February 1942, 120,000 Japanese, most of them citizens by birth, were incarcerated without due process of law. "All of this was done," reported the Commission on Wartime Relocation and Internment of Civilians in 1982, "despite the fact that not a single documented act of espionage, sabotage or fifth column activity was committed by an American citizen of Japanese ancestry or by a resident Japanese alien on the West Coast."[1]

The mass internment of Japanese Americans in 1942 and the atomic bombing of Hiroshima in 1945 followed in the wake of the shocking surprise attack on Pearl Harbor. "Infamy," Roosevelt's term in his call for a declaration of war against Japan, turned out to be a prologue to other infamies.

Reciting the Gettysburg Address in Plantation Hawaii

Shortly after he inspected the still-smoking ruins of the destroyed fleet, Secretary of the Navy Frank Knox issued a statement to the press: "I think the most effective fifth column work of the entire war was done in Hawaii, with the possible exception of Norway." At a Cabinet meeting on December 19, Knox recommended the internment of all Japanese aliens on Oahu on an outer island.[2]

In a radio address aired two days later, however, the military governor of Hawaii, General Delos Emmons, assured Japanese Americans that the authorities would not take general action against them. "There is no intention or desire on the part of the federal authorities to operate mass concentration camps," declared Emmons. "No person, be he citizen or alien, need worry, provided he is not connected with subversive elements. . . . While we have been subjected to a serious attack by a ruthless and treacherous enemy, we must remember that this is America and we must do things the American Way. We must distinguish between loyalty and disloyalty among our people."[3]

A schism in policy was developing between Washington and Honolulu. Pursuant to Secretary Knox's recommendation, the War Department sent General Emmons a letter on January 10, 1942, asking for his view on the question of evacuating the Japanese from Oahu. Emmons replied that the proposed program would be dangerous and impractical. Such an evacuation would require badly needed construction materials and shipping space, and would also tie up troop resources needed to guard the islands. Moreover, the mass evacuation of Japanese would severely disrupt both the economy and defense of Oahu, for the Japanese represented over 90 percent of the carpenters, nearly all of the transportation workers, and a significant proportion of the agricultural laborers. Japanese labor was "absolutely essential" for the rebuilding of Pearl Harbor. Then, on February 9, the War Department ordered General Emmons to suspend all Japanese workers employed by the army. But the order was rescinded after Emmons argued that the Japanese workers were indispensable and that the "Japanese question" should be handled "by those in direct contact with the situation."[4]

On March 13, President Roosevelt, acting on the advice of his

Joint Chiefs of Staff, approved a recommendation for the evacuation of 20,000 "dangerous" Japanese from Hawaii to the mainland. Two weeks later, General Emmons reduced the number drastically to 1,550 Japanese. The War Department then circulated a report received from the Justice Department warning of a Japanese invasion of Hawaii. In a letter to Assistant Secretary of War John J. McCloy, Emmons showed his impatience with Washington: "The feeling that an invasion is imminent is not the belief of most of the responsible people. . . . There have been no known acts of sabotage committed in Hawaii."[5]

Emmons continued to resist pressure from the War Department in Washington to evacuate the Japanese from Hawaii. On October 29, Secretary of War Henry L. Stimson informed President Roosevelt that General Emmons intended to remove approximately 5,000 Japanese from Hawaii as shipping facilities became available. "This, General Emmons believes, will greatly simplify his problem, and considering the labor needs in the islands, is about all that he has indicated any desire to move although he has been given authority to move up to fifteen thousand." Irritated by Emmons, President Roosevelt wrote to Stimson: "I think that General Emmons should be told that the only consideration is that of the safety of the Islands and that the labor situation is not only a secondary matter but should not be given any consideration whatsoever."[6] In the end, still insisting that there was no military necessity for mass evacuation, General Emmons ordered the internment of only 1,444 Japanese (979 aliens and 525 citizens), most of them community leaders, Buddhist priests, and Japanese-language teachers.

Business interests in Hawaii supported General Emmons's resistance to relocation. The president of the Honolulu Chamber of Commerce called for just treatment of the Japanese in Hawaii: "There are 160,000 of these people who want to live here because they like the country and like the American way of life. . . . The citizens of Japanese blood would fight as loyally for America as any other citizen. I have read or heard nothing in statements given out by the military, local police or F.B.I. since December 7 to change my opinion. And I have gone out of my way to ask for the facts." Business leaders in Hawaii were unwilling to permit the mass uprooting of the Japanese. They knew that the evacuation of 158,000 Japanese, constituting over one-third of Hawaii's population, would decimate their labor force and destroy the economy of the islands.[7]

Meanwhile, public officials urged restraint and reason. Hawaii's congressional delegate Sam King advised the military that nothing should be done beyond apprehending known spies. Honolulu police captain John A. Burns refuted rumors of Japanese snipers firing on American soldiers during the attack on Pearl Harbor. "In spite of what . . . anyone . . . may have said about the fifth column activity in Hawaii," stated Robert L. Shivers, head of the FBI in Hawaii, "I want to emphasize that there was no such activity in Hawaii before, during or after the attack on Pearl Harbor. . . . I was in a position to know this fact. . . . Nowhere under the sun could there have been a more intelligent response to the needs of the hour than was given by the entire population of these islands."[8]

The press in Hawaii also behaved professionally and responsibly. Newspapers cautioned their readers not to spread or be influenced by rumors generated by the war situation. Within days after the attack on Pearl Harbor, the *Honolulu Star Bulletin* dismissed reports of Japanese subversion in the islands as "weird, amazing, and damaging untruths." "Beware of rumors always," urged the *Paradise of the Pacific* magazine in February 1942, "avoid them like a plague and, when possible, kill them as you would a reptile. Don't repeat for a fact anything you do not know is a fact."[9]

Meanwhile, through their actions, Japanese Americans were demonstrating their loyalty. During the morning of December 7, two thousand Nisei (American-born Japanese) serving in the U.S. Army stationed in Hawaii battled enemy planes at Pearl Harbor. Japanese civilians participated in the island's defense. They rushed to their posts as volunteer truck drivers for Oahu's Citizens' Defense Committee; they stood in long lines in front of Queen's Hospital, waiting to give blood to the wounded. Many of them were Issei (immigrants). "Most of us have lived longer in Hawaii than in Japan. We have an obligation to this country," they declared. "We are *yoshi* [adopted sons] of America. We want to do our part for America."[10]

Then that night, as the people of the islands tensely waited in the darkness for the expected invasion, thousands of Nisei members of the Hawaii Territorial Guard — youngsters from the high schools and the University of Hawaii ROTC program — guarded the power plants, reservoirs, and important waterfronts. "I jumped into my ROTC uniform and rushed up to the university campus," recalled Ted Tsukiyama. "There were reports that Japanese paratroopers had landed. Our orders were to deploy and meet the enemy and delay their advance into the city. With pounding hearts, we moved to the south end of the campus and scanned for the enemy. To put it bluntly, we were scared! But not for long. As we thought of the sneak attack that morning, a wave of fury and anger swept over us. There was not doubt or decision as we advanced. It was going to be 'either them or us.'"[11]

When General Emmons announced that the Army needed 1,500 Nisei volunteers, 9,507 men responded. "I wanted to show something, to contribute to America," explained Minoru Hinahara, who served as a Japanese language interpreter in the U.S. 27th Army Division and participated in the invasion of Okinawa. "My parents could not become citizens but they told me, 'You fight for your country.'"[12]

Indeed, the United States had become their country. Beginning in the 1880s, 200,000 Japanese immigrants had come to Hawaii. On the sugar plantations, they found themselves pitted against workers of other nationalities. Planters had systematically developed an ethnically diverse labor force in order to create divisions among their workers and reinforce management control. A manager explained the strategy: "Keep a variety of laborers, that is different nationalities, and thus prevent any concerted action in case

of strikes, for there are few, if any, cases of Japs, Chinese, and Portuguese entering into a strike as a unit."[13]

Refusing to be exploited, Japanese plantation workers organized into a union. In 1909, they organized their first major strike
to demand higher wages. Their demands reflected their transformation from sojourning laborers into settlers: "We have decided
to permanently settle here [and] to unite our destiny with that of
Hawaii, sharing the prosperity and adversity of Hawaii with other
citizens of Hawaii." Significantly, Japanese immigrants were fram-
ing their demands in "American" terms. They argued that the
deplorable conditions on the plantations perpetuated an "undemocratic and un-American" society of "plutocrats and coolies." Fair
wages would encourage laborers to work more industriously and
enable Hawaii to enjoy "perpetual peace and prosperity." Seeking
to create "a thriving and contented middle class — the realization
of the high ideal of Americanism," the strikers wanted to share in
the American dream.[14] In 1920, the Japanese went out on strike
again, this time joining Filipino plantation workers. "When we
first came to Hawaii," the strikers proudly declared, "these islands
were covered with ohia forests, guava fields and areas of wild
grass. Day and night did we work, cutting trees and burning grass,
clearing lands and cultivating fields until we made the plantations
what they are today."[15]

The Japanese strikers had decided to settle and raise families in
their adopted country and wanted to give their children opportunities for a better life. Education, they believed, was the key to
freedom from the drudgery of plantation labor. "Father made up
his mind to send his children to school so far as he possibly could,"
said the daughter of a plantation worker. "Yet he had no idea of
forcing us. Instead he employed different methods which made us
want to go to school. We were made to work in the cane fields at
a very early age. . . . After a day's work in the fields dad used to
ask: 'Are you tired? Would you want to work in the fields when
you are old enough to leave school? . . . My father did everything

in his power to make us realize that going to school would be to our advantage."[16]

However, the planters needed the Nisei generation as plantation laborers. In their view, these children should not be educated beyond the sixth or eighth grade, and their education should be vocational training. A visitor from the mainland noticed the presence of Japanese children on the plantations and asked a manager whether he thought the coming generation of Japanese would make intelligent citizens. "Oh, yes," he replied, "they'll make intelligent citizens all right enough, but not plantation laborers — and that's what we want."[17]

Many public schools, however, were not preparing Japanese children to be plantation laborers. The students were reciting the Gettysburg Address and the Declaration of Independence. "Here the children learned about democracy or at least the theory of it," said a University of Hawaii student. They were taught that honest labor, fair play, and industriousness were virtues. But they "saw that it wasn't so on the plantation." Returning from school to their plantation camps, students noticed the wide "disparity between theory and practice." This contradiction was glaring. "The public school system perhaps without realizing it," the student observed, "created unrest and disorganization."[18]

World War II offered the Nisei of Hawaii an opportunity to claim their identity as Americans, entitled to the rights and respect of full citizens. Enlisting in the U.S. Armed Forces, they left the plantations and went off to war. Writing from a European battlefront to a friend in the islands, a Japanese-American soldier explained his purpose for serving in the military: "My friends and my family — they mean everything to me. They are the most important reason why I am giving up my education and my happiness to go to fight a war that we never asked for. But our Country is involved in it. Not only that. By virtue of the Japanese attack on our nation, we as American citizens of Japanese ancestry have been mercilessly flogged with criticism and accusations. But I'm not going to take it sitting down! I may not be able to come back. But that matters little. My family and friends — they are the ones who will be able to back their arguments with facts. They are the ones who will be proud. In fact, it is better that we are sent to the front and that a few of us do not return, for the testimony will be stronger in favor of the folks back home."[19]

"A Tremendous Hole" in the Constitution: Roosevelt's Executive Order 9066

On the day after the attack on Pearl Harbor, Representative John M. Coffee of Washington declared in Congress: "It is my fervent hope and prayer that residents of the United States of Japanese extraction will not be made the victim of pogroms directed by self-proclaimed patriots and by hysterical self-anointed heroes. . . . Let us not make a mockery of our Bill of Rights by mistreating these folks. Let us rather regard them with understanding, remembering they are the victims of a Japanese war machine, with the making of the international policies of which they had nothing to do."[20]

Federal authorities already knew that Japanese Americans could be trusted. The President had secretly arranged to have Chicago businessman Curtis Munson gather intelligence on the Japanese in the United States and assess whether they constituted an internal military threat. In his report submitted to Roosevelt on November 7, 1941, Munson informed the President that there was no need to worry about the Japanese population: "There will be no armed uprising of Japanese [in this country]. . . . For the most part the local Japanese are loyal to the United States or, at worst, hope that by remaining quiet they can avoid concentration camps or irresponsible mobs. We do not believe that they would be at least any more disloyal than any other racial group in the United States with whom we went to war."[21]

A month later the assessment of the Munson report was tested at Pearl Harbor. In his investigation of the Japanese in Hawaii and on the U.S. mainland, Lieutenant Commander K. D. Ringle of the

Office of Naval Intelligence found that the large majority were at least passively loyal to the United States. In late January 1942, Ringle estimated that only about 3,500 Japanese were potential military threats and stated there was no need for mass action against the Japanese. Meanwhile, the FBI had also conducted its own investigation. On December 10, Director J. Edgar Hoover informed Washington that "practically all" suspected individuals were in custody: 1,291 Japanese (367 in Hawaii, 924 on the mainland), 857 Germans, and 147 Italians. In a report to the Attorney General submitted in early February, Hoover concluded that the proposed mass evacuation of the Japanese for security reasons could not be justified.[22]

Despite these intelligence findings, Lieutenant General John L. DeWitt, head of the Western Defense Command, behaved very differently from his counterpart in Hawaii, General Emmons. Within two weeks after the attack on Pearl Harbor, General DeWitt requested approval to conduct search-and-seizure operations in order to prevent alien Japanese from making radio transmissions to Japanese ships. The Justice Department refused to issue search warrants without probable cause, and the FBI determined that the security threat from Japanese Americans was only a perceived one. In January, the Federal Communications Commission, which had been monitoring all broadcasts, reported that the army's fears were groundless. But the army continued pursuing plans based on the assumption of Japanese disloyalty. General DeWitt also wanted authority to exclude both Japanese aliens and Americans of Japanese ancestry from restricted areas. On January 4, 1942, at a meeting of federal and state officials in his Presidio headquarters, DeWitt declared that military necessity justified the exclusion of the Japanese from the West Coast: "We are at war and this area — eight states — has been designated as a theater of operations. . . . [There are] approximately 288,000 enemy aliens . . . which we have to watch. . . . I have little confidence that the enemy aliens are law-abiding or loyal in any sense of the word. Some of them yes; many, no. Particularly the Japanese. I have no confidence in their loyalty whatsoever. I am speaking now of the native born Japanese — 117,000 — and 42,000 in California alone."[23]

California newspapers also pressed for mass evacuation. On January 20, the *San Diego Union* fomented anti-Japanese hysteria: "In Hawaii . . . treachery by residents, who although of Japanese ancestry had been regarded as loyal, has played an important part in the success of Japanese attacks. . . . Every Japanese . . . should be moved out of the coastal area and to a point of safety far enough inland to nullify any inclination they may have to tamper with our safety here." In its call for Japanese removal, the *Los Angeles Times* declared: "A viper is nonetheless a viper wherever the egg is hatched — so a Japanese American, born of Japanese parents — grows up to be a Japanese, not an American."[24]

As the news media mounted its campaign for Japanese removal, it was joined by patriotic organizations. In the *Grizzly Bear,* the Native Sons and Daughters of the Golden West told their fellow Californians: "We told you so. Had the warnings been heeded — had the federal and state authorities been 'on the alert,' and rigidly enforced the Exclusion Law and the Alien Land Law . . . had the legislation been enacted denying citizenship to offspring of all aliens ineligible to citizenship . . . had Japan been denied the privilege of using California as a breeding ground for dual-citizens (Nisei); — the treacherous Japs probably would not have attacked Pearl Harbor December 7, 1941, and this country would not today be at war with Japan."[25]

Demands for the evacuation of the Japanese also came from agricultural interests such as the Grower-Shipper Vegetable Association, the Western Growers Protective Association, and the California Farm Bureau Federation. "We've been charged with wanting to get rid of the Japs for selfish reasons," the Grower-Shipper Vegetable Association stated in the *Saturday Evening Post* in May. "We might as well be honest. We do. It's a question of whether the white man lives on the Pacific Coast or the brown man. They came into this valley to work, and they stayed to take over. . . . If all the Japs were removed tomorrow, we'd never miss them in two weeks, because the white farmers can take over and produce everything the Jap grows."[26]

State politicians joined the clamor for Japanese removal. California attorney general Earl Warren urged federal authorities to evacuate Japanese from sensitive areas on the West Coast. The Japanese "may well be the Achilles heel of the entire civilian defense effort," he warned. "Unless something is done it may bring about a repetition of Pearl Harbor." In letters to the secretary of war and the FBI director, January 16, Congressman Leland Ford of Los Angeles demanded that "all Japanese, whether citizens or not, be placed in concentration camps." Two weeks later, several congressmen from the Pacific Coast states asked President Roosevelt to grant the War Department "immediate and complete control over all alien enemies, as well as United States citizens holding dual citizenship in any enemy country, with full power and authority" to evacuate and intern them.[27]

On February 1, in a telephone conversation with Provost Marshal General Allen Gullion, General DeWitt said that protection against sabotage could only be made "positive by removing those people who are aliens and who are Japs of American citizenship." Shortly after the phone call, General DeWitt sent Gullion a recommendation for the mass exclusion of Japanese Americans: "In the war in which we are now engaged racial affinities are not severed by migration. The Japanese race is an enemy race and while many second and third generation Japanese born on United States soil, possessed of United States citizenship, have become 'Americanized,' the racial strains are undiluted." On February 5, Gullion drafted a War Department proposal for the exclusion of "all persons, whether aliens or citizens . . . deemed dangerous as potential saboteurs" from designated "military areas."[28]

In his diary on February 10, Secretary of War Henry L. Stimson wrote: "The second generation Japanese can only be evacuated either as part of a total evacuation . . . or by frankly trying to put them out on the ground that their racial characteristics are such that we cannot understand or trust even the citizen Japanese. This latter is the fact but I am afraid it will make a tremendous hole in our constitutional system to apply it."[29]

President Roosevelt was willing to risk damage to the Constitution. In fact, he had been considering the internment of Japanese Americans for several years. On August 10, 1936, Roosevelt had written a memorandum to the chief of naval operations: "One obvious thought occurs to me — that every Japanese citizen or noncitizen on the island of Oahu who meets these Japanese ships or has any connection with their officers or men should be secretly but definitely identified and his or her name placed on a special list of those who would be the first to be placed in a concentration camp in the event of trouble." Thus, five years before the attack on Pearl Harbor, Roosevelt was already considering the imprisonment of Japanese aliens and citizens in a "concentration camp" without due process.[30]

On February 19, in Executive Order 9066, Roosevelt directed the secretary of war to prescribe military areas "with respect to which, the right of any person to enter, remain in, or leave shall be subject to whatever restrictions the Secretary of War or the appropriate Military Commander may impose in his discretion." The order did not specify the Japanese as the group to be excluded. But they were the target. A few months later, when President Roosevelt learned about discussions in the War Department to apply the order to Germans and Italians on the East Coast, he wrote to inform Stimson that he considered enemy alien control to be "primarily a civilian matter except in the case of the Japanese mass evacuation on the Pacific Coast."[31]

Immediately, General DeWitt began to implement the executive order. A year later, he told a congressional committee: "You needn't worry about the Italians at all except in certain cases. Also, the same for the Germans except in individual cases. But we must worry about the Japanese all the time until he is wiped off the map. Sabotage and espionage will make problems as long as he is allowed in this area — problems which I don't want to have to worry about." At a press conference after this meeting, DeWitt told reporters that the Japanese should not be allowed to return to the West Coast because "a Jap is a Jap."[32]

Internment: "Huge Dreams" Destroyed

Decades of Japanese struggle to settle in America had come to an abrupt end. Immigrants from Japan had begun arriving in the 1880s, and by 1920, the Japanese population on the U.S. mainland had reached 138,834. They had been drawn here by stories of fantastic American wages. Inota Tawa calculated that as a laborer in America he could save in one year almost 1,000 yen — an amount equal to the income of a governor in Japan. He begged his parents: "By all means let me go to America." To prospective Japanese migrants, "money grew on trees" in the country across the Pacific. They carried an excited expectation:

> Huge dreams of fortune
> Go with me to foreign lands,
> Across the ocean.[33]

Concentrated in the Pacific Coast states, many Japanese immigrants became farmers, growing short-term crops like berries and truck vegetables. Japanese agriculture flourished. In 1900, the Japanese owned or leased twenty-nine farms with a total of 4,698 acres in California. Within five years, the total acreage had jumped to 61,858 and increased again to 194,742 by 1910. Ten years later, the Japanese controlled a total of 458,056 acres. By 1940 they grew 95 percent of fresh snap beans, 67 percent of fresh tomatoes, 95 percent of spring and summer celery, 44 percent of onions, and 40 percent of fresh green peas. Issei men and women had converted the marshes of the San Joaquin Valley, the dusty lands of the Sacramento Valley, and the deserts of the Imperial Valley into lush and profitable agricultural fields and orchards. Pursuing a dream that Jefferson would have admired, they were mixing their labor with the soil and becoming Americans.

But the Japanese were not accepted as Americans. In 1913, the California legislature enacted the Alien Land Law, denying them the right to own land because they were "aliens ineligible to citizenship."

Challenging the 1790 Naturalization Act, Takao Ozawa petitioned the court for his right to naturalized citizenship. On October 14, 1914, he filed an application for United States citizenship. Ozawa was confident he was qualified. After arriving here as a student in 1894, he had graduated from high school in Berkeley, California, and had attended the University of California for three years. He then moved to Honolulu, where he worked for an American company and settled down to raise a family. After his application was denied, Ozawa challenged the rejection in the U.S. District Court for the Territory of Hawaii. But the court ruled that Ozawa was not eligible for naturalized citizenship. The petitioner was, the court declared, "in every way eminently qualified under the statutes to become an American citizen," "except" one — he was not "white."[34]

Six years later, the case went before the Supreme Court. Ozawa informed the Court that he was a person of good character. Honest and industrious, he did not drink liquor, smoke, or gamble. More important, "at heart" he was "a true American." His family belonged to an American church and his children attended an American school. He spoke the "American language" at home, and his children could not speak Japanese. Loyal to the United States, Ozawa stated he was indebted to "our Uncle Sam" for the opportunity the country had given him. But Ozawa lost his petition. Ozawa was not entitled to naturalized citizenship, the Supreme Court held, because he was "clearly" "not Caucasian."[35]

Two years later, Congress enacted the National Origins Act. Under the 2 percent provision for the quota for a nationality group based on the 1890 census, Japan would have been allowed only an insignificant number of forty immigrants annually. But the law included a special provision that prohibited the entry of "aliens ineligible to citizenship," a code phrase for the Japanese. Thus the ban was total. After the Ozawa decision and the 1924 immigration law, Issei felt despair.

> America . . . once
> A dream of hope and longing,
> Now a life of tears.[36]

Facing overwhelming discrimination, immigrant Japanese feared they would have no future in their adopted land, except through their children. Representing a rapidly growing group within the Japanese community, the Nisei constituted 63 percent of the Japanese population on the eve of World War II. Through their children, parents hoped, the Japanese would someday find tolerance in America. English-speaking and educated in American schools, the second-generation Japanese would teach white Americans about the culture of Japan and the hopes of the immigrant generation. As "intermediaries," they would "interpret" the East to the West and the West to the East. The Nisei would be the "bridge" to the larger society.[37]

"You are American citizens," the Issei reminded their children time and again like a litany. "You have an opportunity your parents never had. Go to school and study. Don't miss that opportunity when it comes." The parents were willing to give up their own comforts, even necessities, for the education of their children.

> Alien hardships
> Made bearable by the hope
> I hold for my children.[38]

However, American-born Japanese discovered that education did not make much difference. They graduated from high school with good grades, even honors, and many completed college. The average educational level of Nisei was two years of college, well above the national average. Still they found themselves cut off from employment opportunities. A study of 161 Nisei who graduated from the University of California between 1925 and 1935 found that only 25 percent were employed in professional vocations for which they had been trained. Twenty-five percent worked in family business or trades that did not require a college education, and 40 percent had dead-end jobs. University job placement offices repeatedly reported virtually no employment prospects for Japanese-American graduates.[39] Many became discouraged. "I am a fruitstand worker," wrote one Nisei in a local newspaper. "It is not a very attractive nor distinguished occupation, and most certainly unappealing in print. I would much rather it were doctor or lawyer . . . but my aspirations of developing into such [were] frustrated long ago by circumstances . . . [and] I am only what I am, a professional carrot washer."[40]

The problem for the Nisei generation went far beyond the matter of jobs. It was also profoundly cultural, involving the very definition of who was an American. In his essay "The Rising Son of the Rising Sun," published in *New Outlook* in 1934, Aiji Tashiro explained why Japanese Americans were viewed as strangers. "The Jablioskis, Idovitches, and Johannsmanns streaming over from Europe," he pointed out, "[were able] to slip unobtrusively into the clothes of 'dyed-in-the-wool' Americans by the simple expedient of dropping their guttural speech and changing their names to Jones, Brown or Smith." Tashiro knew it would make no difference if he changed his name to Taylor. He spoke English fluently and had even adopted American slang, dress, and mannerisms. But "outwardly" he "possessed the marked characteristics of the race." To be accepted as American seemed hopeless. "The voice of the flute has long been the unfathomable voice of the East beating upon the West with futility."[41]

But the Nisei did not wish to be completely assimilated, to become simply "American." They felt they were a complex combination of the two cultures, and they should be allowed to embrace their twoness. Everything they had learned at school about the United States had taken "root," and they felt they were Americans. Nevertheless, many of them did not want to reject the culture of their parents. James Sakamoto explained how the Nisei had a "natural love" for the country of their birth as well as for the land of their parents. Deep within, the Nisei stood on the "border line" that separated the "Orient" from the "Occident," the "streams of two great civilizations — the old Japanese culture with its formal traditions and the newer American civilization with its individual freedom."[42]

This hope to be both Japanese and American was suddenly shattered in February 1942. In the view of policymakers like General DeWitt, American-born Japanese were still "Japanese." Under General DeWitt's command, the military ordered a curfew for all persons of Japanese ancestry and posted the following order on telephone poles and storefronts: "Pursuant to the provisions of Civilian Exclusion Order No. 27, this Headquarters, dated April 30, 1942, all persons of Japanese ancestry, both alien and non-alien, will be evacuated from the above area by 12 o' clock noon, P. W. T., Thursday May 7, 1942."[43]

The evacuees were instructed to bring their bedding, toilet articles, extra clothing, and utensils. "No pets of any kind will be permitted." Japanese stood in silent numbness before the notices. Years later, Congressman Robert Matsui, who was a baby in 1942, asked: "How could I as a 6-month-old child born in this country be declared by my own Government to be an enemy alien?" But the order applied to everyone, including children, and even babies were taken out of orphanages.[44]

"Doesn't my citizenship mean a single blessed thing to anyone?" asked Monica Sone's brother in distress. "Several weeks before May, soldiers came around and posted notices on telephone poles," said Takae Washizu. "It was sad for me to leave the place where I had been living for such a long time. Staring at the ceiling in bed at night, I wondered who would take care of my cherry tree and my house after we moved out."[45]

Believing the military orders were unconstitutional, Minoru Yasui of Portland refused to obey the curfew order: "It was my belief that no military authority has the right to subject any United States citizen to any requirement that does not equally apply to all other U.S. citizens. If we believe in America, if we believe in equality and democracy, if we believe in law and justice, then each of us, when we see or believe errors are being made, has an obligation to make every effort to correct them." Meanwhile Fred Korematsu in California and Gordon Hirabayashi in Washington refused to report to the evacuation center. "As an American citizen," Hirabayashi explained, "I wanted to uphold the principles of the Constitution, and the curfew and evacuation orders which singled out a group on the basis of ethnicity violated them. It was not acceptable to me to be less than a full citizen in a white man's country." The three men were arrested and convicted. Sent to prison, they took their cases to the Supreme Court, which upheld their convictions, declaring that the government's policies were based on military necessity.[46]

Most Japanese, however, felt they had no choice but to comply with the evacuation orders. Instructed that they would be allowed to take only what they could carry, they had to sell most of their possessions — their refrigerators, cars, furniture, radios, pianos, farms, and houses. "I remember how agonizing was my despair," recounted Tom Hayase, "to be given only about six days in which to dispose of our property." "It is difficult to describe the feeling of despair and humiliation experienced by all of us," said another evacuee, "as we watched the Caucasians coming to look over our possessions and offering such nominal amounts knowing we had no recourse but to accept whatever they were offering because we did not know what the future held for us."[47]

At control centers, the evacuees were registered and each family was assigned a number. "Henry went to the Control Station to register the family," remembered Monica Sone. "He came home with twenty tags, all numbered '10710,' tags to be attached to each piece of baggage, and one to hang from our coat lapels. From then on, we were known as Family #10710." When they reported at the train stations, they found themselves surrounded by soldiers with rifles and bayonets. "I looked at Santa Clara's streets from the train over the subway," wrote Norman Mineta's father in a letter to friends in San Jose. "I thought this might be the last look at my loved home city. My heart almost broke, and suddenly hot tears just came pouring out. . . ." More than their homes and possessions had been taken from them. "On May 16, 1942, my mother, two sisters, niece, nephew, and I left . . . by train," said Teru Watanabe. "Father joined us later. Brother left earlier by bus. We took whatever we could carry. So much we left behind, but the most valuable thing I lost was my freedom."[48]

When they arrived at assembly centers, the evacuees were shocked to discover that they were to be housed at stockyards, fairgrounds, and race tracks. "The assembly center was filthy, smelly, and dirty. There were roughly two thousand people packed in one large building. No beds were provided, so they gave us gunny sacks to fill with straw, that was our bed." Stables served as housing. "Where a horse or cow had been kept, a Japanese American family was moved in." "Suddenly you realized that human beings were being put behind fences just like on the farm where we had horses and pigs in corrals."[49]

After several weeks in the assembly centers, the evacuees were transported by trains to ten internment camps — Topaz in Utah, Poston and Gila River in Arizona, Amache in Colorado, Jerome and Rohwer in Arkansas, Minidoka in Idaho, Manzanar and Tule Lake in California, and Heart Mountain in Wyoming.

Most of the camps were located in remote desert areas. "We did not know where we were," remembered an internee. "No houses were in sight, no trees or anything green — only scrubby sagebrush and an occasional low cactus, and mostly dry, baked earth." Hundreds of miles of sandy wasteland surrounded them. "We felt as if we were standing in a gigantic sand-mixing machine as the sixty-mile gale lifted the loose earth up into the sky, obliterating everything," recalled Monica Sone. "Sand filled our mouths and nostrils and stung our faces and hands like a thousand darting needles."[50] Twenty-four-year-old Tsuyako "Sox" Kitashima cried her-self to sleep the first night, thinking, "I can't believe I'm in Amer-ica."[51]

The camp was linear, with barracks in orderly rows, bounded by barbed-wire fences with guard towers. Each barrack was about 20 by 120 feet, divided into four or six rooms. Usually a family was housed in one room, 20 by 20 feet. The room had "a pot bellied stove, a single electric light hanging from the ceiling, an Army cot for each person and a blanket for the bed."[52]

Every morning at 7 A.M., the internees were awakened by a siren. In large mess halls, they ate at long tables, parents often sit-ting at separate tables from their children, especially the teenagers. After eating breakfast in a cafeteria, the children went to school, where they began the day by saluting the flag of the United States and then singing "My country, 'tis of thee, sweet land of liberty." Looking beyond the flagpole, they saw the barbed wire, the watch towers, and the armed guards. "I was too young to understand," stated George Takei years later, "but I remember soldiers carrying rifles, and I remember being afraid."[53]

Young married couples worried about having children born in the camps. "When I was pregnant with my second child, that's when I flipped," said a Nisei woman. "I guess that's when the re-ality really hit me. I thought to myself, gosh, what am I doing get-ting pregnant. I told my husband, 'This is crazy. You realize there's no future for us and what are we having kids for?'"[54]

An even greater craziness seemed to crash down on the Nisei when the government decided to force them to serve in the U.S. Armed Forces. In September 1942, the Selective Service had classi-fied all young men of Japanese ancestry as 4-C, enemy aliens. A month later, however, the director of the Office of War Infor-mation recommended that President Roosevelt authorize the enlistment of Nisei: "Loyal American citizens of Japanese de-scent should be permitted, after an individual test, to enlist in the Army and Navy. . . . This matter is of great interest to OWI. Japanese propaganda to the Philippines, Burma, and elsewhere insists that this is a racial war. We can combat this effectively with counter propaganda only if our deeds permit us to tell the truth." Roosevelt understood the need for "counter propaganda." In December the army developed a plan for forming an all Japanese-American combat team.[55]

On February 6, 1943, the government began requiring all internees to answer loyalty questionnaires. Question 27 asked draft-age males: "Are you willing to serve in the armed forces of the United States on combat duty, wherever ordered?" Question 28 asked all internees: "Will you swear unqualified allegiance to the United States of America and faithfully defend the United States from any or all attack by foreign or domestic forces, and forswear any form of allegiance or obedience to the Japanese emperor, or any other foreign government, power or organization?"[56]

Forced to sign the loyalty questionnaire, young men pondered:

Loyalty, disloyalty,
If asked,
What should I answer?[57]

The Divided Soul of the Nisei Generation

Twenty-two percent of the 21,000 Japanese males eligible to register for the draft answered "No," gave a qualified answer, or made no response. "Well, I am one of those that said 'No, no' on the questions, one of the 'No, no' boys," explained Albert Nakai, "and it is not that I was proud about it, it was just that our legal rights were violated and I wanted to fight back." When he was told the Army wanted Japanese to volunteer for a special combat unit, Dunks Oshima retorted: "What do they take us for? Saps? First, they change my army status to 4-C because of my ancestry, run me out of town, and now they want me to volunteer for a suicide squad so I could get killed for this damn democracy. That's going some, for sheer brass!"[58]

At Heart Mountain internment camp, Frank Emi studied the

questionnaire. "The more I looked at it the more disgusted I became," recalled Emi, who at the time was a young father with a wife and two children. "We were treated more like enemy aliens than American citizens. And now this [the loyalty questionnaire]." Emi decided to post his answer on the mess hall door: "Under the present conditions and circumstances, I am unable to answer these questions." Shortly afterward, he attended a mass meeting, where he heard a stirring speech by Kiyoshi Okamoto. An engineer from Hawaii who had moved to the mainland and become a high school teacher, Okamoto declared that as American citizens the internees should stand up for their constitutional rights. "At first we were naive and just felt the questionnaire was unfair," said Emi. "But Okamoto taught us about the Constitution and it came to have great meaning as we began to resist."[59]

Emi and several resisters organized the Fair Play Committee and declared they would not cooperate with the draft unless their citizenship rights first were restored. Three hundred Nisei refused to be inducted, protesting the violation of their constitutional rights.[60]

Worried, government authorities acted quickly to repress the protest. Emi and six other leaders of the Heart Mountain Fair Play Committee were arrested and indicted for conspiracy to violate the Selective Service Act and for counseling others to resist the draft. In court they argued that the draft law as applied to Japanese Americans in the internment camps was morally wrong and unconstitutional. "We, the members of the FPC are not afraid to go to war — we are not afraid to risk our lives for our country," they had declared in their statement of resistance. "We would gladly sacrifice our lives to protect and uphold the principles and ideals of our country as set forth in the Constitution and the Bill of Rights, for on its inviolability depends the freedom, liberty, justice, and protection of all people including Japanese-Americans and all other minority groups."[61] Emi and the others were found guilty and sentenced to four years at Leavenworth Federal Penitentiary.

A citizen by birth, Joseph Kurihara also protested the violation of his constitutional rights. He had grown up in Hawaii, where he had learned what it meant to be an American. "We, the boys of conglomerated races, were brought up under the careful guidance of American teachers, strictly following the principle of American democracy," he wrote in his autobiography. "Let it be white, black, brown, or yellow, we were all treated alike. This glorious paradise of the Pacific was the true melting pot of human races." As a young man, Kurihara decided he wanted to study medicine and moved to California, where he experienced discrimination repeatedly. During World War I, he decided to join the U.S. Armed Forces. While in basic training, Kurihara was befriended by Dr. Homer Knight and William Green. "I made several visits to their homes. On every occasion, I was treated like a prince. I felt happy. I solemnly vouched to fight and die for the U.S. and those good people, whose genuine kindness touched the very bottom of my heart."

Kurihara fought in France and Germany. "For several months I was stationed in Coblenz with the army of occupation. . . . I found out that the German people were just as human as any other race. . . . At every mealtime, the little German girls and boys were lining the walk to the garbage can for whatever scraps the boys were throwing away. I could not bear to see these little ones suffer, so I always made it my duty to ask for as much as my plate would hold and gave it to them." Kurihara reflected on the scenes of destruction. "Wherever I went, I saw the ugly scars of war, reminding me of the cannibalistic deeds of man only more cruel and complete in civilized manner. It was horrible to think that the more the world progresses in science, the more devilish it gets. I shudder from thoughts what the next war would be."

After returning from the war, Kurihara completed degree programs at California Community College in Los Angeles; then he operated a small produce business and studied navigation. In 1941, he was working on a tuna fishing boat. His boat was near the Galapagos Islands when he heard the news of the Japanese attack on Pearl Harbor. The captain decided to return to California.

"On the way above Cedros Islands," Kurihara recalled, "we saw American planes scouting the sea and reporting the movements of all vessels. It was thrilling to see them flying. I felt very proud of them."

When his boat entered San Diego Harbor, it was boarded by F.B.I. agents. One of them yelled at him: "Hey! you Jap, I want some information. You better tell me everything, or I'll kick you in the ———." His blood "boiling," Kurihara replied: "What did you call me? If you want any information from me, you better learn to address a man properly." During the interrogation, Kurihara was asked:

"Have you been a good American citizen?"

"I was and I am."

"Will you fight for this country?"

"If I am needed, I am ready."

"Were you a soldier of any country?"

"Yes, I am a veteran of the Foreign War, U.S. Army."

For security, federal authorities prohibited Japanese from working on boats, but Kurihara applied for a permit to work at sea again. The port master said: "No permit for any Jap." At the end of a heated exchange, Kurihara exploded: "Say officer I wore that uniform when you were still unborn, served in the U.S. Army and fought for Democracy. . . . I may be a Jap in feature but I am an American. Understand!"

Kurihara then experienced a crueler insult: he was removed to the internment camp at Manzanar. There he fumed and agitated against cooperation with the government authorities. He led a movement of workers demanding fair wages for the labor they were doing in camp. Trying to organize them into a union, Kurihara declared that as citizens they were entitled to the same pay they would have received outside of camp. Even behind barbed wire, he argued, Japanese Americans should insist on equal treatment under the law as workers.

When he was released from the internment camp at the end of the war, Kurihara renounced his U.S. citizenship. "America, the standard bearer of democracy had committed the most heinous crime in its history, imprinting in my mind . . . the dread that even democracy is a demon in time of war," he explained. "It is my sincere desire to see this government of the United States some day repair the wrong in full." His renunciation expressed his total disappointment in a country whose ideals he cherished. "This decision was not that of today or that of yesterday," he wrote. "It dates back to the day when General DeWitt ordered evacuation." When General DeWitt declared that "a Jap is a Jap. Once a Jap, always a Jap," "I then swore to become a Jap one hundred percent, and never to do another's day's work to help this country fight this war." In February 1946 Kurihara sailed to Japan, a country he had not yet even visited.[62] For Kurihara, his self-imposed exile was his way of showing his anger at his country for betraying not only him but also its own constitutional principles.

During the war, however, 33,000 Japanese Americans made other choices: they decided to seek equality and justice by serving in the U.S. Armed Forces. "We shared a common commitment to what we perceived to be a right and a duty," said Akiji Yoshimura. "Perhaps most important, each of us in our way looked beyond the 'barbed wires' [of the internment camps] to a better America."[63]

Several thousand Japanese-American soldiers were assigned to the Military Intelligence Service, functioning as interpreters and translators on the Pacific front. Armed with Japanese-language skills, they provided an invaluable service. They translated captured Japanese documents, including battle plans, lists of Imperial Navy ships, and Japanese secret codes. One of their officers described their heroic work with Merrill's Marauders in Burma: "During battles they crawled up close enough to be able to hear Jap officers' commands and to make verbal translations to our soldiers. They tapped lines, listened in on radios, translated documents and papers, made spot translations of messages and field orders."[64]

As members of the MIS, Japanese Americans participated in the invasion of Okinawa. Two of them, Hiroshi Kobashigawa and Frank Higashi were worried about their families living in Okinawa. Both of them had been born in the United States and had parents who had returned to Okinawa before the outbreak of the war. When American soldiers landed in Okinawa, they found the people hiding in caves. Okinawans had been told by the Japanese military that it would be better for them to be dead than to be captured; the people were afraid of being tortured, raped, and killed by the Americans. In his family's home village, Kobashigawa was relieved to find his mother, sister, and three younger brothers safe in a civilian refugee camp. Higashi found his father in the hills of northern Okinawa during a mop-up operation and carried him on his back to the village. Nisei soldiers were also able to persuade many Japanese soldiers to surrender. General Charles Willoughby, chief of intelligence in the Pacific, estimated that the contributions of these Nisei soldiers shortened the war by two years.[65]

Japanese-American soldiers also helped win the war in Europe. In 1942, while General DeWitt was evacuating the Japanese on the West Coast, General Emmons organized a battalion of Hawaiian Nisei — the 100th Battalion. After training in Wisconsin and Mississippi, 1,400 men of the 100th Battalion were sent to North Africa. In September 1943, they participated in the invasion of Italy, where 300 of them were killed and 650 wounded. The 100th was called the "Purple Heart Battalion." In June, the 100th Battalion merged with the newly arrived 442nd Regimental Combat Team, composed of Nisei from Hawaii and also from internment camps. While German Americans and Italian Americans served in integrated military units, Japanese Americans were assigned to a separate fighting team — the 442nd.

In Europe, Japanese-American soldiers experienced bloody fighting at Luciana, Livorno, and the Arno River, where casualties totaled 1,272 men — more than one-fourth of the regiment. After the battle at the Arno River, they were sent to France, where they took the town of Bruyères from the German troops in heavy house-to-house fighting.

Next the 442nd was ordered to rescue the Texan "Lost Battalion," 211 men surrounded by German troops in the Vosges Mountains. "If we advanced a hundred yards, that was a good day's job," recalled a soldier describing the rescue mission. "We'd dig in again, move up another hundred yards, and dig in. That's how we went. It took us a whole week to get to the Lost Battalion. It was just a tree-to-tree fight." At the end of a week of fighting, the 442nd had suffered eight hundred casualties. When the trapped Texans finally saw the Japanese-American soldiers, some broke into sobs. One of the rescued soldiers remembered the moment: "[The Germans] would hit us from one flank and then the other, then from the front and the rear . . . we were never so glad to see anyone as those fighting Japanese Americans."[66] The rescuers had made a tremendous sacrifice in this battle. "Just think of all those people — of the 990 that went over [with me], not more than 200 of them came back without getting hit," said veteran Shig Doi. "If you look at the 442nd boys, don't look at their faces, look at their bodies. They got hit hard, some lost their limbs."[67]

One of the soldiers of the 442nd was Daniel Inouye. His father had emigrated from Japan after a fire had broken out in the Inouye family home and spread to nearby houses. In order to pay for the damage, the family sent their eldest son, Asakichi, to Hawaii to work on the sugar plantations. He planned to return to Japan after the family debt had been paid. But he stayed and made his home in Hawaii, where Daniel was born.

After the attack on Pearl Harbor, Asakichi Inouye asked his son: "You know what *on* means in Japanese?" Daniel answered: "Yes. *On* is at the heart of Japanese culture. *On* requires that when one man is aided by another he incurs a debt that is never canceled, one that must be repaid at every opportunity without stint or reservation." His father then said: "The Inouyes have great *on* for America. It has been good to us. And now . . . it is you who must try to return the goodness of this country."[68]

In the service of his country, Inouye fought in the battle of the Gothic Line in northern Italy, and then in April 1945, he participated in the assault against German troops on Mount Nebbione. "Come on, you guys, go for broke!" his buddies shouted as they charged directly into the fire of enemy machine guns. Captain Inouye crawled to the flank of an emplacement and pulled the pin on his grenade. "As I drew my arm back, all in a flash of light and dark I saw him, that faceless German."

> And even as I cocked my arm to throw, he fired and his rifle grenade smashed into my right elbow and exploded and all but tore my arm off. I looked at it, stunned and unbelieving. It dangled there by a few bloody shreds of tissue, my grenade still clenched in a fist that suddenly didn't belong to me any more. . . . I swung around to pry the grenade out of that dead fist with my left hand. Then I had it free and I turned to throw and the German was reloading his rifle. But this time I beat him. My grenade blew up in his face and I stumbled to my feet, closing on the bunker, firing my tommy gun left-handed, the useless right arm slapping red and wet against my side.[69]

For the seriously wounded Captain Inouye, the war was over. He had given his right arm in defense of his country. On his way back to Hawaii, however, Inouye still experienced racial rejection when he tried to get a haircut in San Francisco. Entering a barbershop with his empty right sleeve pinned to his army jacket covered with ribbons and medals for his military heroism, Captain Inouye was told: "We don't serve Japs here."[70]

Inouye belonged to the most decorated unit in United States military history. They had earned 18,143 individual decorations — including 1 Congressional Medal of Honor, 47 Distinguished Service Crosses, 350 Silver Stars, 810 Bronze Stars, and more than 3,600 Purple Hearts. Japanese-American soldiers had suffered 9,486 casualties, including 600 killed.[71] "They bought an awful hunk of America with their blood," declared General Joseph Stilwell. "You're damn right those Nisei boys have a place in the

American heart, now and forever."[72] When the 442nd regiment returned, President Harry Truman welcomed them by declaring: "You fought for the free nations of the world . . . you fought not only the enemy, you fought prejudice — and you won."[73]

A Mushroom Cloud: The Black Rain of Prejudice

As it turned out, however, prejudice was present in the making of Truman's decision to drop the atomic bomb on Hiroshima.

In his memoirs published in 1955, Truman explained that he had made the decision in order to avoid an invasion of Japan and thus save "half a million" American lives in the final effort to end the war.[74] Repeatedly he denied feeling sorry for dropping the atomic bomb. When asked in an interview whether the decision was a morally difficult one to make, the President shot back: "Hell no, I made it like that," as he snapped his fingers.[75] Reporter Merle Miller observed: "If there was one subject on which Mr. Truman was not going to have any second thoughts, it was the Bomb. If he'd said it once, he said it a hundred times, almost always the same words. The Bomb ended the war. If we had to invade Japan, half a million soldiers on both sides would have been killed. . . . It was as simple as that. That was all there was to it, and Mr. Truman had never lost any sleep over *that* decision."[76]

What actually happened, however, was complicated and also ambiguous. The United States had initiated atomic weapons research in order to counter the possibility of a Nazi nuclear bomb. But on May 7, Germany surrendered, and Truman turned his attention to the Pacific War. In June, Truman ordered the military to calculate the cost in American lives for a planned invasion of Japan. He stated that he wanted to "know how far we could afford to go in the Japanese campaign." Aware of the bloody fighting that had already occurred in the Pacific, Truman hoped to prevent "an Okinawa from one end of Japan to the other." American ground-troop losses in Okinawa had been extremely heavy: 5,309 dead, 23,909 wounded, and 346 missing in action.[77]

On June 18, Truman met with the Joint Chiefs of Staff. In response to his order, the Joint War Plans Committee prepared a report, which gave the following estimates of casualties:

Killed	Wounded	Missing	Total
40,000	150,000	3,500	193,500

This assessment was based on a plan to invade Japan's southern island of Kyushu on November 1, followed by an invasion of the Tokyo Plain on the main island of Honshu in March.[78] The estimate for the total number of soldiers who would die was not "half a million," but forty thousand.[79]

At this meeting, the President was assured that the invasion of Japan would not be another Okinawa. The Kyushu assault, the military chiefs explained, would be different from the deadly battle for the conquest of Okinawa. "There had been only one way to go on Okinawa," said Admiral Ernest King. "This meant a straight frontal attack against a highly fortified position. On Kyushu, however, landings would be made on three fronts simultaneously and there would be much more room for maneuver." The planners calculated that American casualties for the Kyushu invasion would be "relatively inexpensive." According to the minutes of the meeting, Truman said he understood that "the Joint Chiefs of Staff, after weighing all possible alternative plans, were still of the unanimous opinion that the Kyushu operation was the best solution under the circumstances." Then he told the Joint Chiefs of Staff that the Kyushu plan was "all right from a military standpoint" and ordered them to "go ahead with it."[80]

By the end of June, American military leaders determined that Japan had lost the war: the capacity and the will to fight no longer existed within Japan itself. Its cities had been reduced to rubble, work and life had been severely disrupted, and the people themselves were dispirited. On June 29, the Joint Chiefs of Staff discussed plans for the occupation of Japan. One of the items on the meeting's agenda read: "Prepare for sudden collapse of Japan."[81]

A week later, a "top secret" report prepared for the Combined Chiefs of Staff meetings at Potsdam gave an "Estimate of the Enemy Situation": "We believe that a considerable portion of the Japanese population now consider absolute military defeat to be probable. The increasing effects of sea blockade and cumulative devastation wrought by strategic bombing, which has already rendered millions homeless and has destroyed from 25% to 50% of the built-up area of Japan's most important cities, should make this realization increasingly general. An entry of the Soviet Union into the war would finally convince the Japanese of the inevitability of complete defeat. Although individual Japanese willingly sacrifice themselves in the service of the nation, we doubt that the nation as a whole is predisposed toward national suicide." The report also noted that "a conditional surrender by the Japanese Government . . . might be offered by them at any time from now until the time of the complete destruction of all Japanese power of resistance."[82]

Agreeing with this report, Chairman of the Joint Chiefs of Staff William D. Leahy believed that an invasion of Japan was unnecessary. "I was unable to see any justification, from a national-defense point of view, for an invasion of an already thoroughly defeated Japan," he wrote in his autobiography. Leahy calculated that it would be too costly in American lives to invade Japan in order to extract an unconditional surrender. The navy alone, he thought, could bring an end to the war. A completely blockaded Japan would "fall by its own weight."[83] Leahy also pointed out that a conditional surrender which would allow the Japanese people to keep their emperor seemed to be consistent with the Atlantic Charter's promise that Great Britain and the United States would "respect the right of all peoples to choose the form of government under which they will live."[84] Thus Admiral Leahy advised Truman to accept a Japanese surrender, with a provision that would allow the emperor to remain.[85]

The Joint Chiefs of Staff knew that Japan was seeking a way to negotiate a conditional surrender. United States intelligence had intercepted Japanese diplomatic messages asking Russia to mediate the end of the conflict.[86] Japan's primary condition was the maintenance of the emperor.

After the decisive defeat of the Japanese forces at Okinawa on June 23, Secretary of War Henry Stimson advised Truman to pursue a negotiated peace. In a memorandum to the President, July 2, Stimson wrote: "I believe Japan *is* susceptible to reason in such a crisis to a much greater extent than is indicated by our current press and other current comment." As a visitor to Japan in the 1920s who had developed an admiration for the Japanese people, Stimson explained: "Japan is not a nation composed wholly of mad fanatics of an entirely different mentality from ours." Refusing to demonize the enemy, the secretary of war continued: "On the contrary, she has within the past century shown herself to possess extremely intelligent people, capable in an unprecedentedly short time of adopting not only the complicated technique of Occidental civilization but to a substantial extent their culture and their political and social ideas." Then Stimson proposed a strategy: the United States should give "a carefully timed warning to Japan," which would include a conditional surrender. "I personally think that if in [giving such a warning] we should add that we do not exclude a constitutional monarchy under her present dynasty, it would substantially add to the chances of acceptance."[87]

In July 1945, at the Potsdam conference, Stimson worked to include in the declaration a provision for a conditional surrender. On July 24, Stimson was dismayed to learn that the President had deleted his proposal from the final version.[88] In the Potsdam Declaration of July 26, Truman issued an ultimatum to Japan to accept "unconditional surrender," or face the "utter devastation of the Japanese homeland."[89]

Truman's rigid and fierce insistence on unconditional surrender reflected a vengeance-seeking and racialized remembering of Pearl Harbor. Unlike the fighting in Europe, the armed conflict in the Pacific was a race war, powered by mutual hatreds and stereotyping. On the one side, believing they belonged to the superior "Yamato race," many Japanese viewed Americans as "brutes," "wild beasts," monsters, devils, and demons.[90] On the other side, thinking they belonged to an advanced white civilization, many Americans saw the Japanese as "demons," "ungodly," "treacherous," "savages," "subhuman," and "beasts."[91] In July, *Time* magazine declared: "The ordinary unreasoning Jap is ignorant. Perhaps he is human. Nothing . . . indicates it."[92] This negative imaging of the Japanese reflected a cultural bias that Edward Said described as "Orientalism" — the European social construction of representations of Asians as strange, exotic, inferior, different, "the Other."[93] During World War II, "orientalism" conditioned the contrasting ways Americans viewed the Germans and the Japanese.

"We were very patriotic," recalled Peggy Terry, who had worked in a Kentucky defense plant during the war, "and we understood that the Nazis were someone who would have to be stopped." In the movies, however, the Germans were portrayed as tall and handsome. "There'd be one meanie, a little short dumpy bad Nazi," she said. "But the main characters were good-lookin' and they looked like us." On the other hand, Terry noted, "with the Japanese, that was a whole different thing. We were just ready to wipe them out. They sure as heck didn't look like us. They were yellow little creatures that smiled when they bombed our boys."[94]

War correspondent Ernie Pyle noticed how American soldiers felt differently toward the two enemies. In North Africa, he described the relations between American soldiers and German prisoners of war: "German boys were as curious about us as we were of them. Everytime I stopped, a crowd would form quickly. In almost every group was one who spoke English. In all honesty I can't say their bearing or personality was a bit different from that of a similar bunch of American prisoners. . . . The main impression I got, seeing German prisoners, was that they were human like everybody else, fundamentally friendly, a little vain." Later, when Pyle went to the Pacific front, he observed: "And another adjustment I'll have to make is the attitude toward the enemy. In Europe we felt our enemies, horrible and deadly as they were, were still people. But out here I've already gathered the feeling that the Japanese are looked upon as something inhuman and squirmy — like some people feel about cockroaches or mice."[95]

"Remember Pearl Harbor — keep 'em dying," declared a marine motto.[96] Admiral William Halsey gave his men a direct order: "Kill Japs, kill Japs, kill more Japs."[97] A marine captain declared: "We kill yellow rats. If we don't kill 'em, we won't be around for any peace. So we hate and kill — and live."[98] As he ordered his men to go into battle against the Japanese, an American admiral urged his men to go and "get some more Monkey meat."[99]

Some American soldiers followed such orders literally: they sadistically collected battlefield trophies — scalps, skulls, bones, and ears. A marine at Guadalcanal bragged: "I'm going to bring back some Jap ears. Pickled."[100] Robert Lekachman recalled that he "didn't collect ears [of dead Japanese]." But he "knew some others did. We had been fed tales of these yellow thugs, subhumans, with teeth that resembled fangs. If a hundred thousand Japs were killed, so much the better. Two hundred thousand, even better."[101] The gold teeth of corpses became collector's items. One soldier excitedly boasted: "They say the Japs have a lot of gold teeth. I'm going to make myself a necklace."[102] Marine Eugene B. Sledge watched a fellow soldier use his knife to hammer gold teeth from the mouth of a wounded Japanese soldier who could not move his arms.[103]

Comparing the Pacific war with the European war, historian John Dower wrote: "It is virtually inconceivable . . . that teeth, ears, and skulls could have been collected from German or Italian war dead and publicized in the Anglo-American countries without provoking an uproar; and in this we have yet another inkling of the racial dimensions of the war."[104]

The taking of war trophies, especially scalps, was a legacy of an earlier racialized war — the winning of the West. "When I was a young boy," a soldier said, "we always played cowboys and Indians, and when I landed on Guadalcanal that's what I felt like —

I was playing a game, it was not real. Even though I knew it was real. . . ." Marines frequently saw the Japanese attackers as "whooping like a bunch of wild Indians."[105] Jungle combat against the Japanese was often characterized as "Indian fighting," and the perimeter outside American military control was called "Indian country."[106] Commenting on Japanese fighting skills, Colonel Milton A. Hill described the "Japs" as "good at infiltration, too; as good as Indians ever were."[107] Rephrasing an old frontier adage, Admiral Halsey declared: "The only good Jap is a Jap who's been dead six months."[108]

Many soldiers fighting the Japanese on the Pacific "frontier" had fathers and grandfathers who had fought Indians. In an essay, "How We Felt About the War," published shortly after the end of the conflict, historian Allan Nevins noted the connection between the Pacific war and the American frontier experience: "Probably in all our history, no foe has been so detested as were the Japanese. Emotions forgotten since our most savage Indian wars were awakened by the ferocities of Japanese commanders."[109]

Truman himself came from a frontier family. The Trumans had migrated to Missouri, where they participated in the winning of the West. In a letter to Bess, Truman described one of his grandmother's encounters with Indians: "Grandmother once routed a whole band of Indians with a big dog. She was all alone except for a negro woman and her two children. These Indians told her they wanted honey if she didn't give it, they would take it and her too. So they sharpened their knives on the grinding stone and then she turned loose a large dog. Away went Indians, some leaving their blankets."[110] Truman's grandfather Solomon Young ran a wagon train from Independence, Missouri, to San Francisco. When the retired President was asked whether his grandfather had had any trouble with Indians, Truman boasted: "I never heard him say that they bothered him. There were two or three trainmasters that the Indians didn't disturb, and he was one of them. They were afraid of him. That's why. They knew he had the ammunition and the guns, and he would shoot them if they commenced to bother him."[111] From Grandfather Young, Truman had learned a lesson: Let your enemy know you have the guns.

Migrating to Missouri, the Truman pioneers had taken slaves with them. Asked during an interview about his grandparents and slavery, Truman said: "Oh, yes. They all had slaves. They brought them out here with them from Kentucky. Most of the slaves were wedding presents."[112] When the Civil War came, Truman's mother supported the Confederacy. She thought it was "a good thing when Lincoln was shot," Truman told an interviewer.[113] Independence, Missouri, was a segregated town: blacks lived in a neighborhood derisively called "Nigger Neck." The Trumans had black servants. Truman cherished his childhood memories of blacks, especially those of a "good old black woman" who had worked for his family as a cook and washerwoman.[114] On January 6, 1936, Truman joked in a letter to Bess: "He and I and old Senator Coolidge and Barkley were the only ones not dressed, as Jimmy Byrnes said, like nigga preachers."[115]

Truman embraced a vision of a white "manifest destiny" for America. In a letter to Bess, June 22, 1911, Truman wrote: "I think one man is as good as another so long as he's honest and decent and not a nigger or a Chinaman. Uncle Will [Young, the Confederate veteran] says that the Lord made a white man of dust, a nigger from mud, than threw up what was left and it came down a Chinaman. He does hate Chinese and Japs. So do I. It is race prejudice I guess. But I am strongly of the opinion that negroes ought to be in Africa, yellow men in Asia, and white men in Europe and America."[116]

Although Truman did not accept social equality of the races, he believed the Constitution should be the law of the land. As a senator, he supported anti-lynching and anti–poll tax legislation. In 1940, Truman spoke out against the Klan: "I believe in the brotherhood of man, not merely the brotherhood of white men but the brotherhood of all men before the law. I believe in the Constitution and the Declaration of Independence. In giving Negroes the rights which are theirs we are only acting in accord with our own ideals of a true democracy."[117] Truman did not support the internment of Japanese Americans. When asked by interviewer Merle Miller to comment on Japanese-American relocation, the retired President replied: "They were concentration camps. They called it relocation, but they put them in concentration camps, and I was against it. We were in a period of emergency, but it was still the wrong thing to do. It was one place where I never went along with Roosevelt. He never should have allowed it." Referring to the fact that Americans of German and Italian descent had not been interned, Merle asked: "Do you suppose it was because Americans of Japanese descent looked different?" Truman replied: "It may have been. But the reason it happened was just the same as what we've been talking about [hysteria]. People out on the West Coast got scared, and they panicked, and they decided to get rid of the Japanese-Americans."[118]

But Truman also found himself swept into the whirlpool of racial hatreds stirred by the Pacific war. In making his decision to drop the atomic bomb on Hiroshima, Truman was pulled by two different feelings — a racialized rage against the "Japs," but also a recognition of their humanity. In his diary on July 18, Truman wrote that he was certain the "Japs" would surrender when "Manhattan" [the atomic blast] appeared over their homeland. A week later, he entered his decision to drop the bomb: "This weapon is to be used against Japan between now and August 10th. I have told the Sec. of War, Mr. Stimson, to use it so that military objectives and sailors and soldiers are the target and not women and children. Even if the Japs are savages, ruthless, merciless and fanatic, we as the leader of the world for the common welfare cannot drop this terrible bomb on the old capital or the new."[119] But then he unleashed a weapon "without mercy" on women and children in Hiroshima.[120] Justifying the destruction, Truman stated in a private letter written shortly after the atomic attack: "Nobody is more disturbed over the unwarranted attack by the Japanese on Pearl Harbor and their murder of our prisoners of war. The only language they seem to understand is the one that we have been using to bombard them. When you have to deal with a beast you have to treat him as a beast."[121]

Thus, Truman had brought down on Hiroshima what he called "a rain of ruin from the air," the like of which had "never been seen on this earth."[122] Earlier, on that morning of August 6, the people of Hiroshima had started their daily activities. Naoko Masuoka was on a school trip. She and her friends were singing, "Blossoms and buds of the young cherry tree." Around eight o'clock, she heard someone cry out: "A B-29!" "Even as this shout rang in our ears," she said later, "there was a blinding flash and I lost consciousness."[123] Sanae Kano also remembered seeing a "sudden flash of light." She had been eating breakfast and had her chopsticks in her mouth when it happened. Then there was "a big bang" and she almost fainted. Kano ran out of her house. "At the river, I saw people who were burned black and were crying for water. . . . Some people were in the river drinking the water. The fire wardens were shouting at them telling them that it was dangerous to drink the water. But many people went into the river anyway and drank the water and died."[124]

After the horrendous blast, fires were everywhere. Within seconds, the entire city had been reduced to cinders. People were burned, covered with huge blisters. Yoshiaki Wada found many dead people lying on the bridge. "Some were burned black, some had blistered skin that was peeling off, and some had pieces of glass in them all over."[125] After the deadly brilliance, a huge mushroom-shaped cloud rose to the heavens; then a rain descended, but the water that fell from the sky was a black rain. "The wind got stronger," Yohko Kuwabara reported, "and it started raining something like ink. This strange rain came down hard out of the gray sky, like a thundershower and the drops stung as if I were being hit by pebbles."[126] Seventy thousand people were killed instantly. Only 3,243 of them were soldiers.

Three days later, another atomic bomb destroyed Nagasaki. However, the Japanese government still refused to surrender, except on a conditional basis — the retention of the emperor. Meeting with his key policymakers, Truman had to decide whether to continue the atomic bombing or accept a conditional surrender. Admiral Leahy argued strongly for accepting the Japanese terms. "Some of those around the President wanted to demand his [Hirohito's] execution," he wrote in his memoir. "If they had prevailed, we might still be at war with Japan. His subjects would probably have fought on until every loyal Japanese was dead...."[127] Leahy's view prevailed, and in the end, the surrender was not unconditional. Japan was allowed to keep the emperor system. Had this condition been included in the Potsdam Declaration, the war might have been concluded sooner, and the killing of over 200,000 civilians, most of them women and children, could have been avoided.

As the individual ultimately responsible for the horrific destruction, Truman had to face the moral issue of the atomic bombings. Beneath the buck-stops-here facade hid a sensitive interior. Truman knew he had dropped the atomic bomb not on "beasts," but on women and children. At Potsdam, the President had told Stimson he hoped only one bomb would be dropped. He had not expected the second atomic attack to occur so soon after Hiroshima, and immediately ordered the military to halt operations for a third bomb. After the destruction of Nagasaki, Truman confided to Henry Wallace that "the thought of wiping out another 100,000 people was too horrible," and that he did not like the idea of killing "all those kids."[128] When the President complained of terrible headaches, Wallace asked: "Physical or figurative?" Truman replied: "Both."[129]

Several months after the atomic bombings, Truman had a private conversation with J. Robert Oppenheimer. The Los Alamos director said that his work at the weapons laboratory meant he had blood on his hands. Truman offered Oppenheimer his handkerchief: "Well, here, would you like to wipe off your hands."[130] Then Truman declared: "The blood is on my hands. Let me worry about that."[131] After Oppenheimer left the Oval Office, the President told Dean Acheson: "I don't want to see that son of a bitch in this office ever again."[132] On May 3, 1946, he complained again to Acheson about Oppenheimer: "He came to my office five or six months ago, and spent most of his time wringing his hands and telling me they had blood on them because of the discovery of atomic energy."[133] Truman recognized that Oppenheimer was merely the inventor of the bomb, and that he was the one who had made the decision to use the terrible new weapon. The "blood" of the women and "kids" killed in the atomic bombings was on his hands.

Truman's remorse was understandable. Capable of thoughtful reflection and compassion, Truman felt sadness over the horror and suffering of war. On July 16, while waiting for the report of the atomic bomb test at Alamogordo, Truman wrote a diary entry describing the "absolute ruin" he had witnessed in Berlin as he traveled to Potsdam and the sorrowful lines of refugees — old men, old women, children from tots to teens carrying their belongings to nowhere in particular.[134] Deeply moved by these scenes, he pondered the world's grim history of war: "I thought of Carthage, Baalbek, Jerusalem, Rome, Atlantis, Peking, Babylon, Nineveh; Scipio, Rameses II, Titus, Herman, Sherman, Jenghis Khan, Alexander, Darius the Great. But Hitler only destroyed Stalingrad — and Berlin. I hope for some sort of peace — but I fear that machines are ahead of morals by some centuries and when morals catch up perhaps there'll be no reason for any of it. I hope not. But we are only termites on a planet and maybe when we bore too deeply into the planet there'll [be] a reckoning — who knows?"[135]

The technology of atomic weaponry was racing ahead of morals, and the reckoning turned out to be Truman's. Admiral Leahy believed that the dropping of the atomic bomb was not a military necessity. "It is my opinion," he wrote in his memoirs, "that the use of this barbarous weapon at Hiroshima and Nagasaki was of no material assistance in our war against Japan. The Japanese were already defeated and ready to surrender because of the effective sea blockade and the successful bombing with conventional weapons."[136] Moreover, the chairman of the Joint Chiefs of Staff opposed the use of the atomic bomb for a moral reason. As a soldier, he had definite ethical standards on how war should be fought. In July 1944, during a discussion with Roosevelt about the use of biological warfare, Leahy "recoiled" from the idea. "Mr. President," the admiral stated, "this [using germs and poison] would violate every Christian ethic I have ever heard of and all of the known laws of war." Leahy later applied this same religious principle to the atomic attack on Hiroshima. As a former specialist in gunnery and head of the Bureau of Ordnance, he knew how to judge weapons. "'Bomb' is the wrong word to use for this new weapon," he wrote. "It is not a bomb. It is not an explosive. It is a poisonous thing that kills people by its deadly radioactive reaction, more than by the explosive force it develops."[137] Hiroshima filled Leahy with regret. "My own feeling is that in being the first to use it," he wrote in his memoirs, "we had adopted an ethical standard common to barbarians of the Dark Ages. I was not taught to make war in that fashion, and wars cannot be won by destroying women and children." The atomic bomb was an instrument of "uncivilized warfare" — a "modern type of barbarism not worthy of Christian man."[138]

Leahy's moral dismay was widely shared in American society. In a personal letter to the President on August 9, 1945, an anguished citizen protested the use of the bomb. "I think it is a disgrace that America should be involved in such a diabolical thing," wrote Anne Ford. "I had hoped and prayed that America under your leadership would be a good example to the rest of the world. I don't know what to think now."[139] Similarly, a woman from New York wrote to Truman: "I am impelled to write to you now and tell you how stunned and sick at heart I am over what our country has just done to Japan and her people — thousands of them innocent."[140] In letters to the *New York Times*, readers denounced the atomic attack as "a stain upon our national life," and as "simply mass murder, sheer terrorism."[141] "Why," a citizen from St. Paul asked in a letter to NBC news commentator H. V. Kaltenborn, "did we choose to drop our first bomb on a crowded city, where 90% of the casualties would *inevitably be civilian?*"[142] Mexican-American soldier Alex Romandia was in Germany when he heard the news of Hiroshima. In a letter to his sister, he lamented that the atomic bombing made him feel "ashamed of his country for such a savage action." When Romandia returned home from the war, he had a tense conversation with his mother. He told her that he was "angry that this weapon of destruction had been used so callously." She responded that it had helped to end the war. "But, mama," Romandia exclaimed, "it was not necessary."[143] For Walter G. Taylor, a moral line had been crossed: the atomic attack constituted a war crime. "The United States of America has this day become the new master of brutality, infamy, atrocity," he charged in a letter to *Time* magazine. "Bataan, Buchenwald, Dachau, Coventry, Lidice were tea parties compared with the horror which we, the people of the United States of America, have dumped on the world in the form of atomic energy bombs. No peacetime applications of this Frankenstein monster can ever erase the crime we have committed. . . . It is no democracy where such an outrage can be committed without our consent!"[144]

There were also expressions of moral misgivings in the mainstream media. In the *New York Times,* Hanson W. Baldwin wrote: "Yesterday man unleashed the atom to destroy man, and another chapter in human history opened, a chapter in which the weird, the strange, the horrible becomes the trite and the obvious. Yesterday we clinched victory in the Pacific, but we sowed the whirlwind. . . . We have been the first to introduce a new weapon of unknowable effects which may bring us victory quickly but which will sow the seeds of hate more widely than ever. We may yet reap the whirlwind."[145] The editors of *Life* magazine confessed deep disquietude: "The Second World War, which had been tapering off to a whimper is ending instead with a bang." The magazine harshly criticized the sharp rise in the air war's destruction of civilian lives. "From the very concept of strategic bombing, all the developments — night, pattern, saturation, area, indiscriminate — have led straight to Hiroshima, and Hiroshima was, and was intended to be, almost pure *Schrecklichkeit* [terror bombing]."[146]

In December 1945, a poll conducted by *Fortune* found that only 54 percent of the respondents approved of the bombing of Hiroshima and Nagasaki.[147] Even within an American society at war, there was still a sense of fairness and decency based on the belief in the "self-evident truth" of the "unalienable right" of all people to "life."

From minority communities arose protests against the atomic bombing. The fiery mushroom cloud had tragically illuminated the color line as "the Problem of the Twentieth Century." In an essay published in the *Chicago Defender,* W. E. B. DuBois declared that the war in the Pacific had been waged against the "colored" nation of Japan. "No matter how we explain and assess the damage, the result of thinking along the lines of race and color will affect human relations for many years and will excuse contempt and injustice toward colored skins."[148] On August 16, 1945, the editor of the Spanish-language *La Opinión* connected the atomic attacks to the internment of Japanese Americans: "It is painfully difficult to assess the 'effectiveness' of the bomb. Japan surrendered two days ago, but did the means justify the end? We think not. Our sympathies lie with the survivors from Hiroshima and Nagasaki who surely lost everything. This war experience has ironically fostered a bond between the Mexican-American community and the Japanese-American community. The events of internment and the zoot-suit riots share a common pattern of racism that we are all subject to."[149] Indeed, the atomic bombing of Hiroshima had brought the war home, back to the struggle for "double victory."

8

STRUGGLING FOR A WORLD OF
"NO RACE PREJUDICE"
Jewish Americans and the Holocaust

T HE ATOMIC BOMBING of Hiroshima greatly dismayed Robert
Frost. In a burst of moral outrage, he declared that America had
"invented a new Holocaust" and had been "the first with it to win
a war."[1] The poet's reference to the Nazi genocide in his condem-
nation of the instant transformation of a Japanese city into a crematorium revealed a razor-sharp recognition of the role of race in
World War II.

*"The Horror, the Horror": What Should We
Tell the Children?*

For Jews everywhere, the Holocaust was the most horrendous
event in their tragic past of exile and persecution. After the war,
the still molten memory of their near extermination as a people
made the living wonder: what should they tell their children about
the ghastly terror that Jews had experienced in the Nazi "heart of

darkness"?[2] This was the question a father raised in a 1956 letter to the "Bintel Brief," an advice column of the *Jewish Daily Forward:*

> Years have gone by since the sharp fangs of the mad beast destroyed a third of the Jewish people. Thanks to the Allied armies, the beasts in human form were defeated, but with those who were saved by a miracle the nightmares and aftereffects of the destruction remain.
>
> When the living, the lucky ones, began to come out of their hiding places and regained a bit of their normalcy, they began to rebuild their shattered lives. So it was with me and my present wife. The murderers killed my first wife and our two children, and my present wife lost her husband and child. When we met, we decided to marry, establish a home, and start to build a new life, since this was the thing to do.
>
> Now we are here in America, we already have two children . . . and my wife and I often discuss whether we should tell them about the tragic past. I mean, about our personal losses, because I have told them about the general destruction. I feel we should not tell them yet about the loss of our own children, but wait until they are older. My wife, however, thinks the opposite, and sometimes she comes out with a half statement and the children are disturbed.
>
> Now I ask you, who is right, I or my wife? Should the children be told everything now, or is there time yet? I believe you will give us the right answer.
>
> Respectfully,
> H. S., Brooklyn

The editor advised the parents to wait until their children had grown old enough to understand the "horrible massacres" of six million Jews. "Certainly we should tell our children about the holocaust," he answered, "and about the fact that the whole world was silent."[3]

"Preferring to Die on My Feet"

There was another fact the children should know: 550,000 Jewish Americans had fought against the evils of Nazism by serving in the U.S. Armed Forces, proportionately more than Americans as a whole. Their awards included one Medal of Honor, 74 Distinguished Service Crosses, 37 Navy Crosses, 47 Distinguished Service Medals, 344 Legions of Merit, 1,627 Silver Stars, 2,391 Distinguished Flying Crosses, 6,090 Bronze Stars, and 26,009 Purple Hearts.[4]

Jews had a particular reason for serving in the military: they wanted to fight Nazism, with its racist ideology. Writing to the "Bintel Brief" editor in 1943, a mother related a story about her son, "the doctor," who had enlisted in the U.S. Army. After first describing her life as an immigrant, she wrote: "We worked hard to make a living, and we were happy with our children, who were studious and obedient. Even when they went to college they helped us in the store. You can't imagine our joy when our eldest son graduated as a doctor." But because of Hitler, he decided to volunteer for military service. "Our children were always interested in world affairs and were concerned with the Jewish problems. I tried to talk him out of it, and told my husband to discourage him but my husband told me that our son knew what he was doing." Then her second son enlisted. "My heart is breaking, but I know I am not the only mother whose sons went to war. I know they must fight now for our dear country and we must make sacrifices to destroy our enemies. If it were not enough that our sons went away, now our daughter wants to join the Wacs." The editor advised her to recognize that her children were demonstrating the "fact" that "we were all patriotic and loyal to our country."[5]

Another Jewish doctor, Bernard Ehrenpreis, explained his reason for enlisting. "I wanted to fight the Nazis," he said. "Maybe this doesn't sound like a medical man, but ever since 1933, I had been very much aware that I, for one, preferred to die on my feet rather than live on my knees."[6] Dr. Bernard S. Feinberg made the same choice. "You may wonder why I, a practicing dentist, volunteered to go in as a private," he told an interviewer many years after the war. "I was and am a very patriotic American and also a Jew who had no use whatsoever for that Nazi bastard Hitler and his overall plan of genocide for my people."[7]

Fred C. Patheiger joined the army so that he could return to Germany to fight Nazism. A year after he was born in Rastatt, Germany, in 1919, his parents were divorced. "When Hitler got into power, my mother, grandmother, and aunt had to join the [Nazi] party," he recalled. "I discovered one day while a youngster crawling in the living room and listening to them speak that much to my amazement, my grandfather on my mother's side was Jewish." When Patheiger's aunt decided to marry, she confided to her lover that her father was Jewish, and her groom-to-be reported this family background to the Nazi authorities. Worried about her son, Patheiger's mother arranged to have him live with a distant cousin in America. "I had read a lot as a youngster and had always dreamed to come to America. . . . I came over here in April 1938. The others remained over there. We tried to get them over here, but the Nazis kept bringing one obstacle after another. . . . They succumbed in the concentration camps later on." Patheiger tried to join the U.S. Army, but was rejected as an "enemy alien." He then wrote to J. Edgar Hoover, explaining why he wanted to fight the Nazis, and the F.B.I. director encouraged him to appeal his case to the draft board. Patheiger tried again, attaching Hoover's letter, and this time was classified as 1-A. After basic training, he was assigned to military intelligence because he spoke German fluently and could interrogate prisoners of war. In Europe, Patheiger experienced combat action in Normandy, fighting in the Battle of the Bulge.[8]

Many Jews were aware of the need to fight not only anti-

Semitism in Europe but also racism in America. One of them was Murray Shapiro of Los Angeles. In 1943, he decided to leave his studies at U.C.L.A. and join the U.S. Army. At basic training, he was distressed to witness segregation in the military. In a letter to his parents, the young soldier wrote on May 16, 1943: "Camp Roberts is the biggest place you've ever seen. . . . It continuously trained 100,000 men in the West Garrison, which was on one side of US 99 . . . while on the other side of the highway at the East Garrison, 60,000 more Negro troops were being trained in a segregated setting. . . . Looking at the daily camp newspaper, we found a movie we had missed just across the highway in the East Garrison. We knew nothing about the segregated setup. It was not advertised. Jumping off the bus in front of the theater we were immediately met by an MP 1st Sgt. 'Where you men think you're going?' he thundered. 'Right here to the movie,' we responded quietly. 'No you're not. This is a Negro training area. Get right back on the bus and don't come back on this side of the highway.'"[9]

On June 10, Shapiro commented on events back home: "The zoot suit warfare is still going strong. Have you heard that the L.A. City Council was considering a bill to ban zoot suits from the county?" The next day, he wrote to his family: "Glad to hear that Dad [Paul] is defending one of the zoot-suiters. They need someone who is able and brave enough to take their case. There are quite a few stinkers among their group, but there are a lot of innocent ones also and the environment they have been forced to live in all their lives has hardly been conducive to making them honor citizens." On June 14, the son added: "Am very much interested in the zoot-suiters, as I was on the UCLA Committee to Defend American-Mexicans."[10]

On September 17, 1944, Shapiro wrote to tell his family that he had arrived at Liverpool, England. On November 9, the soldier sent a letter from "somewhere in Germany." "Well, here I am knocking on Hitler's doorstep." On May 10, Shapiro wrote: "I guess by now you and Dad will really believe me when I tell you there is nothing to worry about. The Germans are completely defeated."[11]

Like Shapiro, Corporal Harold Katz was also in Germany when he wrote a letter explaining why he was serving in the U.S. Army. Addressing "Dear Mom," he wrote:

> Mom, I want you to know that I asked for a combat assignment. I did so for several reasons. One is that I had certain ideals within my own mind, for which I had often argued verbally. I didn't feel right to sit safe, far behind the lines, while men were risking their lives for principles which I would fight for only with my lips. I felt that I also must be willing to risk my life in the fight for the freedom of speech and thought I was using and hoped to use in the future.
>
> Another reason is the fact that I am Jewish. I felt, again, it wasn't right for me to be safe behind the lines, while others were risking their lives, with one of their goals the principles of no race prejudice. I knew this meant fighting for me and my family because if Hitler won, my family — you, Rolly and Pop — would certainly suffer more than the families of other soldiers who died in the fight.
>
> I felt that I must risk my life, on that point, so that I could earn the right of my family to live in peace and free from race prejudice.[12]

Katz's letter was found on his body after he was killed in action in the German town of Attweilmann on March 30, 1945, only five weeks before the end of the war in Europe. Katz had given his life fighting for a world free of the racial prejudice that had resulted in the Nazi murder of six million Jews.

Were They Their Brothers' Keepers? Jews in America

When Hitler came to power in 1933, four and a half million Jews were living in the United States. Many of them were the descendants of German Jews, who had come in the early nineteenth century. Most, however, had origins in Poland and Russia. As immigrants arriving around the turn of the century, they had fled terrible pogroms — the destruction of their synagogues and the violence of anti-Semitic hatred. "I feel that every cobblestone in Russia is filled with Jewish blood," an immigrant bitterly recalled. "Absolutely every year, there was a *pogrom* before *Pesach* [Passover]." The pogroms, observed Abraham Cahan, had forced Jews to realize that "Russia was not their homeland and that a true home must be found for Jews. But where?"[13]

Spreading from shtetl to shtetl across Russia, a song pointed the way to the "Promised Land":

> As the Russians, mercilessly
> Took revenge on us.
> There is a land, America,
> Where everyone lives free.[14]

After arriving at Ellis Island, the refugees pursued a hopeful dream — to become Americans. "Oysgrinen zikh," the newcomers said, "Don't be a greenhorn."[15] In Russia, few Jews made an effort to speak the dominant language, but in America most of them were eager to learn English. "Today," observed a resident of New York's Jewish community in 1905, "English is more and more the language spoken on the East Side, whereas eight years ago it was rare to hear that tongue." In a letter to the *Jewish Daily Forward,* a mother complained about her daughter who had preceded her family to America: "During the few years she was here without us she became a regular Yankee and forgot how to talk Yiddish. . . . She says it is not nice to talk Yiddish and that I am a greenhorn."[16] Pressures to assimilate also came from mainstream society: the hegemonic idea of the "melting pot" promoted disdain for ethnic cultures and languages as foreign and un-American.

The sites for the transformation of Jewish immigrants from "greenhorns" into Americans were the workplace and the school.

The Jewish colony of the Lower East Side was the industrial center of garment production. From block after block of sweatshops came the "whir of a thousand sewing-machines, worked at high pressure from the earliest dawn till mind and muscle [gave] out together."[17] This work was punishing and humiliating. "We were like slaves," recalled Anzia Yezierska. "You couldn't pick your head up. You couldn't talk. We used to go to the bathroom. The forelady used to go after us, we shouldn't stay too long."[18] Facing exploitation and degradation, the workers resisted. Beginning in 1909, waves of strikes swept through the Lower East Side as laborers organized into unions, demanding higher wages and better working conditions. By 1920, the International Ladies' Garment Workers' Union had 100,000 members. The labor "uprisings" opened doors of economic mobility in the promised land.[19]

In their quest to become Americans, Jewish parents pushed their children to get an education in order to prepare for occupations other than grueling factory work. Describing the Jewish commitment to education, the *Daily Forward* editorialized: "The Jew undergoes privation, spills blood, to educate his child. In [this] is reflected one of the finest qualities of the Jewish people. It shows our capacity to make sacrifices for our children . . . as well as our love for education, for intellectual efforts."[20] Jewish students began crowding into the colleges and universities in New York and elsewhere on the East Coast. "The thirst for knowledge," the *New York Evening Post* reported in 1905, "fills our city colleges and Columbia's halls with the sons of Hebrews who came over in steerage." By 1916, they were ubiquitous on college campuses, especially at New York City College. A government report noted that the school was "practically filled with Jewish pupils, a considerable proportion of them children of Russian or Polish immigrants on the East Side." Jewish students were also entering Harvard, and by 1920, they constituted 20 percent of this elite school's student body.[21]

The increasing presence of Jewish students at Harvard provoked a backlash, however. On campus, anti-Semitic murmurs and complaints swept across the yard. A dormitory at Harvard was labeled "Little Jerusalem" because of its large number of Jewish students. Ethnic epithets circulated: "Jews are an unassimilable race, as dangerous to a college as indigestible food to man." "They are governed by selfishness." "They do not mix. They destroy the unity of the college."[22] President Abbott Lawrence Lowell announced that the college had a "Jewish problem." In a private letter to a member of the Board of Overseers on March 29, 1922, Lowell wrote that Harvard should limit the enrollment of Jewish students by imposing a quota for them. "Experience seems to place that proportion at about 15%."[23]

The very success of Jews in America was fueling anti-Semitism. The Jews "reaped more and more dislike as they bettered themselves," noted historian John Higham. "The more avidly they reached out for acceptance and participation in American life, the more their reputation seemed to suffer." Indeed, as second-generation Jews became educated and began seeking white-collar employment, they often encountered discrimination. Classified job listings sometimes specified "Christians only." Quality hospitals turned away Jewish doctors for internships, and prestigious law firms refused to hire Jewish lawyers. The doors to university faculty appointments were often closed to Jews.[24]

By the early 1930s, the Jewish striving to become American through economic and educational success was contributing to the decline of a Jewish identity. "The cornerstones of Judaism have always been its religion, its culture and its way of life," observed Max Baker and Paul Masserman in *The Jews Come to America* in 1932. "These cornerstones are crumbling in America." The authors predicted the disappearance of Jews as they assimilated into the mainstream. "The future of the Yiddish tongue, of Yiddish literature, of the Yiddish press is dark. The older generation, the Yiddish-speaking generation, is dying out. Yiddish itself, is spoken by a constantly diminishing portion of unassimilated Jewry, and is eschewed almost entirely by the younger generation." The "new Jew" was "entirely an American product," knowing little and caring less about Jewish affairs either in America or abroad.[25]

As they anxiously watched the rise of Nazism in Germany, however, Jewish Americans found themselves facing an agonizing dilemma: how should they respond to the unfolding crisis their brethren were experiencing in Europe?[26] They were also nervously looking over their shoulders at the escalating anti-Semitism in America. In Royal Oak, Michigan, Father Charles E. Coughlin was publishing a weekly tabloid, *Social Justice,* with a circulation in the hundreds of thousands, and broadcasting Sunday radio programs regularly reaching 3.5 million listeners. The Catholic priest was making inflammatory charges, claiming that Jewish-controlled international finances were responsible for the Great Depression and the economic suffering of the American working class. Hostile sentiments also shamelessly surfaced in elite circles. At elegant dinner parties, businessmen joked about the "chosen people" deserving what they were getting in Germany. Financier Jack Morgan, the son of J. P. Morgan, told a friend that he did not like Hitler "except for his attitude toward the Jews," which he considered "wholesome." The presence of Jews in prominent positions in the Roosevelt administration prompted nasty remarks. In a letter to the President written in 1934, a New Yorker complained: "On all sides is heard the cry that you have sold out the country to the Jews, and that the Jews are responsible for the continued depression, as they are determined to starve the Christians into submission and slavery. You have over two hundred Jews, they say, in executive offices in Washington, and Jew bankers run the government and [Bernard] Baruch is the real President." Roosevelt's New Deal was being characterized as the "Jew Deal."[27]

For many Jews in the United States, the Nazi persecutions underscored the need for a Jewish nation in Palestine. Before the rise of Hitler, the immigrants and their children had little interest in Zionism. They viewed their ethnic identity as religious, not political. In 1898, the Union of American Hebrew Congregations articulated this view when it declared: "We are unalterably opposed to political Zionism. The Jews are not a nation, but a religious community. Zionism was a precious possession of the past, the early home of our faith, where our prophets uttered their world-subduing thoughts, and our psalmists sang their world-enchanting hymns. As such it is a holy memory, but it is not our hope of the future. America is our Zion." In 1930, the Zionist Organization of America had such a dwindling membership that Rabbi Stephen Wise observed: "There is a complete lull in things Zionistic in America."[28]

But the lull was not to last. The "dire developments" of Nazism, historian Henry Feingold noted, would do for "the Zionist movement what it had been unable to do for itself."[29] "Many . . . young Jews, as myself," wrote a contributor to *New Palestine,* "have been startlingly awakened to the threat to our existence by the horribly persistent forward march of Hitlerism abroad and by the rise of American Hitlerism through the medium of Coughlinism. . . . We should like to be some sort of American Zionists enjoying Zionism in an American way."[30] They were not necessarily thinking of following Theodore Herzl's call for mass emigration to Palestine. Rather they would remain here: their citizenship would be American and their ethnic identity would be Jewish.

One of the intellectual leaders of this newly aroused ethnic nationalism was Chaim Zhitlowsky, author of *The Future of Our Youth in This Country and Assimilation,* published in 1935. The Nazi persecution of Jews, he argued, was demonstrating that assimilation as a remedy against anti-Semitism was a "bankrupt" strategy for acceptance. In Europe, Jews had been "swallowed up" by assimilation, only to find themselves "vomited up and thrown out on the Jewish shore, battered up, injured, robbed of [their] economic means of existence, and [their] human esteem deeply insulted and degraded." Zhitlowsky criticized Jews for embracing an "American" rather than a "Jewish" identity. Anxious to be accepted into the larger society, many of them had smothered their Jewishness and even tried to hide behind non-Jewish names. But the "catastrophic collapse of assimilation in Hitlerized Germany,"

Zhitlowsky argued, had sent a grim message: "Everywhere" there was "one Jewish problem, everywhere one great danger." There was only one solution — the restoration of a Zionist nation. A separate state for Jews, Zhitlowsky concluded, would allow them to become again "a normal respectable people, worthy of being a member of equal standing in the family of nations constituting humanity."[31]

In growing numbers, Jewish Americans began embracing Zhitlowsky's view: membership in the Zionist Organization of America jumped from 18,000 in 1929 to 52,000 in 1939, and would reach 136,000 by 1945. The Zionists focused on the 1917 Balfour Declaration, the British government's promise to create "a national Jewish home for the Jewish people" in the British mandate of Palestine. However, the effort to resettle Jews in their ancient homeland was suddenly stalled in 1939 when the British government, responding to Arab pressure, announced that it would allow only 75,000 Jews to enter Palestine over a five-year period.[32] American Zionists denounced this change in British policy. At the Extraordinary Zionist Conference in New York in May 1942, Rabbi Abba Hillel Silver argued that the foundation of anti-Semitism in Europe and elsewhere, including America, had been Jewish statelessness. He pointed out that Hitler was the most recent example of an affliction that had begun with the Roman destruction of the Jewish state. The basic fact in the Jewish tragedy was their "national homelessness." Thus, Silver concluded, the establishment of a Jewish nation in Palestine would be the "ultimate solution."[33]

Meanwhile, however, Jews in America had been forced to turn their attention to the Nazi darkness descending on their brethren in Europe. In 1933, representative Samuel Dickstein of New York offered a Congressional resolution for the admission of all German Jews who were related to American citizens and were fleeing from Hitler's persecution. The resolution called for the suspension of the 1924 Immigration Act's quota of 27,370 immigrants from Germany and also the requirement that prospective immigrants prove they were not likely to become public charges.

However, Dickstein encountered opposition from Jews themselves. The American Jewish Committee voiced the strongest criticism of his resolution for the admission of Jewish refugees. Founded in 1906 by wealthy German-Jewish immigrants, the Committee believed that Jews in this country should simply be loyal Americans. Representing the committee, Max J. Kohler warned that Dickstein's proposal was provoking the anti-Semitic charge that Jews in America were willing to sacrifice American interests in order to help Jews in Germany. Defending the immigration quotas, B'nai B'rith agreed that the restrictions should be enforced to protect American labor. The American Jewish Congress also called for keeping the gates closed. Composed of Eastern European Jews, the Congress was led by Rabbi Stephen Wise of New York City. In his testimony in Congress on March 22, 1933, he spoke against the passage of "special amendments to American immigration laws" or "new legislation" for Jewish victims of Nazi Germany. He argued that the existing restrictions were needed to keep out immigrants who would take jobs away from American workers. Jews in this country, Wise declared, were "Americans, first, last, and all the time."34

In *Opinion,* published by the American Jewish Congress, Harold Fields explained: "To allow aliens, Jew or non-Jew, to enter this country without funds, seeking employment where no employment is to be found, or coming to families already destitute, would be economical folly and unfair to the alien, his family and to us as Americans." But a more important concern, Fields added, was not economic. The admission of "too many" Jews would agitate anti-Semitism in America. "Is it desirable," he frankly asked, "to insist upon the admission of possibly 25,000 more Jews from Germany (and later from Poland, Austria, etc.) and thus give fuel to the claims of anti-Semites here that we, the Jews, were seeking to bring all the unfortunates to this country in these unfortunate times, or is the wiser policy to safeguard the mental, physical, and social happiness of the four million Jews now in the United States by refraining from bringing too many more Jews here?"35

Worried about the rising resentment against American Jews, Wise advised Representative Donald O'Toole of New York not to introduce legislation offering asylum to refugees. "I wish I thought that it were possible for this measure to be passed without repercussions upon the Jewish community in this country," the leader of the American Jewish Congress wrote in 1937. "I have reason to believe, unfortunately, that any effort that is made at this time to waive the immigration law will result in a serious accentuation of what we know to be a rising wave of anti-Semitic feeling in this country." Similarly, the American Jewish Committee warned in 1938: "While humanitarian accomplishments in bringing . . . victims of persecution to the United States and finding work for them cannot be highly enough praised, this is helping to intensify the Jewish problem here. Giving work to Jewish refugees while so many Americans are out of work, has naturally made bad feelings." The plight of the refugees was debated at a meeting of the General Jewish Council, an umbrella organization composed of representatives from the American Jewish Committee, the American Jewish Congress, B'nai B'rith, and the Jewish Labor Committee. Unable to choose between "the imperative necessity" of mass immigration and "the fundamental wrong of such a policy," the Council decided "that, at least for the time being, nothing should be done with regard to this matter."[36]

But many other American Jews felt that to do "nothing" was morally wrong. After seizing power in Germany, the Nazis had begun excluding Jews from government and professional employment. Then, in 1935, they enacted the racist Nuremberg laws. "A citizen of the Reich," the legislation declared, "is only a subject of the state who is of German or related blood, who demonstrates by his behavior that he is determined and suited to serve faithfully the German *Volk* and Reich."[37] Now "blood" determined citizenship in Germany.

This escalating persecution generated an urgent call for action to rescue the victims of Nazi hate. "The Jews of Germany are doomed!" concerned Protestant minister John Hayes Holmes warned members of the American Jewish Congress in *Opinion.* "There is only one thing that can be done about the Jews in Germany, and that is to *get them out.* They must be rescued, as the residents of a burning house, trapped by devouring flames, are rescued by firemen."[38]

Roosevelt's Rescue-Through-Victory Strategy

In July 1938, the U.S. government responded to the cry for help by convening representatives from thirty-three Western nations in Evian, France. The purpose of this conference was to help facilitate the emigration of political refugees from Germany. Two days before the opening, Anne O'Hare McCormick of the *New York Times* made a passionate moral appeal: "It is heartbreaking to think of the queues of desperate human beings around our consulates in Vienna and other cities waiting in suspense for what happens at Evian. But the question they underline is not simply humanitarian. It is not a question of how many unemployed this country can safely add to its own unemployed millions. It is a test of civilization. . . . Can America live with itself if it lets Germany get away with this policy of extermination, allows the fanaticism of one man to triumph over reason, refuses to take up this gage of battle against barbarism?"[39]

The conference, however, was designed to fail. The idea for the meeting had originated in the U.S. State Department. Worried that "certain Congressmen with metropolitan constituencies" were trying to revise the restrictionist immigration policies, Secretary of State Cordell Hull and Undersecretary Sumner Welles decided that the administration should "get out in front and attempt to guide the pressure, primarily with a view toward forestalling attempts to have the immigration laws liberalized." In his invitation for the conference, President Roosevelt stated that "no nation would be expected or asked to receive a greater number of emigrants" than would be permitted by its existing laws. Little wonder the delegates did nothing to assist the victims of Nazi persecution. Commenting on the Evian Conference, Vienna's *Volkischer Beobachter* stated: "We cannot take seriously President Roosevelt's appeal to the nations of the world as long as the United States maintains racial quotas for immigrants."[40]

Four months after the effete effort at Evian, Jews in Germany suddenly became the targets of hate violence. During one terrifying night, rampaging mobs murdered scores of Jews. According to the *New York Times,* in Berlin "raiding squads of young men roamed unhindered through the principal shopping districts, breaking shop windows with metal weapons, looting or tossing merchandise into the streets or into passing vehicles and leaving the unprotected Jewish shops to the mercy of vandals who followed in this unprecedented show of violence." After the night of fear and breaking glass, known as "Kristallnacht," the Nazis arrested thirty thousand Jews and assembled them at a depot. "At the station a train arrived to collect the Jews from our area," one of them recalled. "After Karlsruhe, when the train branched off toward Stuttgart, the only word to be heard was the terrible name Dachau."[41]

At a press conference, Roosevelt condemned the night of mayhem and murder: "The news of the past few days from Germany has deeply shocked public opinion in the United States. . . . I myself could scarcely believe that such things could occur in a twentieth century civilization." The President announced that he had ordered the American ambassador in Berlin to return immediately and report on the grave situation. Asked if he had considered a possible mass transfer of Kristallnacht victims to the United States, Roosevelt replied: "I have given a great deal of thought to it." Then he added: "The time is not ripe for that." Roosevelt was also asked if he would relax the immigration laws for Jewish refugees. "That is not in contemplation," he answered; "we have the quota system."[42] A Gallup poll conducted in November 1938, after Kristallnacht, showed that 77 percent of the Americans surveyed opposed increasing the immigration quota for Germany.[43] Although Roosevelt extended the visas for twelve thousand refugees already in the United States, he refused to open the gates to new refugees. The *Nation* observed that the liberalization of immigration legislation was an idea that most politicians regarded as "too hot to handle."[44]

Seeking an alternative to revising immigration policies, Congressman Dickstein offered a proposal for the resettlement of Jewish refugees in Alaska, still an undeveloped frontier region. This idea had been suggested to Roosevelt in 1938, but he had rejected it, saying that the project would "in effect make Alaska a foreign territory for immigration purposes, which would obviously be out of the question." In 1940, Dickstein and Senator William King introduced legislation for the admission of European laborers to help develop Alaska. Refugees, King explained, would be willing to relocate in this harsh, underpopulated wilderness in order to escape Nazi savagery.[45]

Reactions from the Jewish-American community were mixed. Major Jewish organizations rejected the Alaska rescue project. Rabbi Wise feared that the plan would give a "wrong and hurtful impression" that Jews were taking over a region of the country for settlement. On the other hand, support for the bill came from the Labor Zionists of America: "As Jews, we are especially interested that the government should allow a larger number of European refugees to enter if not the United States, at least Alaska."[46] The proposed legislation for refugee resettlement in Alaska died in the subcommittees.

Meanwhile, Senator Robert Wagner of New York and Representative Edith Nourse Rogers of Massachusetts hoped that Americans would at least have the heart to save Jewish children. In January 1939, they jointly introduced a bill that would allow the non-quota entry of twenty thousand refugee children from Germany over a two-year period. The children would be admitted on the condition that they would be supported by responsible private agencies or individuals and would not become public charges. The bill quickly came under attack from restrictionists. John B. Trevor of the American Coalition of Patriotic Societies scolded Wagner and Rogers for sponsoring such legislation in view of the needs of

a million "neglected boys and girls, descendants of American pioneers, undernourished, ragged and ill."[47]

The Wagner-Rogers bill needed support from the President.
While on a Caribbean cruise in February 1939, Roosevelt received
a cable from Mrs. Roosevelt: "Are you willing I should talk to
Sumner [Welles] and say we approve passage of Child Refugee
Bill. Hope you are having grand time. Much love. Eleanor."[48]
Roosevelt replied: "It is all right for you to support the child
refugee bill, but it is best for me to say nothing till I get back."[49]
After he returned, Roosevelt maintained his silence. Trying to get
the President to issue a statement on the proposed legislation, Representative Caroline O'Day wrote to ask him for his view on the
bill. Instead, Roosevelt penciled on her letter the following in-
structions to Secretary "Pa" Watson: "File, no action. FDR."[50]

Roosevelt was aware of widespread public opposition to the
bill. A Gallup poll revealed that 66 percent of those questioned did
not want the government to admit the children.[51] Roosevelt realized that the situation was desperate. "But it was one thing to sym-
pathize with the plight of the Jewish refugees," wrote historian
Doris Kearns Goodwin, "and quite another to pit his presidency
against the xenophobic, anti-Semitic mood of his country in the
late 1930s and early '40s. This Roosevelt was unwilling to do."[52]
Eleanor Roosevelt understood her husband's sensitivity to the
pulse of the people. "While I often felt strongly on various subjects," she wrote in *This I Remember*, "Franklin frequently re-
frained from supporting causes in which he believed, because of
political realities."[53]

The Wagner-Rogers proposal also turned out to be an extremely
sensitive political issue for Jewish-American leaders. During the
congressional hearings on the legislation, Rabbi Wise stated that he
would be willing to admit "a rather limited number of children," but
that he wanted the immigration restrictions to remain. "If there is
a conflict between our duty to those children and our duty to our
country, speaking for myself as a citizen, I should say, of course,
that our country comes first; and if children cannot be helped, they

cannot be helped, because we should not undertake to do anything that would be hurtful to the interests of our country."[54] The Wagner-Rogers bill failed to leave the committees, and even terrified refugee children would not be saved.

A few months later, 907 German-Jewish refugees tried to rescue themselves. They boarded the steamship *St. Louis* bound for Cuba, where they expected to find asylum. When their ship reached Havana, however, the Cuban government suddenly invalidated their immigration visas. Turned away at the dock, they remained on board while their ship steamed in circles between Cuba and Florida. The passengers saw the lights and beaches of Miami, but the U.S. Coast Guard escorted their ship out of American waters. Frantically, they pleaded for permission to land in the United States. Describing the *St. Louis* as "the saddest ship afloat today," carrying a "cargo of despair," the *New York Times* editorialized: "We can only hope that some hearts will soften somewhere and some refuge found. The cruise of the *St. Louis* cries high to heaven of man's inhumanity to man." The *Jewish Daily Forward* printed a scream for help from the passengers: "We appeal to world Jewry. We are being sent back. How can you be peaceful? How can you be silent? Help! Do everything you can! Some on the ship have committed suicide. Help! Do not allow the ship to go back to Germany!"[55]

As the ship sailed along the U.S. coastline, a Jewish-American organization, the Joint Distribution Committee, tried to post a bond of $500,000 guaranteeing that the refugees would not become public charges in Cuba. The Cuban government refused the offer. The rejected refugees now focused all of their hope on Roosevelt. "The desperate passengers on the *St. Louis* telegraphed the President," wrote historian Arthur Hertzberg, "but he ignored them."[56] Forced to sail back across the Atlantic, the passengers were resettled in the United Kingdom, France, the Netherlands, Belgium, and Denmark. Many of them would again face the threat of Nazi extermination. One of the passengers was Ilse Marcus, who would be taken to a Nazi concentration camp. Years later, living in New York, she recalled that she had found it incredible that the passengers of the *St. Louis* had not been permitted to land. "This country was built on immigrants," declared Marcus, "and there was no room in this country for 900 people who were in danger of death."[57] The American-born daughter of Jewish immigrants remembered following the tragic fate of the ship through the newspapers. "It's something we should always be ashamed of," remarked Lena Friedman. "We should have given Roosevelt holy hell."[58]

The *St. Louis* incident unleashed a sense of frustration within Jewish communities. "Let our leaders lead!" demanded Samuel Margoshes impatiently in the Yiddish daily *The Day*. "Let them not delay and postpone. Let the General Jewish Council meet and deliberate immediately. The Jewish masses are waiting to go out into the streets, to close their places of business, to stop all work, to declare a fast and to demonstrate to the entire world that we will no longer allow ourselves to be slaughtered by a barbaric regime." In the same newspaper, B. Z. Goldberg took readers to the razor's edge: "How can one sit quietly when one's flesh and blood is beaten? . . . Aren't [Jews] people too? Aren't they also Americans? Can't they also scream of their pain?"[59]

The anguish intensified in September 1939 when Germany occupied Poland and three million more Jews came under Nazi rule. "In the matter of the treatment of Jews in Nazi-over-run Poland," Rabbi Wise wrote in *Opinion* in February 1940, "we face a spectacle of daily torture and horror such as men have not beheld since the days of Genghis Khan."[60]

But what awaited the Jews of Europe would surpass the atrocities of Genghis Khan. When Hitler began his anti-Semitic campaign, he had declared that his goal was Jewish expulsion. In a 1939 circular sent to its consular officials, the German Foreign Ministry stated that the government's policy was to remove all Jews from German territory. Two years later, however, Hitler reversed this policy: suddenly, the Nazi government prohibited Jews from leaving German-held territory.

Hitler's homicidal plan was unshrouded during the German invasion of Russia. Following the advancing German army, Nazi execution squads, known as the Einsatzgruppen, had begun murdering Jews by the hundreds of thousands. The atrocities were reported in newspapers throughout the West. The shocking revelations forced Wise to reassess his reluctance to give special consideration to the Jewish victims. Only a year earlier, the Jewish-American leader had argued: "The greatest crime against the Jewish victims of Hitler would be to treat the crimes against the Jews differently from the treatment of crimes against French, Czechs, or Poles or Greeks."[61] Now he was forced to recognize that Hitler was treating Jews "differently," and that the crimes against them were "different." In August 1941, Wise editorialized in *Opinion*: "Time may pass before the ghastly details come to be known. But certain it is . . . that the Nazis have most ruthlessly set the torch to the homes of all Jews in their martial path. Apparently Jews have suffered most, according to their own grisly tale, in such places in Roumania as Jassy, where, according to one report 700 Jews were led out and shot."[62]

The purpose of the executions was extermination. "The discovery of the Jewish virus," Hitler told Heinrich Himmler in 1942, "is one of the greatest revolutions that have taken place in the world. The battle in which we are engaged today is of the same sort as the battle waged, during the last century, by Pasteur and Koch. How many diseases have their origin in the Jewish virus. . . . We shall regain our health only by eliminating the Jew."[63]

News of the Einsatzgruppen mass murders continued to reach the United States, and on July 21, 1942, twenty thousand people gathered at Madison Square Garden to protest the Nazi atrocities. In a message sent to the rally, Roosevelt urged the people there to support his rescue-through-victory strategy. "Americans who love justice and hate oppression," he declared, "will hail the solemn commemoration in Madison Square Garden as an expression of the determination of the Jewish people to make every sacrifice for victory over the Axis powers. Citizens, regardless of religious allegiance, will share in the sorrow of our Jewish fellow citizens over the savagery of the Nazis against their helpless victims."[64] At the mass meeting, Rabbi Wise endorsed Roosevelt's strategy when he declared that the "salvation of our people" could come only through a "speedy and complete" victory.[65] On August 12, in the Philharmonic Auditorium in Los Angeles, three thousand concerned citizens gathered at a meeting sponsored by the American Jewish Congress. Speakers denounced the Nazis for murdering more than one million Jews, and urged the United States to do everything it could to "insure that human liberty and human decency may once again triumph."[66]

At this point, Americans were still unaware of the extent of the Nazi extermination effort — the systematic and complex apparatus of trains, barracks, factories, gas chambers, and crematoria.[67] But within weeks, they would no longer be able to claim that they did not know. On August 28, 1942, Wise received a cable from Gerhart Riegner, the World Jewish Congress representative in Geneva. The message stated:

> Received alarming report that in Fuhrer's headquarters plan discussed and under consideration according to which all Jews in countries occupied or controlled by Germany numbering 3½–4 millions should after deportation and concentration in East be exterminated at one blow to resolve once for all the Jewish question in Europe stop the action reported planned for autumn methods under discussion including prussic acid stop we transmit information with all necessary reservation as exactitude cannot be confirmed stop informant stated to have close connections with highest German authorities and his reports generally speaking reliable.[68]

The Riegner report made one thing absolutely clear: there was no longer a reason for doubting the genocide, or an excuse for hesitating to make every effort to rescue Jews. Hitler had, in fact, unleashed his ultimate pogrom — the "Final Solution."

Wise took the incriminating cable to Undersecretary of State Sumner Welles, only to be told that he should wait until the information could be confirmed. Wise agreed, but he shared Riegner's report with representatives of the major Jewish-American organizations. The wait for Welles's response was agonizing for Wise. "I don't know whether I am getting to be a Hofjude [court Jew]," he confided in a letter to a friend, "but I find that a good part of my work is to explain to my fellow Jews why our government cannot do all the things asked or expected of it."[69] Remaining silent tormented Wise, for he knew that Jews were being murdered by the thousands daily. "I have had the unhappiest days of my life," the rabbi wrote to the Reverend John Hayes Holmes. "Think of what it means to hear, as I have heard, through a coded message — first from Geneva, then from Berne, through the British Foreign Office, — that Hitler plans the extermination at one time of the whole Jewish population of Europe; and prussic acid is mentioned as the medium." Wise wrote in anguish: "I don't want to turn my heart inside out, but I am almost demented over my people's grief."[70]

Three months later, after the Nazis had murdered an additional one million Jews, Wise was finally summoned by Welles. "I hold in my hands documents which have come to me from our legation in Berne," the undersecretary of state said. "I regret to tell you, Dr. Wise, that these documents confirm and justify your deepest fears." Welles suggested that Wise release the Riegner report to the press. "For reasons you will understand," he said, "I cannot give these to the press, but there is no reason why you should not. It might even help if you did."[71]

At once, Wise held a press conference to announce the confirmed evidence of the official Nazi policy of genocide. Incredibly, the press did not cover the shocking news as a major story. In order to arouse the American public from its moral lethargy, Jewish leaders organized a Day of Mourning and Prayer on December 2, 1942. In New York City, half a million Jewish union laborers stopped production for ten minutes, and special services were held in synagogues. NBC broadcast a quarter-hour memorial service. "In every country where Hitler's edicts run, every day is a day of mourning for Jews," editorialized the *New York Times*. "Today has been set aside, by action of the chief Rabbinate of Palestine, supported by the Jewish organizations of the United States, as a day of mourning, prayer and fasting among Jews throughout the free countries of the world."[72]

That day, Wise requested a meeting with President Roosevelt: "Dear Boss: I do not wish to add an atom to the awful burden which you are bearing with magic and, as I believe, heaven-inspired strength at this time. But you do know that the most overwhelming disaster of Jewish history has befallen Jews in the form of the Hitler mass-massacres . . . and it is indisputable that as many as two million civilian Jews have been slain."[73]

Six days later, Wise and delegates from major Jewish organizations met with Roosevelt. The meeting turned out to be a great disappointment. The meeting lasted twenty-nine minutes, and Roosevelt engaged in casual conversation for nearly the entire time. Near the end of the meeting, the discussion finally turned to the Jewish crisis in Europe. But this "entire conversation [on the urgent issue] lasted only a minute or two," wrote one of the frustrated participants in his diary.[74]

A few months later, in April 1943, American and British representatives met in Bermuda to discuss the Jewish emergency, but they simply reaffirmed Roosevelt's rescue-through-victory strategy. The inaction of the Bermuda conference angered Szmul Zygielbojm, a Jewish Socialist member of the Polish National Council. In a searing letter, he condemned the United States and Great Britain for their complicity in the mass murder of Jews:

> The responsibility for this crime of murdering the entire Jewish population of Poland falls in the first instance on

the perpetrators, but indirectly it is also a burden on the whole of humanity, the people and the governments of the Allied States which thus far have made no effort toward concrete action for the purpose of curtailing this crime.

By the passive observation of the murder of defenseless millions and of the maltreatment of children, women, and old men, these countries have become the criminals' accomplices. . . .

As I was unable to do anything during my life, perhaps by my death I shall contribute to breaking down that indifference.[75]

Shortly after writing this letter, Zygielbojm committed suicide.

The utter failure of the Bermuda Conference to address the refugee crisis provoked anger as well as action within the Jewish-American community. In a letter to Sumner Welles, the Joint Emergency Committee on European Jewish Affairs charged that relegating the fate of the Jews to "the day of victory" was "virtually to doom them to the fate" that Hitler had designed for them. At the August 10 meeting of the Joint Emergency Committee, Lillie Shultz of the American Jewish Congress declared: "The time has come . . . to be critical of lack of action and in view of the fact that this is the eve of a presidential election year, ways can be found to indicate to the administration, and possibly through the political parties that the large and influential Jewish communities will find a way of registering at the polls its dissatisfaction over the failure of the administration to take any effective steps to save the Jews of Europe."[76]

Wise also criticized the Bermuda Conference as "a woeful failure." He had come to believe that the refugee crisis demanded action beyond the military effort to defeat Nazi Germany. "Children must be saved," Wise wrote in *Opinion*. "Havens of refuge must be provided for those who are able to escape. Immigration regulations must for a time be waived or suspended." In Detroit, he declared in a speech: "I do not believe my country is so poor in spirit as to deny refuge to such handfuls as may escape the Hitler morgue and come to our shores."[77]

The most militant criticism of Roosevelt's rescue-through-victory strategy came from the Committee for a Jewish Army of Stateless and Palestinian Jews. In an advertisement in the *New York Times* on May 3, 1943, the committee pointed to the Allied commitment to the Four Freedoms and then blasted them for their hypocrisy: "Wretched, doomed victims of Hitler's tyranny! Poor men and women of good faith the world over! You have cherished an illusion. Your hopes have been in vain. Bermuda was not the dawn of a new era, of an era of humanity and compassion, of translating pity into deed. Bermuda was a mockery and cruel jest."[78]

To stir the moral conscience of America, the Committee for a Jewish Army turned to drama as a weapon of protest. Theater would be their fire bell in the night to break the screaming silence. In March 1943, they sponsored a tour of Ben Hecht's pageant "We Will Never Die." Forty thousand people attended the opening presentation at Madison Square Garden. The performance presented an enactment of the history of Jews, their contributions to civilization, and the genocide they were experiencing. Hecht's powerful dramatization of Hitler's war against the Jews conveyed a passionate plea to Americans: everything possible should be done to rescue the remaining four million Jews.[79] Moved by the pageant, Eleanor Roosevelt wrote in her "My Day" column: "No one who heard each group come forward and give the story of what had happened to it at the hands of a ruthless German military, will ever forget those haunting words: 'Remember us.'"[80]

But, for Peter Bergson, a leader of the Committee for a Jewish Army, Americans had to do much more than remember the victims of Nazism. What was desperately needed was action — the transfer of Jews from Hitler-dominated countries to places of refuge or to Palestine. In October 1943, Bergson took his campaign directly to Washington. Seeking to confront Roosevelt, he led several hundred Orthodox rabbis to the White House. Shortly before their arrival, however, Roosevelt slipped away, first to attend a ceremony and then to retreat for a five-day weekend at Hyde Park. Meeting instead with Vice President Henry Wallace, the rabbis presented a petition calling for a special intergovernmental agency with powers and means to rescue the remaining Jews under Hitler's control. But Wallace only reaffirmed Roosevelt's rescue-through-victory strategy.

Only a Remnant Remained

By then, an ominous question had emerged: after the Allied triumph would there be any Jews left alive?

Unwilling to wait for an Allied victory, Representative Will Rogers and Senator Guy Gillette decided to press for a rescue program. In November 1943, they introduced resolutions that urged the President to create a commission of diplomatic, economic, and military experts that would create and implement a plan of action to save the remainder of the Jews in Europe. During a hearing on the issue before a House committee in December 1943, Breckenridge Long of the State Department testified that the United States was already doing everything it could to rescue Jews, and that the government had admitted approximately 580,000 refugees from Nazi-controlled countries.

Long's figures, however, represented the number of refugees who were theoretically eligible. In fact, less than half of this number had been admitted. Long himself had been actively working to exclude refugees. Claiming that they represented a security threat, he had helped to erect a maze of bureaucratic requirements and procedures that effectively limited refugee immigration. Protesting the State Department's immigration practices, Albert Einstein had written to Eleanor Roosevelt in 1942: "A policy is now being pursued which makes it all but impossible to give refuge in America to many worthy persons who are the victims of Fascist cruelty in Europe. Of course this is not openly avowed by those responsible for it. The method which is being used, however, is to make immigration impossible by creating a wall of bureaucratic measures alleged to be necessary to protect America against subversive, dangerous elements."[81]

Long's misleading testimony provoked a storm of protest as the resolution headed toward Senate committee hearings. In its report, the Senate Foreign Relations Committee urged action for a moral reason: "The problem is essentially a humanitarian one. It is not a Jewish problem alone. It is a Christian problem and a problem for enlightened civilization. . . . We have talked; we have sympathized; we have expressed our horror; the time to act is long past due."[82] Secretary of the Treasury Henry Morgenthau recognized that the controversy over the resolution was "a boiling pot on the Hill," and that it was "going to pop": either Roosevelt would have to do something very fast or the Congress would do it for him.[83]

Morgenthau decided to nudge Roosevelt into action. At a meeting with the President on January 16, 1944, he presented a report on the mass murders of Jews. The opening sentence expressed moral indignation: "One of the greatest crimes in history, the slaughter of the Jewish people in Europe, is continuing unabated." Morgenthau called for immediate action. "The matter of rescuing the Jews from extermination is a trust too great to remain in the hands of men who are indifferent, callous and perhaps even hostile. The task is filled with difficulties. Only a fervent will to accomplish, backed by persistent and untiring effort, can succeed where time is so precious."[84] The concerned Jewish secretary of the treasury warned the President that "a growing number of responsible people and organizations" believed that there was "plain anti-Semitism motivating the actions of these State Department officials, and, rightly or wrongly, it [would] require little more in the way of proof for this suspicion to explode into a nasty scandal."[85]

A scandal was exactly what Roosevelt wished to avoid in an election year. Six days later, he signed an executive order establishing the War Refugee Board, a government agency that would be responsible for "the development of plans and programs and the inauguration of effective measures for a) the rescue, transportation and maintenance and relief of the victims of enemy oppression, and b) the establishment of havens of temporary refuge for such victims."[86] Morgenthau's assistant in the Treasury Department, John W. Pehle, was appointed executive director of the new agency.

Welcoming the creation of the War Refugee Board, Jewish leaders urged the government to create havens of refuge in the United States. "Every surviving Jewish man, woman and child who can escape from the Hitlerite fury into the territories of the United Nations," the American Jewish Congress declared, should have "the right of temporary asylum." Making an analogy between refugees and goods stored temporarily in ports free from custom duties, the *Congress Weekly* called for the establishment of "free ports." Supporting a Senate resolution favoring "free ports," Bergson's committee published a full-page advertisement in the *Washington Post*: "25 Square Miles or Two Million Lives, Which Shall It Be?"[87]

Roosevelt rejected these proposals. He defended the administration's policies by explaining that the government was transporting to North Africa all of the refugees who had been able to escape from Nazi control. The President also argued that it would be "wasteful and unnecessary to bring these refugees across the ocean from Europe only to return them later."[88] However, Pehle bluntly informed the President: "The necessity for unilateral action by this Government lies in the fact that we cannot expect others to do what we ourselves will not do and if we are to act in time we must take the lead." In the end, Roosevelt offered a small concession: he agreed to create an emergency shelter near Oswego, New York, for one thousand refugees representing "a reasonable proportion of various categories of persecuted people."[89]

One thousand was not even a token number. By then, Hitler had seized control of Hungary, and the Nazis had begun shipping that country's 800,000 Jews to the death camps in Poland. At Auschwitz the gas chambers were murdering 12,000 people daily. German scientists had designed and built a state-of-the-art processing plant for genocide. A firsthand account of the killing fac-

tory was given by Sarah Cender, who was twenty-five years old
when she was taken to the death camp.

> Upon arrival we were separated from the males and
> brought in front of a building where heaps of clothing
> were lying on the ground. We were ordered to undress
> quickly and naked we were pushed into a pitch dark
> chamber (what we naively and hopefully thought to be a
> bath facility — although no soap or towel were given
> to us).
>
> The doors closed behind us. Anxious seconds and min-
> utes passed. Nothing seemed to happen for a while. Only
> cries and laments and hysterical screams were heard
> from every corner of the chamber. . . .
>
> Suddenly a tremendous rumble shook the place. In the
> few minutes we could not understand what had happened,
> but soon enough we recognized the familiar sound of
> over-flying bombers. The shattering noises and rumblings
> continued throughout the night. Exhausted, neither dead
> nor alive, holding on to each other, cramped and entrapped
> we waited in darkness for the inevitable to come.[90]

Those "rumblings" were American bombers. What was urgently
needed to end the carnage was the immediate destruction of the
machinery of genocide — the Allied bombing of the rail lines leading to Auschwitz and even the death camp itself. On July 6, 1944,
representatives of the Jewish Agency for Palestine asked the British
air force to carry out the bombings; a day later, Winston Churchill
responded favorably. "Get anything out of the Air Force that you
can," he wrote to Anthony Eden.[91] But Churchill was informed
that British air bases were too far away for their planes to reach
the targeted rail lines or Auschwitz. American planes, however,
were within striking distance.

On July 24, the Emergency Committee to Save the Jewish People of Europe asked Roosevelt to order the bombing of the railways and the gas chambers. The destruction of the railways, the committee argued, would disrupt not only the transportation of Jews but also military traffic. Roosevelt did not respond. A week later, a rally of forty thousand people at Madison Square Garden demanded that the United States stop the genocide by making every effort to destroy the Nazi extermination facilities.

On August 8, the World Jewish Congress forwarded to the War Refugee Board an urgent message from Czechoslovakian leader Ernest Frischer: "Germans are now exhuming and burning corpses in an effort to conceal their crimes. This could be prevented by destruction of crematoria and then Germans might possibly stop further mass exterminations especially since so little time is left to them."[92] The next day, A. Leon Kubowitzki of the World Jewish Congress forwarded this plea to Assistant Secretary of War John J. McCloy. Five days later, McCloy replied:

> Dear Mr. Kubowitzki:
> I refer to your letter of August 9 in which you request consideration of a proposal made by Mr. Ernest Frischer that certain installations and railroad centers be bombed.
> The War Department has been approached by the War Refugee Board, which has raised the question of the practicality of this suggestion. After a study it became apparent that such an operation could be executed only by the diversion of considerable air support essential to the success of our forces now engaged in decisive operations elsewhere and would in any case be of such doubtful efficacy that it would not warrant the use of our resources. There has been considerable opinion to the effect that such an effort, even if practicable, might provoke even more vindictive action by the Germans.
> The War Department fully appreciates the humanitarian motives which prompted the suggested operation,

but for the reasons stated above, it has not been felt that it can or should be undertaken, at least at this time.

> Sincerely,
> John J. McCloy[93]

But how could German actions be "even more vindictive"? And would bombing the rail lines and crematoria have been much of a "diversion"? At that time, American planes were dropping bombs near the death camp itself. On August 20, they attacked munitions factories in the city of Auschwitz less than five miles east of the gas chambers. On the ground, Shalom Lindenbaum and a group of Jews were being moved into a "bath house," which he knew was a gas chamber. "I remember how I ran ahead of my father in order to be together in what seemed to be our last hour," he later wrote. "At that time Allied bombers appeared in the sky. It will be difficult to describe our joy. We prayed and hoped to be bombed by them, and so to escape the helpless death in the gas chambers. To be bombed meant a chance that also the Germans will be killed. Therefore we were deeply disappointed and sad when they passed over, not bombing."[94]

Hitler's factories of death continued to emit their sorrow-filled smoke. Determined to do what they could to destroy the killing facilities, a group of desperate prisoners blew up one of the crematorium buildings in a suicidal uprising. They used some explosives stolen by Jewish women working at one of the munitions factories that American planes were trying to bomb.[95] By then, as Roosevelt's rescue-through-victory strategy was coming to a conclusion, only a remnant of the Jews in Europe remained alive.

"Scratches" on the Door: Remember Us, Please

Rescue came, finally, when Allied troops advanced into Germany in April 1945. The first death camp liberated was Ohrdruf. On April 12, General Omar Bradley and General Dwight Eisenhower toured the extermination facility. Bradley was overwhelmed, physically sickened by the smell of death. "More than 3,200 naked, emaciated bodies had been flung into shallow graves," he recalled. "Others lay on the streets where they had fallen. Lice crawled over the yellowed skin of their sharp, bony frames." Eisenhower thought his troops should see the gruesome evidence, and ordered all nearby units that were not engaged in combat to tour Ohrdruf. "We are told that the American soldier does not know what he is fighting for," he declared. "Now, at least, he will know what he is fighting *against*."96

At Dachau, Japanese-American soldiers of the 442nd saw directly the ghastliness of ethnic cleansing rooted in the Nazi ideology of racial hatred. "When the gates swung open, we got our first good look at the prisoners," Ichiro Imamura wrote in his diary. "Many of them were Jews. They were wearing black and white striped prison suits and round caps. A few had shredded blanket rags draped over their shoulders. . . . The prisoners struggled to their feet [and] shuffled weakly out of the compound. They were like skeletons — all skin and bones."97

Initially, the Jewish prisoners were surprised and confused to see soldiers of Japanese ancestry. "When they first came in, we thought they were [the Japanese] allies of the Germans," a survivor recalled. "We believed they were there to torture us." The inmates thought that their liberators did not look like "Americans." When she saw the Nisei soldiers, Janina Cywinska, a Catholic woman who had been sent to Dachau when her family was caught smuggling weapons to Jewish resisters, exclaimed: "Oh, no, you're a Japanese and you're going to kill us." And a Nisei soldier replied: "We are *American* Japanese. You are free."98

The gaze into Hitler's chamber of horrors was particularly dreadful for Jewish-American soldiers. Entering one of the barracks at Buchenwald, Chaplin Rabbi Herschel Schacter saw hundreds of survivors lying on shelves from the floor to the ceiling. They were "strewn over scraggly straw sacks," looking down at him out of dazed eyes. Schacter then shouted in Yiddish, "Sholem

Aleychem, Yiden, yir zent frey!" "You are free." Schacter felt a special empathy for this pitiful humanity before him: "If my own father had not caught the boat on time, I would have been there."[99]

David Malachowsky of the 104th Infantry Division was stunned when he saw "row upon row of bodies just stacked like cordwood maybe five feet high." The rotting bodies had created a smell that saturated the countryside for miles around. Then Malachowsky came across the living — emaciated souls with huge sunken eyes. One of them, looking like an old woman, turned out to be a seventeen-year-old girl. Speaking Yiddish, she kept asking for water, "wasser." Malachowsky recalled the rage he felt: "I know that as a Jew, I was more incensed, I feel, than many of the other soldiers, even though they also were terribly upset by this regardless of what religion they had. I heard that there were special camps just for Jews like myself. And I could just visualize what had happened to them. And so seeing this, I mean, just the bestiality — what kind of mentality would permit this?"[100]

Dr. Philip Lief of the 3rd Auxiliary Surgical Group, First Army, wondered how this murderous madness could come out of a highly civilized society. "I had studied German literature while an undergraduate at Harvard College," he told an interviewer. "I knew about the culture of the German people and I could not, could not really believe that this was happening in this day and age; that in the twentieth century a cultured people like the Germans would undertake something like this. It was just beyond our imagination."[101] In the apartment of Buchenwald's commandant, Lief had seen a pocketbook and a lampshade made out of human skin.

At Dachau, Walter J. Fellenz realized that the Nazi facility represented "an organized scheme of destruction of a whole race of people!" During an inspection of the camp, he had entered a storage warehouse. "This large building contained the naked, dead bodies of over 4,000 men, women and children, thrown one on top of the other like sacks of potatoes," he reported. "The odor was terrific. I vomited three times in less than five minutes; it was the most revolting smell I have ever experienced." Fellenz then visited the gas chamber. Over its entrance, written in Yiddish, was the word "Showers." The room itself was inlaid with high-quality brown tile and had 200 chrome shower nozzles. How could the Nazi guards have lived with themselves, asked Fellenz, after herding people into the chambers, turning on what appeared to be showers, and then piling the bodies in stacks to be burned? The executioners, he thought, must have initially found their actions abhorrent, but then the killing had become "an everyday thing."[102]

Chaplin Judah Nadich tried to picture what it was like to be in the gas chamber. The rabbi had noticed thousands of scratches on the inside of the door, "scratches that must have been made by the fingernails of so many men and women and children." Outside of the crematorium, he inspected what looked like potato sacks, stamped with the German word for fertilizer. Suddenly, Nadich realized that the sacks were filled with human ash from the furnaces, ready for shipment to German farms. "I plunged my arm into one of the sacks up to the elbow," he recalled, "and pressed the 'fertilizer,' the human ash, with the fingers of my hand into my palm and ground it into my palm so that I might never forget what I had seen there."[103]

Also witnessing what they would never forget were African-American soldiers. When they entered the Nazi killing fields of Buchenwald and Dachau, many of them broke down emotionally. "I was seventeen, and my life was almost extinguished," recalled Buchenwald prisoner Ben Bender. "For me, it was an instant awakening of life after a long darkness. . . . I was seeing black soldiers for the first time in my life, crying like babies, carrying the dead and the starved and trying to help everybody." "It was the morning of April 11," recalled Elie Wiesel, an inmate of Buchenwald. "I will always remember with love a big black soldier. He was crying like a child — tears of all the pain in the world and all the rage."[104]

At Dachau, black soldier Paul Parks experienced a sickening sensation as he scanned the horror — the survivors looking like ghosts, the ovens still warm. "Why Jews?" asked Parks, who three years earlier had witnessed the sadistic murder of a fellow black soldier in Louisiana. "It doesn't make sense. Why were they killed?" A prisoner explained: "They were killed because they were Jews." Parks commented: "I understand that." Then he added: "I understand that because I've seen people lynched just because they were black." Parks compared the experiences of African Americans and Jews: "There's one other great incident of humanity that I'm very familiar with, the three hundred years of slavery in my own country, where people for generations were not allowed to be free, subject to the dictates of another race. Held in bondage, forced to work, and forced to do what another person wanted you to do. And if you didn't obey, there were no laws against killing you and destroying your family. So I said, 'As you talk, I see there's a close parallel between the history of my people in America and what's happened to the Jews in Europe.'"[105]

At Dachau, African-American soldiers like Parks understood a valuable lesson: the war for "double victory" was a cross-stitched struggle for victory over anti-Semitism in Europe and over racism in America.

9

A MULTICULTURAL "MANIFEST DESTINY"
We Are "Not a Narrow Tribe"

A Rising Wind: Toward the Civil Rights Revolution

INALLY, WITH THE DEFEAT of Germany, Italy, and Japan, peace came. However, the war against "ugly prejudices" at home remained yet to be won.[1] During the international conflict, this internal "enemy" had revealed itself in the jim crow army, the internment of Japanese Americans, the desolation of the Pima reservation of Ira Hayes, the refusal to admit Jewish refugees, the exclusion of minority workers from the defense industries, the Detroit race riot, the Los Angeles "zoot-suit" riot, and the "rain of ruin" on Hiroshima.

The fight for the "Four Freedoms" would now focus on the home front. A teenager at the time, Maya Angelou asked: "Hadn't we all, black and white, just snatched the remaining Jews from the hell of concentration camps?" Black soldiers, however, were returning home only to hang out "on the ghetto corners like forgotten laundry left on a back yard fence." Their futures, brightened by the war, had suddenly clouded over again. "Thus we lived through a major war," Angelou wrote. "The question in the ghettos was, Can we make it through a minor peace?"[2]

Angelou knew the answer: African Americans would have to struggle for "victory" in America. She had personally learned this lesson during the war. Encouraged by the demand for labor, Angelou applied for a job as a streetcar operator in San Francisco. "I'd picture myself, dressed in a neat blue serge suit, my money changer swinging jauntily at my waist, and a cheery smile for the passengers which would make their own work day brighter," she recalled. At the Market Street Railway Company office, the receptionist told Angelou that they were accepting applicants only from agencies. Suspicious, Angelou pointed to a job listing in that morning's *San Francisco Chronicle;* demanding to see the manager, she was told that he was out of the office. Angelou refused to be denied. "I WOULD HAVE THE JOB. I WOULD BE A CONDUCTORETTE AND SLING A FULL MONEY CHANGER FROM MY BELT. I WOULD," she declared, determined. Returning time and again, she was finally allowed to fill out an application. "I was given blood tests, aptitude tests, physical coordination tests, and Rorschachs, then on a blissful day I was hired as the first Negro on the San Francisco streetcars."[3] Angelou had discovered a spirit within her that would soar after the war. She would become a literary conductorette, slinging poems and stories from her heart.

Ermelinda Murillo also reinvented herself during the war. In 1923, when she was a child, her family had emigrated from Jalisco, Mexico, to Chicago. Twenty years later, Murillo was hired by Inland Steel Company in Indiana, where she worked as a heat chaser, hot shear expediter, hot bed operator, and stocker at the 10-inch Bar Mill. "I speak some Spanish, Polish, Serbian, Croatian," Murillo said. "I learned bits of each language by working with people with various ethnic backgrounds. If I can't get a point across in one language, I simply try another. We worked hard, argued, shared a sandwich and had coffee together. To me it was a real world inside the mill." After the war, Murillo continued working for Inland Steel until she retired. Her hard hat read: MELA — QUEEN OF THE 12-INCH.[4]

One of the first Chinese-American women to volunteer for the

Army Nurse Corps, Helen Pon Onyett had also earned respect during the war. She was twenty-five years old with four years of nursing experience when she enlisted in 1942. Assigned to duty in the European war, Onyett nursed wounded soldiers on transports off North Africa. "I can't swim, so I wore my Mae West [life jacket] twenty-four hours a day. It was very scary, especially when some of the ships you would be traveling with would be sunk right under your nose." Her experience as an army nurse was so affirming that she continued her service in the military as a reservist for more than thirty years. "I wouldn't have done half the things I did if I hadn't been in the service. . . . I had a chance to go to school on the G.I. bill and to improve my standing." In 1971, Onyett was promoted to the rank of full colonel. "When I spoke before audiences, people gawked at me, saying, 'Oh, my God, she's a colonel,' not 'She's Oriental.' "[5]

For Dalip Singh Saund, the war also offered a passage into America: he was one of the 1,772 Asian Indians who became naturalized citizens between 1947 and 1965. Since his arrival in 1919, Saund had wanted to become a citizen. "I had married an American girl, and was the father of three American children," he explained in his autobiography. "I was making America my home. Thus it was only natural that I felt very uncomfortable not being able to become a citizen of the United States." During the war, Saund and his compatriots petitioned Congress to grant them eligibility for citizenship. To gain support for their proposal, they directed war-bond drives among Asian Indians, hoping to "earn" the "confidence" of Americans. "I saw that the bars of citizenship were shut tight against me," Saund remarked. "I knew if these bars were lifted I would see much wider gates of opportunity open to me, opportunity as existed for everybody else in the United States of America." Three years after successfully helping to lobby their proposal through Congress, Saund became a naturalized citizen. He went on to be elected to the House of Representatives in 1956, serving for three terms.[6]

The war also opened opportunities for Mary Daniels Williams. When Japan attacked Pearl Harbor, she was a house cleaner with only a ninth-grade education. "I had no skills. I was going nowhere fast. I was getting older and I could just see us living in the slum forever. I could see myself living in two or three rooms for the rest of my life, and I decided for myself I wasn't going to do it." At a post office, a military recruiter promised her "education, new places to go and to visit — well, just a totally new life." Williams enlisted in the Women's Army Corps and served in England and France. After the war, she completed her bachelor's degree under the G.I. bill and worked for twenty years as a social worker in Cincinnati. "I knew what I wanted," said the African-American veteran, "and I knew that I was never gonna scrub another floor."[7]

Indeed, there was no turning back. "A wind *is* rising," declared Walter White of the NAACP in 1945, "a wind of determination by the have-nots of the world to share the benefits of freedom and prosperity which the haves of the earth have tried to keep exclusively for themselves. That wind blows all over the world. Whether that wind develops into a hurricane is a decision which we must make now and in the days when we form the peace."[8]

One of the first racial exclusions to be swept away by this rising wind of determination was segregation in the military. Demanding the end of this shameful practice, A. Philip Randolph threatened to lead massive civil disobedience. At a meeting with the President in 1948, Randolph declared: "Negroes are in no mood to shoulder guns for democracy abroad, while they are denied democracy here at home." Under pressure, Truman did what Roosevelt had failed to do: he issued an executive order requiring "equality of treatment and opportunity for all persons in the armed services."[9]

Also stirred by this wind of freedom, Japanese Americans wondered what would happen to them in postwar society. At a press conference on November 21, 1944, Roosevelt was asked whether the internees would be free to return to the West Coast. In his jocular speaking style, the President replied:

A good many of them . . . [have already left the camps and] have re-placed themselves, and in a great many parts of the country. And the example that I always cite, to take a unit, is the size of the county, whether it's the Hudson River or in western "Joe-gia" (Georgia) which we all know, in one of those counties, probably half a dozen or a dozen families could be scattered around on the farms and worked into the community. After all, they are American citizens, and we all know that American citizens have certain privileges. And they wouldn't — what's my favorite word? — discombobulate — [Laughter] — the existing population of those particular counties very much. After all — what? — 75 thousand families scattered all around the United States is not going to upset anybody.[10]

However, Japanese Americans were determined to make their own choices: they refused to allow Roosevelt to relocate them again — this time by scattering them across the country so as not to "discombobulate" America. Most of the internees returned to California.

Home again, Kajiro and Kohide Oyama decided to petition the court to overturn California's alien land law, which denied land-ownership to Japanese immigrants because they were not "white." In 1948 the Supreme Court ruled that this law was "nothing more than outright racial discrimination" and therefore "unconstitutional." The Fourteenth Amendment was "designed to bar States from denying to some groups, on account of race or color, any rights, privileges, and opportunities accorded to other groups." Referring to the war against Nazi Germany, the Court declared that the alien land law was "an unhappy facsimile, a disheartening reminder, of the racial policy pursued by those forces of evil whose destruction recently necessitated a devastating war."[11]

Four years later, another "unhappy facsimile" was abolished. Under pressure from lobbying groups including Japanese-American veterans, Congress rescinded the 1790 Naturalization Law, which stipulated that applicants for naturalized citizenship had to be "white." Winning citizenship for the immigrant generation "was the culmination of our dreams," exclaimed Harry Takagi. "The bill established our parents as the legal equal of other Americans; it gave the Japanese equality with all other immigrants."[12] By 1965, forty-six thousand Japanese immigrants had taken their citizenship oaths. Finally attaining legal acceptance, one of them rejoiced:

> Going steadily to study English,
> Even through the rain at night,
> I thus attain,
> Late in life,
> American citizenship.[13]

Seeking a fair share for the "have-nots," the rising wind of determination also swept through the barrios. "Mexican-American soldiers," declared veteran Balton Llanes, "shed at least a quarter of the blood spilled at Bataan. . . . What they want now is a decent job, a decent home, and a chance to live peacefully in the community."[14] The war had transformed Mexican Americans. "Those of us who went to war didn't return the same," observed Sabine R. Ulibárri. "We left something over there, or we picked up something over there. . . . Not only were we changed but we, in turn, have affected and changed all the people around us. War is not something you hang in the closet and forget about. War is something you carry with you under your skin." Ulibárri explained what he and many fellow veterans were carrying: "We had earned our credentials as American citizens. We had paid our dues on the counters of conviction and faith. We were not about to take any crap."[15]

Military service during the war had opened the way to opportunities in skilled employment. "Before the war," recalled Manuel Fraijo, a worker in a Southwestern copper mine, "all good jobs, —

hoistman, mechanic, pumpman, and timekeeper, — were all held by Anglo-Americans. The low-bracket, common jobs were held by Mexicans. . . . When the war came, millions of men were drafted and sent overseas. The majority of those drafted from our town were 'Mexicans.' Curiously enough, a good percentage of these supposedly stupid Mexicans became pilots, radio operators, and radarmen."[16]

Returning from the battlefields, however, the soldiers of "la raza" found that they were still forced to stay on the other side of the tracks. Even after death, Mexican Americans faced discrimination. In Three Rivers, Texas, the director of a funeral home refused to allow services for the remains of Félix Longoría, who had died fighting in the Philippines. "Well, you see, it's this way," Tom Kennedy told Dr. Héctor García, representing the widow, "this is a small town and you know how it is. . . . I am the only funeral home here, and I have to do what the white people want. The white people just don't like it." Dr. García replied: "Yes, but Mr. Kennedy, this man is a veteran, I mean, a soldier who was killed in action, and he is worthy of all our efforts and our greatest honors. Doesn't that make a difference?"[17] After protests from Mexican-American veterans, Senator Lyndon B. Johnson sent a telegram to Longoría's widow: "I deeply regret to learn that the prejudices of some individuals extend even beyond this life. I have no authority over civilian funeral homes. Nor does the federal government. However, I have today made arrangements to have Félix Longoría buried with full military honors at Arlington Cemetery. . . . This injustice and prejudice is deplorable. I am happy to have a part in seeing that this Texas hero is laid to rest with the honor and dignity his service deserves."[18]

The struggle to win dignity for Longoría reflected a fervent refusal to return to the prewar status quo. "During the war," stated defense worker Juana Caudillo, "there was a lessening of discrimination by some public places because they needed our money. . . . After the war, some restaurants, stores, and taverns again refused to serve us on an equal basis with whites. We knew this was totally unfair because we had worked hard to win the war."[19] Equality had become an earned entitlement. "When our young men came home from the war," recalled Eva Hernández, "they didn't want to be treated as second-class citizens anymore. . . . We women didn't want to turn the clock back either regarding the social positions of women before the war. The war had provided us the unique chance to be socially and economically independent, and we didn't want to give up this experience simply because the war ended. We, too, wanted to be first-class citizens in our communities."[20]

The Mexican-American struggle for justice expanded to the right to equal education. In the 1946 case of *Méndez v. Westminister School District of Orange County,* the U.S. Circuit Court of Southern California declared that the segregation of Mexican children violated their right to equal protection of the law guaranteed to them under the Fourteenth Amendment and therefore was unconstitutional.[21] To support the *Méndez* case, *amicus curiae* briefs were filed by the American Jewish Congress, the National Association for the Advancement of Colored People, and the Japanese American Citizens League. Together, they won a victory over prejudice in education.

The *Méndez* decision set a precedent for the historic 1954 *Brown v. Board of Education* decision. As chief counsel for the NAACP, Thurgood Marshall presented the legal argument against the 1896 "separate but equal" doctrine of *Plessy v. Ferguson.* Marshall's passion for social justice was spurred by his memory of World War II. "War is hell in every place and time," he told Carl T. Rowan, "but it was a special hell for people who were forced to fight for freedoms they had never known, for liberties that thousands of them would die without knowing it." Marshall was certain, however, that there would be a reckoning after the war. "I watched the bravery and patriotism of blacks, of the Japanese [Americans] in World War Two, and I couldn't believe white Americans would continue to treat them as semislaves. People who died flying fighter planes in an Air Force that didn't welcome them. Japanese boys who fought valiantly even though their parents . . . were behind the barbed wire of our concentration camps." Marshall was willing to bet "a bundle" that white Americans would respect the Fourteenth Amendment after the war, and "that this country would move to place the colored race, in respect to civil rights, upon a level equal to whites."[22]

Marshall won his bet: the Supreme Court ruled that separate educational facilities were "inherently unequal" and that school segregation was "a denial of the equal protection of the laws." The decision was hailed as a triumph for all Americans. "We look upon this memorable decision not as a victory for Negroes alone," the NAACP announced, "but for the whole American people and as a vindication of America's leadership in the free world." Robert Williams recalled the elation he experienced when the Court announced its decision: "I felt that at last the government was willing to assert itself on behalf of first-class citizenship, even for Negroes. I experienced a sense of loyalty that I had never felt before. I was sure that this was the beginning of a new era of American democracy."[23]

But the Supreme Court's ruling was the beginning of true democracy on paper only; the real initiative would come from a people's movement. On December 1, 1955, Rosa Parks boarded a bus in Montgomery, Alabama; ordered by the driver to give up her seat to a white man, she refused. The seamstress was not, as historian Fred Powledge noted, "just a simple black woman whose feet were tired from working all day for the white folks."[24] Her civil rights activism was rooted in World War II: Parks had been the secretary of the local NAACP and the organizer of the NAACP Youth Council chapter in Montgomery. In 1954, she had attended an interracial meeting at Highlander Folk School, led by Myles Horton, who had been active in union and civil rights organizing during the war. A year later Parks was ready to commit her great refusal — an act that ignited the Montgomery Bus Boycott.

Although African Americans were dependent on the buses to get to and from work, thousands of them sang:

Ain't gonna ride them buses no more
Ain't gonna ride no more
Why in the hell don't the white folk know
That I ain't gonna ride no more.

Instead they shared rides, rode in black-owned taxis, and walked. "My feets is tired," a woman said, "but my soul is rested." Another walker, an elderly woman, explained: "I'm not walking for myself. I'm walking for my children and my grandchildren."[25]

Swept into the protest, a young minister discovered he had a rendezous with destiny. In his first speech at a boycott rally, Reverend Martin Luther King, Jr., found within himself a militant voice — powerful, poetic, prophetic. "There comes a time when people get tired," he declared. "We are here this evening to say to those who have mistreated us so long that we are tired — tired of being segregated and humiliated; tired of being kicked about by the brutal feet of oppression."[26]

The boycott ended more than a year later when the court ordered the desegregation of the bus system. The victory affirmed the power of African Americans to transform the conditions of their lives through a grassroots movement. Their courageous action inspired an inner transformation — a hard-won sense of self-esteem. "We got our heads up now," exclaimed a janitor proudly, "and we won't ever bow down again — no, sir — except before God."[27]

After the success of the Montgomery Bus Boycott, black students in Greensboro, North Carolina, staged the 1960 sit-in at a Woolworth's lunch counter. "We're trying to eradicate the whole stigma of being inferior," the students explained. "We do not picket just because we want to eat. We do picket to protest the lack of dignity and respect shown us as human beings." Out of these sit-ins emerged the Student Non-Violent Coordinating Committee (SNCC). "A generation of young people," King observed, "has come out of decades of shadows to face naked state power; it has lost its fears, and experienced the majestic dignity of a direct struggle for its own liberation. These young people have connected up with their own history — the slave revolts, the incomplete revolution of the Civil War, the brotherhood of colonial colored men in Africa and Asia. They are an integral part of the history which is reshaping the world, replacing a dying order with a modern democracy."[28]

Then came the "freedom rides" — acts of civil disobedience to integrate the interstate buses and bus terminals of the South. Led by the Congress of Racial Equality (CORE), which had been founded by James Farmer during World War II, black and white civil rights activists courageously rode together in buses, singing:

> Hallelujah, I'm traveling
> Hallelujah, ain't it fine,
> Hallelujah, I'm traveling
> Down Freedom's main line.

In the South, freedom riders were yanked from the buses and beaten by white mobs. On television, the whole world watched the brutality and racialized hatred. "Every Freedom Rider on that bus was beaten pretty bad," recalled Isaac Reynolds. "I'm still feeling the effect. I received a damaged ear."[29]

In 1963, the cry for civil rights reached a crescendo with the March on Washington. The idea that had originally been proposed during World War II became a reality. On August 28, addressing a gathering of 200,000 people at the Lincoln Memorial, A. Philip Randolph reiterated the 1941 demands he had submitted to President Roosevelt: "We are the advance guard of a massive moral revolution for jobs and freedom. All who deplore our militancy, who exhort patience in the name of false peace, are in fact supporting segregation and exploitation. They would have social peace at the expense of social and racial justice."[30]

After his speech, Randolph introduced Martin Luther King as the man who personified "the moral leadership of the civil rights revolution." Speaking to the marchers, the nation, and the world,

King shared his vision of freedom in America. "Five score years ago, a great American, in whose symbolic shadow we stand, signed the Emancipation Proclamation," King declared. "I say to you today, my friends, that in spite of the difficulties and frustrations of the moment I still have a dream. It is a dream deeply rooted in the American dream. I have a dream that one day this nation will rise up and live out the true meaning of its creed: 'We hold these truths to be self-evident; that all men are created equal.'"[31]

Also speaking at the March on Washington, Joachim Prinz wove together King's dream and the painful memory of the Holocaust. A refugee from the Nazis in 1937, the rabbi shared a lesson he had learned from the world's failure to respond to Hitler's murderous rampage against Jews. The "most urgent" problem was not bigotry and hatred; "the most urgent, the most disgraceful, the most shameful and the most tragic problem [was] silence." Prinz appealed to his listeners: "America must not become a nation of onlookers."[32] His message was clear: Remembering the Holocaust required the lifting of every voice against racial injustice.

Nazi genocide had given Jews a unique understanding of what it meant to be victimized as a people. "We shall overcome, black and white together," sang the marchers, many of them Jewish. Over half of the white students who went South to organize voter-registration drives during the 1964 Freedom Summer were Jewish. The two civil rights workers who were murdered with James Chaney in Mississippi were Jewish — Andrew Goodman and Michael Schwerner. One of Martin Luther King's closest personal advisers was Stanley Levison; Howard Zinn, a professor at Spelman College, was a counselor to SNCC. The NAACP's labor director was Herbert Hill, a graduate of an orthodox yeshiva. The head of the NAACP Legal Defense and Education Fund was Jack Greenberg. As a ten-year-old kid who had cheered Jackie Robinson when he broke the major league baseball's color line in 1947, Greenberg understood what the black struggle for equality meant for Jews. Robinson was "adopted as the surrogate hero by many of us growing up at the time," he recalled. "He was the way we

saw ourselves triumphing against the forces of bigotry and igno-
rance."[33]

This unrelenting and passionate interracial movement compelled Congress to pass the 1964 Civil Rights Act, which prohibited discrimination in public accommodations and employment. A
year later, the demand for equality pushed President Lyndon Johnson to issue Executive Order 11246, which required firms with
federal contracts to take "affirmative action." Companies had to
set "good faith goals and timetables" for employing "underutilized"
qualified minority workers. In his 1966 speech at Howard University, Johnson declared: "This is the next and more profound stage
of the battle for civil rights. We seek . . . not just equality as a right
and a theory but equality as a fact and equality as a result."[34] Reflecting A. Philip Randolph's vision of an interventionist government, Johnson's executive order advanced minority hiring far
beyond Roosevelt's Executive Order 8802 and its ineffective Fair
Employment Practices Committee.

In the wake of civil rights legislation for African Americans, a
question surfaced: if discrimination is immoral and illegal, why
was there an immigration law that excluded Asians? "Just as we
sought to eliminate discrimination in our land through the Civil
Rights act," declared a congressman, "today we seek by phasing
out the national origins quota system to eliminate discrimination
in immigration to this nation composed of the descendants of immigrants." Agreeing that people of all ethnicities should have an
equal opportunity to enter America, Attorney General Robert
Kennedy told Congress: "Everywhere else in our national life, we
have eliminated discrimination based on national origins. Yet, this
system is still the foundation of our immigration law."[35] In 1965,
Congress abolished the prohibition of immigration from Asia —
an injustice that Asian Americans had struggled to overcome during World War II.

The civil rights movement inspired young Japanese Americans
to address another past injustice. The time had come to confront
World War II's "years of infamy."[36] Born after the war, the Sansei,

or third-generation Japanese Americans, asked their elders to tell them about the internment experience. "Why? Why!" their parents would respond defensively. "Why would you want to know about it? It's not important, we don't need to talk about it." Insisting that they were entitled to this memory, the young people made pilgrimages to the internment camps of World War II.[37]

Rising from these pilgrimages came a call for redress and reparations for the mass incarceration of Japanese Americans without due process. In their demand for justice, Japanese Americans had a broader purpose: they wanted to repair the "tremendous hole" in the Constitution created by Roosevelt's Executive Order 9066. In 1988, they persuaded Congress to approve legislation for a national apology and a payment of $20,000 to each of the internment survivors. When President Ronald Reagan signed the bill, he admitted that the United States had committed "a grave wrong." He pointed out that Japanese Americans had remained "utterly loyal" to this country during World War II. "Indeed, scores of Japanese Americans volunteered for our Armed Forces — many stepping forward in the internment camps themselves. The 442nd Regimental Combat Team, made up entirely of Japanese Americans, served with immense distinction — to defend this nation, their nation. Yet, back at home, the soldiers' families were being denied the very freedom for which so many of the soldiers themselves were laying down their lives." The nation needed, the President acknowledged, to end "a sad chapter in American history."[38]

A "Ceremony" for America: Remembrance of the War

There were other sad chapters in World War II — acts of injustice and inhumanity that had been committed during America's war for democracy.

In her novel *Ceremony,* Leslie Marmon Silko of the Laguna Pueblo tribe wove several of those chapters into her story of Tayo. Like many young Indians, he had enlisted in the marines and was sent to the Pacific war. Returning home shell-shocked, he faints in a train station and wakes up to find a Japanese-American woman helping him. Tayo looks at the kind stranger, and remembers how the government had "locked up" her people in an internment camp near his reservation in Arizona. Memories of the hate war that marines had fought in the Pacific sweep through Tayo when he sees fellow veteran Emo show off "his war souvenirs, the [gold] teeth he had knocked out of the corpse of a Japanese soldier."

Haunted by nightmares of the sadistic fighting, Tayo visits his totally blind grandmother. She tries to comfort him by telling him a story about a strange experience she had one night in July 1945. She saw a flash filling the whole southeastern sky like a bursting sunrise. His grandmother's story is a disturbing epiphany for Tayo. "Trinity Site, where they exploded the first atomic bomb," he realizes, "was only three hundred miles to the southeast, at White Sands."

Tayo finally understands the horror of Hiroshima, depicted in the sand painting of the ceremony that had been performed to help him recover from the trauma of the war. The painting traced "the point of convergence where the fate of all living things, and even the earth, had been laid." The lines of cultures were drawn in "flat dark lines on fine light sand, converging in the middle of witchery's final ceremonial sand painting. From that time on, human beings were one clan again, united by the fate the destroyers had planned for them, for all living things; united by a circle of death that devoured people in cities twelve thousand miles away, victims who had never known these mesas, who had never seen the delicate colors of rock which boiled up their slaughter."[39] The people of the mesas and the victims across the Pacific had been hurled together by a destructive fate.

But, while artistic and powerful, Silko's remembrance of the war did not tell the whole story. What actually happened in history was more dialectical and varied. Victimization was only a part of the national narrative. As we have learned throughout this study, there was also resistance against the "circle of death" — collective and individual struggles to unite human beings into "one clan again" by reconciling the war's moral incongruities.

Wrestling with these contradictions was the secretary of war himself. In early 1945, Henry L. Stimson opposed the expansion of the air war, with its indiscriminate mass killings of civilians. He advised Truman that the American air force should confine the bombings to precision targets because he "did not want to have the United States acquire the reputation of outdoing Hitler in atrocities."[40] On May 16, 1945, Stimson informed Truman that "the reputation of the United States for fair play and humanitarianism is the world's biggest asset for peace in the coming decades. . . . The same rule of sparing the civilian population should be applied as far as possible to the use of any new weapon."[41]

As it turned out, however, this humanitarian rule was not applied to the atomic bombing of Hiroshima. In his essay "The Decision to Use the Atomic Bomb," published in *Harper's Magazine* in 1947, Stimson wrote a startling and revealing final note. He confessed that he was unwilling to "pretend" that war was anything else than what it was: "the face of war" was "the face of death." "Now, with the release of atomic energy," Stimson anxiously warned, "man's ability to destroy himself is very nearly complete. The bombs dropped on Hiroshima and Nagasaki ended a war. They also made it wholly clear that we must never have another war," and that international violence in the twentieth century had become "more barbarous, more destructive, more debased in all its aspects."[42]

In his diary the day after the destruction of Nagasaki, Stimson recalled that at Potsdam he had advocated the "continuance" of the emperorship with certain conditions. "The President and Byrnes struck that out." Then Stimson noted the tragic consequences of cultural stereotypes.

> There has been a good deal of uninformed agitation against the Emperor in this country mostly by people who know no more about Japan than has been given

them by Gilbert and Sullivan's "Mikado," and I found out today that curiously enough it had gotten deeply embedded in the minds of influential people in the State Department.[43]

At eye level on the battlefield of the Pacific war, marine Guy Louis Gabaldon also confronted the moral inconsistency of the way the Pacific war was fought. In the Mexican barrio of East Los Angeles, Gabaldon was one of seven children crowded into a small house. On the streets, he was befriended by two Japanese-American brothers, Lane and Lyle Nakano. "More and more I was with them than I was with my natural parents," recalled Gabaldon. Living with the Nakano family for six years, he learned Japanese. But then the war came, and the Nakanos were taken away to an internment camp.

Only seventeen years old at the time, Gabaldon joined the marines and was sent to the Pacific. On his first day of combat on Saipan, he killed thirty-three Japanese soldiers. Perhaps they reminded him of the sons of his Japanese foster family. Filled with remorse, Gabaldon decided he would go out alone and try to persuade the Japanese soldiers to surrender, for they were completely surrounded and cut off from the Japanese navy. He captured six soldiers. Speaking in Japanese, he told them that they would be given medical care and food. "I'm keeping three of you here," Gabaldon said. "The other three can leave and bring some friends back." But he warned them that if they did not return, he would shoot his hostages. The three came back with six more soldiers. Gabaldon kept repeating this tactic, and within seven hours, he had eight hundred prisoners.[44]

Praising Gabaldon's humanitarian heroism, veteran Pete Limon commented: "He used their own language and he didn't kill them. In the process, he saved the lives of the Japanese but also probably thousands of GIs who would have had to face them in battle." For his bravery, Gabaldon was awarded the Navy Cross. "Working alone in the front of the lines," read his citation, "he daringly entered enemy caves, pillboxes, buildings and jungle brush, frequently in the face of hostile fire, and succeeded not only in obtaining vital military information but in capturing well over 1,000 civilians and troops."[45] Gabaldon was indeed a unique war hero — a Japanese-speaking, Mexican-American humanitarian soldier!

Fighting in the European war, black soldier Leon Bass shuddered at the moral incongruity he faced in Buchenwald. After entering the death camp, he saw "the walking dead," reduced to skin, bone, and "skeletal faces with deep-set eyes." Bass went into a building where body parts from "medical experiments" had been stored in jars of formaldehyde. "I saw fingers and eyes and the hearts and genitals." Then the young soldier noticed mounds of little children's clothing — sweaters, caps, and booties. "But I never saw a child." The residue inside the ovens showed what had happened to the children and their parents: they had become rib cages, skulls, and ashes. "What did these people do," Bass asked, "that merited this kind of treatment?" Then he leaped to the question of moral responsibility: "And it boggles the mind when you think that it had gone on for almost ten years before we got into the war! Why wasn't it dealt with? Why did nobody scream and shout, 'Stop!'" Bass reflected: "If this could happen here, it could happen anywhere. . . . It could happen to black folks in America. . . . And I thought about how many times my people were lynched and maltreated across the country, and nobody raised a voice."[46] For in both the Holocaust in Europe and lynchings in America, the war for freedom from fear had lost the battle against the silence of apathy and prejudice.

Although the war was not altogether "good," to borrow Studs Terkel's term, the fierce fight against fascism helped to teach Americans of an ethnically diverse society how to accept one another and live together as one people. This spirit of *"E Pluribus Unum"* was expressed in a poem by Belle S. Vankin. In "Epitaph to My Son, Michael," published in a U.S. Army pamphlet in June 1945, she commemorated the lives of three soldiers.

I, Dorie Miller, brown-skinned and eyed
My heritage that of the Robesons, the Carvers, the
    Douglasses,
My forebears the once proud citizens of a proud Africa.
I, Dorie Miller, laid down my life
Fighting the lynch laws that threatened all mankind.
Now that my job is done, are you with me, brother?
I manned a gun that was not meant for hands like mine,
For Liberty is dearly bought and once man struggles for it
It's his who pays the bitter price.
My people are richer by those moments of battle,
Their march is ahead, their destiny inevitable.

I, Meyer Levin, olive-skinned, dark-eyed,
Growing up in a world where power-hungry men toyed with
    our fate,
Loving the instruments of flight which were created for
    progress
But which they in their greed turned into missiles of death.
I felt the roaring motor under my eager hands,
And my missions were many and rewarding
Against the fascist enemies.
As I saw the bombs drop, I exulted
For I was bringing an end to the beasts
Who had vowed extermination to my noble people.
Einstein, Heifitz, Heine,
I cried your names in defiance
While the shrieks of those who would enchain us
Died away in the distance.

I, Colin Kelley, fair-skinned, blue-eyed, Irish,
Mind with but a single purpose,
Having all to live for, wife, baby, joy.
Gave it up so that they might not be enslaved,

Now that my job is done, are you with me, brother?
I saw that battleship, Haruna,
I saw it only as a triumph of force over democracy.
So I dived straight at its heart and force and democracy
Went up in flames, only democracy
Rose victorious from out of the bitter ashes.

Miller, Levine, Kelly,
Dorie, Meyer, Colin,
All are fused in one, the dark skin, the brown eyes, the blue.
And the face that appears is the face of Freedom
Forever enshrined in the hearts of all men.
Sleep well, little brothers,
We're with you.[47]

The war for "double victory" offered Americans a truth about themselves that Herman Melville had observed over a hundred years ago. America was settled by "the people of all nations," he wrote. "All nations may claim her for their own. You can not spill a drop of American blood, without spilling the blood of the whole world. We are not a narrow tribe." In this new society, Melville hoped, the "prejudices of national dislikes" would be "forever extinguish[ed]."[48] During World War II, Americans originating from all over the world had spilled their blood as they fought to extinguish prejudices abroad and also in their own society. For all of them, as W. E. B. DuBois applauded, the war was a struggle for "democracy not only for white folks but for yellow, brown, and black."[49]

Divided by segregation in the military, by discrimination in the war industries, and by race riots in the cities, Americans from many different communities nevertheless fought to form "a more perfect union." Out of their protests against injustices such as a jim crow army and internment came a rising wind, a relentless refusal to allow equality to be a "dream deferred."[50] Out of their defense of a democracy that failed to include all the people emerged a hopeful rededication to the principles of the Declaration of Independence. Out of their fervent demand for full citizenship arose a renewed determination to "discombobulate" society, if necessary, in order to "let America be America," where equality would be "in the air we breathe."[51] Indeed, during this great turning point in American history, the nation's "destiny" had become "manifestly" multicultural. Fighting to make the "Four Freedoms" a reality not only overseas but also in our own society, a diverse people had created "ties that bind" for all of us in our still unfinished struggle for "victory" at home.

NOTES

Chapter 1. Introduction

1. William Faulkner, quoted in Vincent G. Harding, "Healing at the Razor's Edge: Reflections on a History of Multicultural America," *Journal of American History,* vol. 81, no. 2 (September 1994), pp. 571–584.

2. Joseph Kurihara, autobiography, in Japanese Evacuation and Relocation Study, Bancroft Library, University of California, Berkeley; Fred Smith, interview, August 30, 1998; Roberto Haro, brother of Alex Romandia, interview, July 25, 1998; Penny Colman, *Rosie the Riveter: Women Working on the Home Front in World War II* (New York, 1955), p. 29; Murray Shapiro, letter to his father, November 9, 1944, in Murray Shapiro Papers, Eisenhower Center, University of New Orleans.

3. Walt Whitman, *Leaves of Grass* (New York, 1958), p. 9.

4. Studs Terkel, *"The Good War": An Oral History of World War Two* (New York, 1984), "Note," opening statement.

5. Pearl Buck, *American Unity and Asia* (New York, 1942), p. 29.

6. Ruth Benedict, *The Races of Mankind* (New York, 1943), p. 31.

7. Whitman, *Leaves of Grass,* p. 284.

8. Francis L. Broderick, *W. E. B. Du Bois: Negro Leader in a Time of Crisis* (Stanford, 1959), p. 196.

9. Herman Melville, *Moby-Dick* (Boston, 1956), pp. 325–329.

Chapter 2. A Declaration of War

1. John Morton Blum, *V Was for Victory: Politics and American Culture During World War II* (New York, 1976), p. 3.

2. Seichin Nagayama, interview, in Ethnic Studies Oral History Project, *Uchinanchu: A History of Okinawans in Hawaii* (Honolulu, 1981), p. 479.

3. John Garcia, interview, in Studs Terkel, *"The Good War": An Oral History of World War Two* (New York, 1984), p. 17.

4. Poem published in the *Boston Herald,* April 12, 1942, reprinted in William M. Tuttle, Jr., *"Daddy's Gone to War": The Second World War in the Lives of America's Children* (New York, 1993), pp. 3–4.

5. Tuttle, *"Daddy's Gone to War,"* p. 5.

6. Mary Tsukamoto, interview, in John Tateishi, *And Justice for All: An Oral History of the Japanese American Detention Camps* (New York, 1984), p. 6.

7. Stephen Fox, *The Unknown Internment: An Oral History of the Relocation of Italian Americans During World War II* (Boston, 1990), p. 169.

8. Carlos Bulosan, *America Is in the Heart: A Personal History* (Seattle, 1981; originally published in 1943), pp. 315–316.

9. Tom Bradley, interview, in Terkel, *"The Good War,"* p. 25.

10. Bong-Youn Choy, *Koreans in America* (Chicago, 1979), p. 172.

11. Socorro Diáz Blanchard, *Recuerdos (Memories),* vol. 1, December 1992, unpublished manuscript, loaned to the author by her grandson, Sean O'Shea, pp. 47–48.

12. Raul Morín, *Among the Valiant: Mexican-Americans in WW II and Korea* (Alhambra, Calif., 1966), p. 15.

13. Bruce Watson, "Navajo Code Talkers: A Few Good Men," *Smithsonian,* vol. 24, no. 5 (August 1993), p. 35; Keith Little, Navajo-Code Talkers Symposium, University of California, Berkeley, November 17, 1995.

14. Brenda L. Moore, *To Serve My Country, to Serve My Race: The Story of the Only African American Wacs Stationed Overseas during World War II* (New York, 1996), p. 34.

15. Timuel Black, interview, in Terkel, *"The Good War,"* p. 275.

16. Rubye Seago, letter, December 7, 1941, reprinted in Judy Barrett Litoff and David C. Smith (eds.), *Since You Went Away: World War II Letters from American Women on the Home Front* (New York, 1991), p. 9.

17. Moore, *To Serve My Country, to Serve My Race,* pp. 34–35.

18. Lonnie Quan, interview, October 15, 1982, Chinese Women of America Research Project, Chinese Culture Foundation of San Francisco, p. 11.

19. Robert Dallek, *Franklin D. Roosevelt and American Foreign Policy, 1932–1945* (New York, 1979), pp. 267, 307.

20. Dallek, *Roosevelt,* p. 311.

21. Jonathan Marshall, *To Have and Have Not: Southeast Asian Raw Materials and the Origins of the Pacific War* (Berkeley, 1995), p. xi.

22. Ibid., pp. 14, 181.

23. Waldo Heinrichs, *Threshold of War: Franklin D. Roosevelt and American Entry into World War II* (New York, 1988), p. 38.

24. Dallek, *Roosevelt,* pp. 242–243.

25. Heinrichs, *Threshold of War*, pp. 7, 10, 133, 141, 179.

26. Dallek, *Roosevelt*, pp. 274–275.

27. Christopher Thorne, *Allies of a Kind: The United States, Britain and the War against Japan, 1941–1945* (London, 1978), pp. 52–53.

28. George Kennan, "World War II: 30 Years After," in *Survey*, vol. 21 (winter-spring 1975), p. 30.

29. James Rusbridger and Eric Nave, *Betrayal at Pearl Harbor: How Churchill Lured Roosevelt into World War II* (New York, 1992), pp. 72, 82, 83, 88, 90.

30. Ibid., pp. 138–139, 146.

31. Ibid., p. 144; John Costello, *Days of Infamy: MacArthur, Roosevelt, Churchill — The Shocking Truth Revealed* (New York, 1994), pp. 320–327. At the FECB Singapore station, Commander Malcolm Burnett and his wife, Mary, had deciphered this critical Japanese military message, and knew that the attack would be on Pearl Harbor. Transmitting the message to Churchill, Burnett assumed that the prime minister would forward it to Roosevelt in time to alert the U.S. Navy in Hawaii. When Commander Burnett learned that the U.S. Navy had been caught by surprise on December 7, 1941, re-called Mary vividly many years later, he was astonished. See Costello, pp. 320–327.

32. Rusbridger and Nave, *Betrayal at Pearl Harbor*, p. 153.

33. Costello, *Days of Infamy*, p. 329.

34. Winston Churchill, *The Second World War*, 6 volumes (London, 1948–1954), vol. 3, p. 539.

35. Dallek, *Roosevelt*, p. 307.

36. "Navy Secretary Commends Dorie Miller for Bravery," *Pittsburgh Courier*, April 11, 1942.

37. "'I Downed Four Enemy Planes' — Dorie Miller," *Pittsburgh Courier*, January 2, 1943.

38. *New York Times*, December 22, 1941.

39. *Militant*, December 27, 1941, reprinted in C. L. R. James, et al. (eds.), *Fighting Racism in World War II* (New York, 1980).

40. James G. Thompson, letter to the editor, *Pittsburgh Courier*, January 31, 1942.

41. "Private James Gratz Thompson of Wichita, Kansas, originator of The Pittsburgh Courier's 'VV,' symbolic of the fight for Victory at Home and Victory Abroad," the *Pittsburgh Courier* reported on March 13, 1942, "is now working in the U.S. armed forces as a supply office typist with the 395th Coast Artillery Battalion in the Headquarters, Battery Camp, N.C."

Chapter 3. *"Bomb the Color Line"*

1. Bernice Reagon, "World War II Reflected in Black Music," *Southern Exposure*, vol. 1, nos. 3 & 4 (winter 1974), p. 173.

2. Philip McGuire (ed.), *Taps for a Jim Crow Army: Letters from Black Soldiers in World War II* (Lexington, Ky., 1993), p. xxiii.

3. Brenda L. Moore, *To Serve My Country, to Serve My Race: The Story of the Only African American Wacs Stationed Overseas During World War II* (New York, 1996), p. 29.

4. McGuire (ed.), *Taps for a Jim Crow Army*, pp. 127–128.

5. Herbert Shapiro, *White Violence and Black Response: From Reconstruction to Montgomery* (Amherst, Mass., 1988), p. 303.

6. Richard Polenberg, *One Nation Divisible: Class, Race, and Ethnicity in the United States Since 1933* (New York, 1980), p. 76; Harvard Sitkoff, *A New Deal for Blacks: The Emergence of Civil Rights as a National Issue* (New York, 1978), p. 324.

7. *Crisis,* October 9, 1940.

8. Adam Clayton Powell, Jr., "Is This a White Man's War?" *Common Sense,* April 1942, p. 112.

9. George Schuyler, quoted in Sitkoff, *New Deal for Blacks,* p. 301.

10. *Chicago Defender,* quoted in Gunnar Myrdal, *An American Dilemma: The Negro Problem and Modern Democracy* (New York, 1944), p. 1007; Sitkoff, *New Deal for Blacks,* pp. 301, 324.

11. Private Bert Babero, letter to Truman K. Gibson, February 13, 1994, reprinted in McGuire (ed.), *Taps for a Jim Crow Army*, p. 50.

12. Quoted in Lucille B. Milner, "Jim Crow in the Army," *New Republic,* vol. 110 (March 13, 1944), p. 339.

13. Horace R. Cayton, "Fighting for White Folks?" *Nation,* vol. 155 (September 26, 1942), p. 268.

14. Poem in African-American newspaper, quoted in Howard Zinn, *A People's History of the United States* (New York, 1980), p. 411.

15. Malcolm X, with the assistance of Alex Haley, *The Autobiography of Malcolm X* (New York, 1966), pp. 71, 105–107.

16. Dwight MacDonald, "The Novel Case of Winfred Lynn," *Nation,* vol. 156 (February 20, 1943), pp. 268–270; Dwight MacDonald, "The Supreme Court's New Moot Suit," *Nation,* vol. 159 (July 1, 1944), pp. 13–14; S. P. Breckinridge, "The Winfred Lynn Case Again," *Social Service Review,* vol. 18 (September 1944), pp. 369–371.

17. Letter to the editor of the *Pittsburgh Courier,* April 10, 1944, by "A Private," reprinted in McGuire (ed.), *Taps for a Jim Crow Army*, pp. 28–29.

18. Letter to the *Pittsburgh Courier,* February 10, 1943, reprinted in McGuire (ed.), *Taps for a Jim Crow Army*, p. 13.

19. Letter to the *Baltimore Afro-American,* November 4, 1943, reprinted in McGuire (ed.), *Taps for a Jim Crow Army*, p. 20.

20. Letter to the *Pittsburgh Courier,* April 10, 1944, from "A Private," reprinted in McGuire (ed.), *Taps for a Jim Crow Army*, pp. 28–29.

21. Letter to the *Richmond Afro-American,* November 22, 1943, from the 328th

Aviation Squadron, reprinted in McGuire (ed.), *Taps for a Jim Crow Army,* pp. 67–69.

22. Letter to the *Pittsburgh Courier,* October 28, 1942, from "A Lone Soldier," reprinted in McGuire (ed.), *Taps for a Jim Crow Army,* p. 63.

23. Letter to the *Pittsburgh Courier,* November 4, 1943, from Private Laurence W. Harris, p. 21; letter to the Afro-American Newspapers, February 18, 1944, from Samuel A. Conner, reprinted in McGuire (ed.), *Taps for a Jim Crow Army,* p. 21, pp. 75–76.

24. Fred Smith, interview with author, August 30, 1998.

25. Editorial, *Crisis,* June 1941, p. 183.

26. *Pittsburgh Courier,* January 3, 1942.

27. Lou Potter, with William Miles and Nina Rosenblum, *Liberators: Fighting on Two Fronts in World War II* (New York, 1992), p. 68–69.

28. Memorandum #40, February 13, 1943, Lucien Warner, Special Services Division, to James D. Secrest, Bureau of Intelligence, Master File, National Archives, Washington, D.C. Other incidents of black soldiers killed by police in 1943 were reported in the *Chicago Defender,* April 24 and May 8, 1943.

29. Walter White, *A Rising Wind* (Garden City, N.Y., 1945), p. 143.

30. Herbert Shapiro, *White Violence and Black Response: From Reconstruction to Montgomery* (Amherst, Mass., 1988), pp. 308–309.

31. Letter to President Franklin Delano Roosevelt, May 9, 1944, from Charles F. Wilson, private 36794590, Air Corps, reprinted in McGuire (ed.), *Taps for a Jim Crow Army,* pp. 134–139.

32. Langston Hughes, "Lennox Avenue Mural," in Langston Hughes, *The Langston Hughes Reader* (New York, 1958), p. 123.

33. "Harriet M. Waddy, WAC Officer, Dies at 94," *New York Times,* March 8, 1999.

34. Timuel Black, interview, in Studs Terkel, *"The Good War": An Oral History of World War Two* (New York, 1984), pp. 274–279.

35. Joseph Small, interview, Terkel, *"The Good War,"* p. 395.

36. Robert Allen, *The Port Chicago Mutiny: The Story of the Largest Mass Mutiny Trial in U.S. Naval History* (New York, 1993), p. 64.

37. Small, interview, Terkel, *"The Good War,"* p. 397.

38. Allen, *Port Chicago Mutiny,* pp. 42, 85, 130.

39. Small, interview, Terkel, *"The Good War,"* p. 397.

40. Abraham Lincoln, First Inaugural Address, reprinted in Richard Hofstadter (ed.), *Great Issues in American History,* vol. 1 (New York, 1958), pp. 396–397.

41. Fred Smith, interview with author, August 30, 1998.

42. *Pittsburgh Courier,* January 31, 1942.

43. *Crisis,* February 1941, p. 39.

44. Stanley Sandler, *Segregated Skies: All-Black Combat Squadrons of WW II* (Washington, D.C., 1992), p. 60.

45. Coleman Young, interview, Terkel, *"The Good War,"* p. 344.
46. Potter, *Liberators,* p. 111.
47. Ibid., pp. 195–196.
48. Philip W. Latimer, reprinted in Potter, *Liberators,* pp. 196–197.
49. Moore, *To Serve My Country,* pp. 8–13.
50. Shapiro, *White Violence and Black Response,* p. 308.
51. Charity Adams Early, *One Woman's Army: A Black Officer Remembers the WAC* (College Station, Tex., 1989), p. 62.
52. Lucia M. Pitts, *One Negro Wac's Story* (Los Angeles, 1968, privately published), copy in the Bancroft Library, University of California, Berkeley, p. 4.
53. Margaret Y. Jackson, to Martha S. Putney, August 26, 1986, in Putney, *When the Nation Was in Need: Blacks in the Women's Army Corps During World War II* (Metuchen, N.J., 1992), pp. 100–101.
54. Early, *One Woman's Army,* p. 151.
55. Pitts, *One Negro Wac's Story,* pp. 20–21.
56. White, *A Rising Wind,* pp. 123–124.
57. Hughes, *Hughes Reader,* p. 383.
58. Sitkoff, *New Deal for Blacks,* pp. 35, 36.
59. Ibid., pp. 37, 39.
60. Raymond Wolters, *Negroes and the Great Depression: The Problem of Economic Recovery* (Westport, Conn., 1970), pp. 91, 92.
61. Sitkoff, *New Deal for Blacks,* pp. 54, 55, 56–57.
62. Doris Kearns Goodwin, *No Ordinary Time: Franklin and Eleanor Roosevelt: The Home Front in World War II* (New York, 1994), p. 247.
63. Paula Giddings, *When and Where I Enter: The Impact of Black Women on Race and Sex in America* (New York, 1984), p. 235.
64. Sitkoff, *New Deal for Blacks,* p. 300.
65. "47 Branches Picket Defense Industries," *Crisis,* May 1941, p. 164.
66. Sitkoff, *New Deal for Blacks,* p. 314; Jacqueline Jones, *Labor of Love, Labor of Sorrow: Black Women, Work, and the Family from Slavery to the Present* (New York, 1985), p. 233.
67. A. Philip Randolph, "Let the Negro Speak," *Black Worker,* March 1941.
68. A. Philip Randolph, "The Call to the March on Washington," *Black Worker,* July 1941.
69. Ibid.
70. Sitkoff, *New Deal for Blacks,* p. 320.
71. Jervis Anderson, *A. Philip Randolph: A Biographical Portrait* (Berkeley, 1986), pp. 256–257.
72. Franklin D. Roosevelt, Executive Order 8802, in *The Federal Register,* vol. 6 (July 27, 1941).
73. Miriam Frank, Marilyn Ziebarth, and Connie Field, *The Life and Times of Rosie the Riveter: The Story of Three Million Working Women During World War II* (Emeryville, Calif., 1982), p. 51.

74. Reports from Special Service Division, April 28, 1942, Office of War Information, National Archives, Washington, D.C.

75. George E. DeMar, "Negro Women Are American Workers, Too," in *Opportunity: Journal of Negro Life,* vol. 21, 1943, p. 42.

76. "An Open Letter to President Roosevelt — An Editorial," *Crisis,* January 1943, p. 8.

77. Karen Tucker Anderson, "Last Hired, First Fired: Black Women Workers During World War II," in *Journal of American History,* vol. 69, no. 1, June 1982, pp. 84–85.

78. Polenberg, *One Nation Divisible,* p. 75.

79. Interview with Ella Johnson, in Carl Nolte, "Infamy, War — And a Sea Change," *San Francisco Chronicle,* May 9, 1999, p. 5.

80. Maya Angelou, *I Know Why the Caged Bird Sings* (New York, 1971), p. 178.

81. Eugene Katz to Cornelius Du Bois, July 14, 1942, Special Services Division, Office of War Information, National Archives, Washington, D.C.

82. Frank, et al., *Rosie the Riveter,* p. 49.

83. Anderson, "Last Hired, First Fired," pp. 82, 87.

84. Mary Anderson, "Negro Women on the Production Front," *Opportunity: Journal of Negro Life,* vol. 21, 1943, p. 38.

85. Frank, et al., *Rosie the Riveter,* p. 54.

86. Sherna Berger Gluck, *Rosie the Riveter Revisited: Women, the War, and Social Change* (New York, 1987), pp. 37, 38, 23.

87. Frank, et al., *Rosie the Riveter,* pp. 57–58.

88. Amy Kesselman, *Fleeting Opportunities: Women Shipyard Workers in Portland and Vancouver during World War II and Reconversion* (Albany, N.Y., 1990), pp. 41–42.

89. George E. DeMar, "Negro Women Are American Workers, Too," in *Opportunity: Journal of Negro Life,* vol. 21, 1943, p. 77.

90. Jones, *Labor of Love, Labor of Sorrow,* p. 236.

91. Frank, et al., *Rosie the Riveter,* p. 68.

92. Leotha Hackshaw, "What My Job Means to Me," *Opportunity: Journal of Negro Life,* vol. 21, 1943, p. 553.

93. Carey McWilliams, *Brothers Under the Skin* (Boston, 1964), p. 9.

94. Jones, *Labor of Love, Labor of Sorrow,* p. 257.

95. Reagon, "World War II Reflected in Black Music," pp. 181, 183.

96. Frank, et al., *Rosie the Riveter,* p. 54.

97. Social Science Institute, Fisk University, *Monthly Summary of Events and Trends in Race Relations,* vol. 1 (1944), p. 2.

98. "What We Ought to Find Out in Detroit," August 14, 1942, Office of War Information, National Archives, Washington, D.C.

99. *Pittsburgh Courier,* March 6, 1942.

100. Earl Brown, "The Truth about the Detroit Riot," *Harper's,* vol. 187 (November 1943), p. 495.

101. Report No. 19, "White Attitudes Toward Negroes," July 21, 1942, Special Service Division, Bureau of Intelligence, Office of War Information, National Archives, Washington, D.C., p. 11.

102. Ibid., p. 12.

103. Report No. 109, March 15, 1943, Bureau of Intelligence, Office of War Information, National Archives, Washington, D.C., p. 3.

104. Brown, "The Truth about the Detroit Riot," p. 492.

105. L. Alex Swan, "The Harlem and Detroit Riots of 1943: A Comparative Analysis," in *Berkeley Journal of Sociology,* vol. 16 (1971–72), pp. 80–81. A memorandum, August 12, 1942, to Cornelius Du Bois, Special Services Division, Office of War Information, National Archives, Washington, D.C., reported that the housing needs of both whites and blacks in Detroit were "desperate."

106. Report No. 19, "White Attitudes Toward Negroes," p. 16.

107. "Sojourner Truth Homes," *Crisis,* April 1942, p. 111.

108. Brown, "The Truth about the Detroit Riot," pp. 495–496.

109. *Detroit Tribune,* June 26, 1943, quoted in Potter, *Liberators,* pp. 94–95.

110. Brown, "The Truth about the Detroit Riot," p. 492.

111. "The Riots," *Crisis,* July 1943, p. 199.

112. Carl T. Rowan, *Dream Makers, Dream Breakers: The World of Thurgood Marshall* (New York, 1993), pp. 98–99.

113. "Special Report on Negro Housing Situation in Detroit," March 5, 1942, marked "Confidential," prepared by Nelson Foote, Office of Facts and Figures, Bureau of Intelligence, National Archives, Washington, D.C.

114. Report No. 109, March 15, 1943, Bureau of Intelligence, Office of War Information, Master Files, National Archives, Washington, D.C., p. 1.

115. Shapiro, *White Violence and Black Response,* p. 311.

116. *Chicago Defender,* June 26, 1943.

117. Nat Brandt, *Harlem at War: The Black Experience in WW II* (Syracuse, 1996), p. 151.

118. Goodwin, *No Ordinary Time,* p. 447.

119. "Detroit — The Storm Bursts," *Christian Century,* vol. 60 (June 30, 1943), pp. 759–761.

120. White, *A Rising Wind,* pp. 124–125.

121. Claude Brown, *Manchild in the Promised Land* (New York, 1965), pp. 12–14.

122. Richard Wright, *New York PM,* August 3, 1943.

123. Adam Clayton Powell, Jr., *Marching Blacks* (New York, 1945), pp. 171–172.

124. Ibid., p. 125.

Chapter 4. The Original Americans

1. Keats Begay, interview, in Broderick H. Johnson (ed.), *Navajos and World War II* (Tsaile, Navajo Nation, Ariz., 1977), pp. 17–18, 23, 25.

2. Bruce Watson, "Navajo Code Talkers: A Few Good Men," *Smithsonian*, vol. 24, no. 5 (August 1993), p. 40.

3. Harold Foster, interview, number 1164, American Indian History Project, Western History Center, University of Utah, p. 11.

4. Jere Franco, "Bringing Them Alive: Selective Service and Native Americans," *Journal of Ethnic Studies*, vol. 18, no. 3 (fall 1990), p. 18.

5. Ibid., pp. 17–18.

6. Tom Holm, "Fighting a White Man's War: The Extent and Legacy of American Indian Participation in World War II," *Journal of Ethnic Studies*, vol. 9, no. 2, pp. 73, 74.

7. Franco, "Bringing Them Alive," p. 18.

8. Evon Z. Vogt, *Navaho Veterans: A Study of Changing Values* (Cambridge, Mass., 1951), p. 64.

9. Alison R. Bernstein, *American Indians and World War II: Toward a New Era in Indian Affairs* (Norman, Okla., 1991), p. 42.

10. John Collier, "The Indian in a Wartime Nation," *Annals of the American Academy of Political and Social Science*, vol. 223 (September 1942), p. 30.

11. Bernstein, *American Indians*, p. 45; Holm, "Fighting a White Man's War," p. 71; Harold Ickes, "Indians Have a Name for Hitler," *Collier's*, January 1944, p. 58.

12. Holm, "Fighting a White Man's War," pp. 71, 72.

13. Bernstein, *American Indians*, pp. 70, 68, 86; Collier, "Indian in a Wartime Nation," p. 31.

14. Penny Colman, *Rosie the Riveter: Women Working on the Home Front in World War II* (New York, 1995), p. 29, with illustration of the photograph.

15. Irene Stewart, *A Voice in Her Tribe: A Navajo Woman's Own Story* (Socorro, N.Mex., 1980), p. 39.

16. Agnes R. Begay, interview, in Johnson (ed.), *Navajos and World War II*, p. 48.

17. Bernstein, *American Indians*, p. 76.

18. Nancy Shoemaker, "Urban Indians and Ethnic Choices: American Indian Organizations in Minneapolis, 1920–1950," *Western Historical Quarterly*, vol. 19, no. 4 (November 1988), p. 443.

19. Ignatia Broker, *Night Flying Woman: An Ojibway Narrative* (St. Paul, Minn., 1983), pp. 3–4.

20. Ibid., p. 5.

21. Peter Nabokov (ed.), *Native American Testimony* (New York, 1978), p. 203; Richard White, *The Roots of Dependency: Subsistence, Environment, and Social Change among the Choctaws, Pawnees, and Navajos* (Lincoln, Neb., 1983), pp. 212–215.

22. Peter Iverson, *The Navajo Nation* (Westport, Conn., 1981), p. 9.

23. John Collier, *The Indians of the Americas* (New York, 1947), p. 280; Graham D. Taylor, *New Deal and American Indian Tribalism: The Administration of the Indian Reorganization Act, 1934–1945* (Lincoln, Neb., 1980), p. 32.

24. Phelps-Stokes Fund, *The Navajo Indian Problem* (New York, 1939), pp. 8–9; David F. Aberle, *The Peyote Religion Among the Navaho* (Chicago, 1966), pp. 55–64; Collier, *Indians of the Americas,* p. 276; Iverson, *Navajo Nation,* pp. 27, 28.
25. White, *Roots of Dependency,* pp. 251, 258; Edward H. Spicer, "Sheepmen and Technicians: A Program of Soil Conservation on the Navajo Indian Reservation," in Edward H. Spicer (ed.), *Human Problems in Technological Change* (New York, 1952), p. 185.
26. Walter Dyk (ed.), *Son of Old Man Hat: A Navajo Autobiography* (New York, 1938), pp. 78, 103.
27. White, *Roots of Dependency,* pp. 265, 313; Spicer, "Sheepmen and Technicians," p. 193; Peter Nabokov (ed.), *Native American Testimony* (New York, 1991), p. 330.
28. White, *Roots of Dependency,* pp. 229, 313.
29. Phelps-Stokes Fund, *Navajo Indian Problem,* pp. 8–9; David F. Aberle, *The Peyote Religion Among the Navaho* (Chicago, 1966), pp. 55–64; Collier, *Indians of the Americas,* p. 276; Iverson, *Navajo Nation,* pp. 27, 28.
30. "Navajo Poem," in John Collier, *On the Gleaming Way* (Chicago, 1962), p. 45.
31. Kenji Kawano, *Warriors: Navajo Code Talkers* (Flagstaff, 1990), p. 56.
32. S. McClain, *Navajo Weapon* (Boulder, Colo., 1994), p. 38.
33. Philip Johnston to the Commandant, United States Marine Corps, September 14, 1942, Navajo Tribal Museum, Window Rock, Arizona.
34. Commanding General Clayton B. Vogel to Commandant U.S. Marine Corps, March 6, 1942, Navajo Tribal Museum, Window Rock, Arizona.
35. McClain, *Navajo Weapon,* pp. 45–46.
36. Cozy Stanley Brown, interview, in Johnson (ed.), *Navajos and World War II,* p. 54.
37. Isabel Simmons, "The Unbreakable Code," *Marine Corps Gazette,* November 1971, pp. 4–6.
38. Interview with Jimmy King, tape number 2, p. 6, American Indian Oral History Project, Western History Center, University of Utah.
39. Ibid., pp. 8–9.
40. Ibid., p. 7.
41. Kawano, *Warriors,* p. 75.
42. Ibid., p. xvi.
43. Symposium on the Navajo Code Talkers, University of California, Berkeley, November 17, 1995.
44. Kawano, *Warriors,* p. 72.
45. McClain, *Navajo Weapon,* p. 89.
46. Interview with Jimmy King.
47. Watson, "Navajo Code Talkers," p. 40.
48. Kawano, *Warriors,* p. 28.
49. McClain, *Navajo Weapon,* p. 180.

50. Watson, "Navajo Code Talkers," p. 35.
51. Ibid., p. 40.
52. McClain, *Navajo Weapon,* p. 183.
53. Kawano, *Warriors,* p. 23.
54. Bernstein, *American Indians,* pp. 58, 60.
55. William Bradford Huie, *The Hero of Iwo Jima and Other Stories* (New York, 1959), pp. 10–12.
56. Hayes to parents, August 29, 1942; Hayes to parents, September 8, 1942; Hayes to parents and brothers, September 20, 1942; Hayes to parents, January 28, 1943; Hayes to parents, April 9, 1943, reprinted in Hule, *Hero of Iwo Jima,* pp. 14–15, 16, 18, 23, 24.
57. Albert Hemingway, *Ira Hayes: Pima Marine* (Lanham, Md., 1988), pp. 23, 31.
58. Ibid., p. 33.
59. Huie, *Hero of Iwo Jima,* pp. 26–27.
60. Ibid., p. 27.
61. McClain, *Navajo Weapon,* p. 181.
62. Karal Ann Marling and John Wetenhall, *Iwo Jima: Monuments, Memories, and the American Hero* (Cambridge, Mass., 1991), p. 111.
63. Huie, *Hero of Iwo Jima,* p. 36.
64. Ibid., p. 37.
65. Hayes to parents, May 10, 1945, reprinted in Huie, *Hero of Iwo Jima,* p. 38; Hayes, speech, in Huie, *Hero of Iwo Jima,* p. 40.
66. Huie, *Hero of Iwo Jima,* p. 41.
67. Marling and Wetenhall, *Iwo Jima,* p. 116.
68. Huie, *Hero of Iwo Jima,* p. 43.
69. Ibid., p. 51.
70. Quoted in Joe Rosenthal with W. C. Heinz, "The Picture That Will Live Forever," *Collier's,* February 18, 1955, p. 67; also quoted in Marling and Wetenhall, pp. 120–121.
71. Quoted in Marling and Wetenhall, *Iwo Jima,* p. 125.
72. Thomas H. Begay, interview, number 1166, American Indian History Project, Western History Center, University of Utah, p. 16.
73. Huie, *Hero of Iwo Jima,* p. 64.
74. Watson, "Navajo Code Talkers," p. 41.
75. Claude Hatch, interview, in Johnson (ed.), *Navajos and World War II,* pp. 124–125.
76. Watson, "Navajo Code Talkers," p. 42.
77. Interview with Dan Akee, number 1159, American Indian History Project, pp. 14–15.
78. Interview with Sidney Bedoni, number 1168, American Indian History Project, p. 18.
79. Keats Begay, interview, in Johnson (ed.), *Navajos and World War II,* p. 44.
80. Letter from Mrs. B, reprinted in Doris A. Paul, *The Navajo Code Talkers* (Bryn Mawr, Pa., 1973), p. 112.

81. Oliver La Farge, "They Were Good Enough for the Army," *Harper's*, November 1947, p. 445.
82. Bernstein, *American Indians,* p. 152.
83. McClain, *Navajo Weapon,* p. v.

Chapter 5. A Dream of El Norte

1. Roberto Haro, interview with author, July 25, 1998.
2. Beatrice Griffith, *American Me* (Boston, 1948), p. 321.
3. Raul Morín, *Among the Valiant: Mexican Americans in WW II and Korea* (Alhambra, Calif., 1966), p. 30.
4. Mario García, *Mexican-Americans: Leadership, Ideology & Identity, 1930–1960* (New Haven, 1989), p. 166.
5. Richard Santillán, "Rosita the Riveter: Midwest Mexican American Women during World War II," in *Perspectives in Mexican American Studies,* vol. 2, 1989 (Tucson), p. 120.
6. Carlos Muñoz, Jr., *Youth, Identity, Power: The Chicano Movement* (London, 1989), pp. 38–39.
7. Morín, *Among the Valiant,* p. 21.
8. Ibid., p. 91.
9. Ricard Griswold del Castillo and Richard A. García, *César Chávez: A Triumph of Spirit* (Norman, Okla., 1995), pp. 12, 19.
10. Socorro Diáz Blanchard, *Recuerdos (Memories),* vol. 1, December 1992, unpublished autobiography, loaned to the author by her grandson, Sean O'Shea, p. 108.
11. Maria Louisa Hernandez to Nicholas Ortiz, October 12, 1942, reprinted in Judy Barrett Litoff and David C. Smith (eds.), *Since You Went Away: World War II Letters from American Women on the Home Front* (New York, 1991), p. 40.
12. Patricia Preciado Martin, *Songs My Mother Sang to Me: An Oral History of Mexican-American Women* (Tucson, 1996), p. 70.
13. Santillán, "Rosita the Riveter," p. 124.
14. Ibid., p. 135.
15. *La Opinión,* July 12, 1944; February 25, 1945.
16. *La Opinión,* May 2, 1944; June 27, 1944.
17. *La Opinión,* June 1, 1945; August 15, 1945; March 25, 1945.
18. *La Opinión,* June 24, 1942; April 1, 1945; May 27, 1945.
19. Autobiographical statement, November 12, 1994, José D. Carrasco, in the Eisenhower Center, University of New Orleans.
20. Morín, *Among the Valiant,* pp. 24, 89, 100, 111–112, 136–137, 153–154, 192–193, 255.
21. Quoted in Carey McWilliams, *North from Mexico: The Spanish-Speaking People of the United States* (New York, 1968), p. 260.
22. Ricardo Romo, *East Los Angeles: History of a Barrio* (Austin, Tex., 1983),

p. 48; Lawrence A. Cardoso, *Mexican Emigration to the United States, 1897–1931* (Tucson, 1980), p. 80.

23. Albert Camarillo, *Chicanos in a Changing Society: From Mexican Pueblos to American Barrios in Santa Barbara and Southern California, 1848–1930* (Cambridge, Mass., 1979), p. 146; Manuel Gamio, *The Mexican Immigrant: His Life Story* (Chicago, 1931), p. 15.

24. Carey McWilliams, *Factories in the Field: The Story of Migratory Farm Labor in California* (Santa Barbara, 1971), pp. 127–128, 131; Abraham Hoffman, *Unwanted Americans in the Great Depression: Repatriation Pressures, 1929–1939* (Tucson, 1974), p. 10; Cardoso, *Mexican Emigration*, p. 25.

25. Mark Reisler, *By the Sweat of Their Brow: Mexican Immigrant Labor in the United States, 1900–1940* (Westport, Conn., 1976), p. 13.

26. Hoffman, *Unwanted Americans*, pp. 47, 84.

27. Albert Camarillo, *Chicanos in a Changing Society*, p. 163; Hoffman, *Unwanted Americans*, p. 95.

28. Cardoso, *Mexican Emigration*, p. 146.

29. Carey McWilliams, "Getting Rid of the Mexican," in Wayne Moquin (ed.), *A Documentary History of the Mexican Americans* (New York, 1971), p. 297.

30. *La Opinión*, March 21, 1942.

31. Maria Herrera-Sobek, *Northward Bound: The Mexican Immigrant Experience in Ballad and Song* (Bloomington, 1993), pp. 147–148.

32. McWilliams, *North from Mexico*, pp. 266–267.

33. Matt S. Meier and Felicino Ribera, *Mexican Americans/American Mexicans* (New York, 1993), p. 175.

34. Erasmo Gamboa, *Mexican Labor and World War II: Braceros in the Pacific Northwest, 1942–1947* (Austin, 1990), p. 62.

35. Herrera-Sobek, *Northward Bound*, p. 155.

36. Marilyn P. Davis, *Mexican Voices, American Dreams: An Oral History of Mexican Immigration to the United States* (New York, 1990), pp. 171, 126.

37. Herrera-Sobek, *Northward Bound*, p. 168.

38. Braceros, interviews, in Henry Anderson, *Fields of Bondage: The Mexican Contract Labor System in Industrialized Agriculture* (Martinez, Calif., 1963), p. 34a.

39. Bracero, interview, in Anderson, *Fields of Bondage*, p. 53.

40. Herrera-Sobek, *Northward Bound*, p. 165.

41. Bracero, interview, in Anderson, *Fields of Bondage*, p. 53.

42. Gonzalo B. García, interview, oral history number 604, Mexican-American Oral History Project, California State University, Fullerton, California.

43. Bracero, interview, in Anderson, *Fields of Bondage*, p. 34d.

44. Ibid., p. 34b.

45. Erasmo Gamboa, *Mexican Labor and World War II: Braceros in the Pacific Northwest, 1942–1947* (Austin, 1990), p. 115.

46. Ibid., pp. 82–90.

47. Report No. 24, "Spanish-Americans in the Southwest and the War Effort," August 18, 1942, Special Services Division, Bureau of Intelligence, Office of War Information, National Archives, Washington, D.C., p. 11.

48. Clete Daniel, *Chicano Workers and the Politics of Fairness: The FEPC in the Southwest, 1941–1945* (Austin, 1991), pp. 38–41.

49. Daniel, *Chicano Workers,* pp. 50, 49.

50. *La Opinión,* November 2, 1943; February 12, 1943.

51. Ibid., January 23, 1944.

52. Ibid., April 1, 1942.

53. Richard Santillán, "Midwestern Mexican American Women and the Struggle for Gender Equality," in *Perspectives in Mexican American Studies,* vol. 5 (1995), p. 95.

54. Santillán, "Rosita the Riveter," p. 125.

55. Sherna Berger Gluck, *Rosie the Riveter Revisited: Women, the War, and Social Change* (New York, 1987), pp. 85–86.

56. Santillán, "Rosita the Riveter," p. 127.

57. Ibid., p. 129.

58. Gluck, *Rosie the Riveter Revisited,* pp. 85–86.

59. Santillán, "Rosita the Riveter," p. 128.

60. Ibid., p. 127.

61. Martin, *Songs My Mother Sang to Me,* p. 115.

62. Gluck, *Rosie the Riveter Revisited,* pp. 208, 211.

63. Díaz Blanchard, *Recuerdos (Memories),* pp. 105–108.

64. Vicki Ruiz, *From Out of the Shadows: Mexican Women in Twentieth-Century America* (New York, 1998), p. 82.

65. Santillán, "Rosita the Riveter," pp. 123–124.

66. Santillán, "Midwestern Mexican American Women," pp. 98–99.

67. Octavio Paz, *The Labyrinth of Solitude: Life and Thought in Mexico* (New York, 1961), pp. 9–28.

68. Emory S. Bogardus, "Gangs of Mexican-American Youth," *Sociology and Social Research,* vol. 23, no. 1 (September-October 1943), pp. 55, 57.

69. Gluck, *Rosie the Riveter Revisited,* p. 84.

70. Ruth D. Tuck, "Behind the Zoot Suit Riots," *Survey Graphic,* August 1943, p. 316.

71. Mario García, "Americans All: The Mexican American Generation and the Politics of Wartime Los Angeles, 1941–45," *Social Science Quarterly,* vol. 65, no. 2 (June 1984), p. 282.

72. Report No. 24, "Spanish-Americans in the Southwest and the War Effort," August 18, 1942, p. 18.

73. Díaz Blanchard, *Recuerdos (Memories),* pp. 73–76.

74. Romo, *East Los Angeles,* p. 166.

75. David G. Gutiérrez, *Walls and Mirrors: Mexican Americans, Mexican Immigrants, and the Politics of Ethnicity* (Berkeley, 1995), p. 125.

76. *Los Angeles Times,* August 5, 1942.

77. Ibid., August 6, 1942.

78. Ibid., August 5, 1942.

79. Anthony Quinn, *One Man Tango* (New York, 1995), pp. 16–17.

80. George J. Sánchez, *Becoming Mexican American: Ethnicity, Culture and Identity in Chicano Los Angeles, 1900–1945* (New York, 1993), p. 253.

81. Carey McWilliams, "Los Angeles' Pachuco Gangs," *New Republic*, January 18, 1943, pp. 76–77.

82. "Zoot-Suit War," *Time*, June 21, 1943, p. 18; Stuart Cosgrove, "The Zoot-Suit and Style Warfare," *History Workshop*, issue 18 (autumn 1984), p. 81.

83. Griffith, *American Me*, p. 8.

84. "Zoot-Suit War," *Time*, June 21, 1943, p. 18.

85. Griffith, *American Me*, pp. 10, 11.

86. "Zoot-Suit War," *Time*, June 21, 1943, p. 18.

87. "Zoot Suiters Learn Lesson in Fights with Servicemen," *Los Angeles Times*, June 7, 1943.

88. Ibid.

89. Mauricio Mazón, *The Zoot-Suit Riots: The Psychology of Symbolic Annihilation* (Austin, 1984), pp. 78–79.

90. Carey McWilliams, "The Zoot-Suit Riots," *New Republic*, June 21, 1943, p. 820.

91. Mazón, *Zoot-Suit Riots*, p. 75.

92. "Jurors Hear 'Zooters' Defend Right to Garb," *Los Angeles Times*, June 16, 1943.

93. "First Lady Traces Zoot Riots to Discrimination," *Los Angeles Times*, June 17, 1943.

94. "Murray Appeals to Roosevelt in Zoot Rioting," *Los Angeles Times*, June 20, 1943.

95. *Chicago Defender*, June 19, 1943.

96. Chester B. Hines, "Zoot Riots Are Race Riots," *Crisis*, vol. 50, no. 7, July 1943, p. 222.

97. David Rojas Gaytán, "Pachucos in the Wartime Mexican Angeleno Press," unpublished M.A. thesis, California State University, Hayward, 1996, p. 98.

98. Gutiérrez, *Walls and Mirrors*, pp. 128–129.

Chapter 6. Diversity and Its Discontents

1. *Time*, December 22, 1941, p. 33.

2. Lee Chew, interview, "Life Story of a Chinaman," in Hamilton Holt (ed.), *The Life Stories of Undistinguished Americans as Told by Themselves* (New York, 1906), pp. 287–288.

3. *Debates and Proceedings in the Congress of the United States, 1789–1791*, 2 vols. (Washington, D.C.), vol. 1, pp. 998, 1284; vol. 2, pp. 1148–1156, 1162, 2264.

4. "Life History and Social Document of Andrew Kan," August 22, 1924, pp.

2, 11, Survey of Race Relations, Stanford University, Hoover Institution Archives.

5. "Life History and Social Document of Albert King," July 31, 1924, p. 7, Survey of Race Relations, Stanford University, Hoover Institution Archives.

6. Ling-chi Wang, *Politics of Assimilation and Repression: History of the Chinese in the United States, 1940 to 1970,* unpublished manuscript, Asian American Studies Library, University of California, Berkeley, pp. 167–168; Nellie Wong, *Dreams in Harrison Railroad Park* (Berkeley, 1977), p. 16.

7. James Low, oral history, in Victor and Brett De Bary Nee, *Longtime Californ': A Documentary Study of an American Chinatown* (New York, 1972), p. 170.

8. Diane Mei Lin Mark and Ginger Chih, *A Place Called Chinese America* (Dubuque, Iowa, 1982), pp. 88, 89; "Life History and Social Document of Fred Wong," August 29, 1924, p. 6, Survey of Race Relations; "Interview with Peter Soohoo," August 7, 1925, p. 1, Survey of Race Relations; Flora Belle Jan, "An American-Born Looks at Young Chinatown," *Chinese Christian Student,* January 1931, p. 7, in Julia I. Hsuan Chen, "The Chinese Community in New York: A Study in Their Cultural Adjustment, 1920–1940," unpublished Ph.D. thesis, American University, Washington, D.C., 1941, p. 92.

9. *Chung Sai Yat Po,* August 17, 1933, and June 25, 1935, translated and quoted in Richard Kock Dare, "The Economic and Social Adjustment of the San Francisco Chinese for the Past Fifty Years," unpublished M.A. thesis, University of California, Berkeley, 1959, p. 62; "Interview with Louise Leung," August 13, 1924, Survey of Race Relations.

10. Victor Wong, "Childhood II," in Nick Harvey (ed.), *Ting: The Cauldron: Chinese Art and Identity in San Francisco* (San Francisco, 1970), p. 70.

11. "A Memo to Mr. Hitler, Hirohito & Co.," *Chinese Press,* May 8, 1942.

12. Peter Kwong, *Chinatown, N.Y.: Labor & Politics, 1930–1950* (New York, 1979), pp. 114–115.

13. "First Chinese WAAC: New York's Emily Lee Shak," *Chinese Press,* September 25, 1942.

14. De Bary Nee, *Longtime Californ',* pp. 154–155; Mark and Chih, *A Place Called Chinese America,* pp. 97–98.

15. Kamin Chin, statement, "Allies and Enemies: The Dilemma of Asian Americans during World War II," symposium sponsored by the Museum of Chinese in America, New York, March 2, 1996.

16. Rose Hum Lee, "Chinese in the United States Today: The War Has Changed Their Lives," *Survey Graphic,* October 1942, p. 419; "Give 'Em Wings: The Story of the Part Played in Aircraft by L.A. Chinese," *Chinese Press,* April 2, 1943.

17. Arthur Wong, oral history, in Joan Morrison and Charlotte Fox Zabusky,

American Mosaic: The Immigrant Experience in the Words of Those Who Lived It (New York, 1980), p. 78.

18. Jade Snow Wong, *Fifth Chinese Daughter* (New York, 1965, originally published in 1945), p. 189; "Chinese Career Girls: They Help Run the Vital 'Behind-the-Line' Business of the United States at War," *Chinese Press,* May 29, 1942; "Women in the War," *Chinese Press,* March 26, 1943.

19. Lee, "Chinese in the United States Today," pp. 419, 444.

20. Fred Riggs, *Pressures on Congress: A Study of the Repeal of Chinese Exclusion* (New York, 1950), pp. 111, 112, 116; "A Chinese Youth Meeting," *Chinese Press,* October 1, 1943.

21. Franklin D. Roosevelt, "Message from the President of the United States Favoring Repeal of the Chinese Exclusion Laws," October 11, 1943, in appendix, Riggs, *Pressures on Congress,* pp. 210–211.

22. John W. Dower, *War Without Mercy: Race and Power in the Pacific War* (New York, 1986), p. 167; Riggs, *Pressures on Congress,* pp. 161–162.

23. Dower, *War Without Mercy,* pp. 164–169; *Congressional Record,* 78th Congress, 1st Session, 1943, vol. 89, part 6, pp. 8580, 8581, 8597.

24. Dolores Quinto, "Life Story of a Filipino Immigrant," *Social Process in Hawaii,* vol. 4, 1938, p. 71; Carlos Bulosan, *America Is in the Heart* (Seattle, 1981), p. 88.

25. U.S. Supreme Court, in Sonia Wallovits, *The Filipinos in California* (San Francisco, 1972), p. 3.

26. "I Am Only a Foreigner — So This Is America," letter written by a Filipino to an Americanization teacher in Los Angeles, circa 1924, p. 1, Survey of Race Relations.

27. Manuel Buaken, *I Have Lived with the American People* (Caldwell, Idaho, 1948), pp. 321–323; Carlos Bulosan, "The Voice of Bataan," in Susan Evangelista, *Carlos Bulosan and His Poetry: A Biography and Anthology* (Seattle, 1985), p. 121.

28. Buaken, *I Have Lived with the American People,* pp. 322–323; James G. Wingo, "The First Filipino Regiment and Its Racial Strains," *Asia,* October 1942, p. 562; see also R. T. Feria, "War and the Status of Filipino Immigrants," *Sociology and Social Research,* vol. 31 (1946–1947), p. 52.

29. Bienvenido Santos, "Filipinos in War," *Far Eastern Survey,* vol. 11 (November 30, 1942), p. 249.

30. Doroteo Vite, "A Filipino Rookie in Uncle Sam's Army," *Asia,* October 1942, p. 564.

31. Iris Brown Buaken, "My Brave New World," *Asia,* May 1943, p. 269; F. A. Taggaoa, "No Cause for Regret," *Asia,* October 1942, p. 567.

32. Manuel Buaken, "Life in the Armed Forces," *New Republic,* vol. 100 (August 30, 1943), p. 278.

33. Manuel Buaken, "Our Fighting Love of Freedom," *Asia,* October 1942, p. 88.

34. R. T. Feria, "War and the Status of Filipino Immigrants," *Sociology and Social Research*, vol. 31 (1946–1947), pp. 50, 51, 53.

35. Bong-Youn Choy, *Koreans in America* (Chicago, 1979), p. 170; *Korean National Herald-Pacific Weekly*, February 25, 1942, in Lauriel Eubank, "The Effects of the First Six Months of World War II on the Attitudes of Koreans and Filipinos toward the Japanese in Hawaii," unpublished M.A. thesis, University of Hawaii, 1943, p. 73.

36. Alice Chai, "A Picture Bride from Korea: The Life History of a Korean American Woman in Hawaii," in *Bridge* (winter 1978), p. 37.

37. H. Brett Melendy, *Asians in America: Filipinos, Koreans, and East Indians* (Boston, 1977), p. 136.

38. Harold Sunoo and Sonia Sunoo, "The Heritage of the First Korean Women Immigrants in the United States: 1903–1924," paper presented at the 10th Annual Conference of the Association of Korean Christian Scholars of North America, Chicago, 1976, p. 21.

39. Hyung June Moon, "The Korean Immigrants in America: The Quest of Identity in the Formative Years, 1903–1918," unpublished Ph.D. thesis, University of Nevada, Reno, 1976, p. 161.

40. Jean Park, in Christopher Kim, "Three Generations of Koreans in America," Asian American Studies 199 paper, University of California, Berkeley, 1976, section on Park, pp. 46–47.

41. Melendy, *Asians in America*, pp. 156–158.

42. Eubank, "Effects of the First Six Months of World War II on the Attitudes of Koreans," pp. 73, 86.

43. Melendy, *Asians in America*, p. 157; Choy, *Koreans in America*, p. 326.

44. Choy, *Koreans in America*, pp. 173–175.

45. Ibid., p. 280.

46. "Biographical Sketch of Deal Singh Madhas," based on interviews, in appendix, Allan Miller, "An Ethnographic Report on the Sikh (East) Indians of the Sacramento Valley," Anthropology 299 paper, University of California, Berkeley, 1950, pp. 106–107; Sucha Singh, interview, August 8, 1924, Survey of Race Relations.

47. H. A. Millis, "East Indian Immigration to the Pacific Coast," in *Survey*, vol. 28 (1912), p. 379; Herman Scheffauer, "The Tide of Turbans," *Forum*, vol. 43 (June 1910), pp. 616–618; Bruce La Brack, "The Sikhs of Northern California: A Socio-historical Study," unpublished Ph.D. thesis, Syracuse University, 1980, p. 130.

48. *Survey*, vol. 25 (1910), p. 3; Melendy, *Asians in America*, p. 223.

49. *United States v. Bhagat Singh Thind*, 261 U.S. (Washington, D.C., 1923), pp. 204–215; Gurdial Singh, "East Indians in the United States," *Sociology and Social Research*, vol. 30 (January-February 1946), p. 212.

50. Melendy, *Asians in America*, pp. 224, 225.

51. Riggs, *Pressures on Congress*, pp. 164–165; David Reimers, *Still the Golden Door: The Third World Comes to America* (New York, 1985), p. 15.

52. S. Chandrasekhar, "Indian Immigration in America," *Far Eastern Survey,* July 26, 1944, pp. 142, 143.

53. Ken Scharnberg, *Voices: Letters from World War II* (Nashville, Tenn., 1993), p. 63.

54. Commission on Wartime Relocation and Internment of Civilians, *Personal Justice Denied: Report of the Commission on Wartime Relocation and Internment of Civilians* (Washington, D.C., 1982), pp. 290–291; La Verne J. Rippley, *The German-Americans* (Boston, 1976), see pp. 180–213.

55. Victor Von Borosini, "Home-Going Italians," *Survey,* September 28, 1912, p. 792.

56. John Higham, *Strangers in the Land* (New York, 1966), pp. 66, 183.

57. Stephen Fox, *The Unknown Internment: An Oral History of the Relocation of Italian Americans During World War II* (Boston, 1990), pp. xiii, 63.

58. Ibid., p. 71.

59. Ibid., p. 106.

60. Stephen C. Fox, "General John DeWitt and the Proposed Internment of German and Italian Aliens during World War II," *Pacific Historical Review,* vol. 57, no. 4 (November 1988), p. 424.

61. Commission on Wartime Relocation, *Personal Justice Denied,* p. 287.

62. Fox, *Unknown Internment,* pp. xiii, 136.

63. Harry Paxton Howard, "Americans in Concentration Camps," *Crisis,* September 1942, p. 284.

64. Fox, *Unknown Internment,* p. 55.

65. Ibid., pp. 74, 147.

66. Michi Weglyn, *Years of Infamy: The Untold Story of America's Concentration Camps* (New York, 1976).

Chapter 7. Remembering Pearl Harbor

1. Commission on Wartime Relocation and Internment of Civilians, *Personal Justice Denied: Report of the Commission on Wartime Relocation and Internment of Civilians* (Washington, D.C., 1982), p. 3.

2. Robert A. Wilson and Bill Hosokawa, *East to America: A History of the Japanese in the United States* (New York, 1980), p. 154; Commission on Wartime Relocation, *Personal Justice Denied,* p. 264.

3. Commission on Wartime Relocation, *Personal Justice Denied,* p. 265.

4. Ibid., pp. 269, 270.

5. Ibid., pp. 270, 272.

6. Ibid., p. 274.

7. Lawrence Fuchs, *Hawaii Pono: A Social History* (New York, 1961), p. 302; Andrew Lind, *Hawaii's Japanese: An Experiment in Democracy* (Princeton, 1946), p. 64.

8. Jacobus tenBroek, Edward Barnhart, and Floyd Matson, *Prejudice, War and the Constitution: Causes and Consequences of the Evacuation of the Japan-

ese Americans in World War II (Berkeley, 1970), p. 117; Lind, *Hawaii's Japanese,* p. 63.

9. Dennis Ogawa, *Kodomo no tame: For the sake of the children* (Honolulu, 1978), pp. 279–280; Lind, *Hawaii's Japanese,* p. 42.

10. Lind, *Hawaii's Japanese,* p. 122.

11. Lyn Crost, *Honor by Fire: Japanese Americans at War in Europe and the Pacific* (Novato, Calif., 1994), p. 10.

12. Minoru Hinahara, interview, July 3, 1988.

13. George H. Fairfield, in Republic of Hawaii, *Report of the Labor Commission on Strikes and Arbitration* (Honolulu, 1895), p. 36.

14. *The Higher Wage Question,* reprinted in Bureau of Labor Statistics, *Report of the Commissioner of Labor on Hawaii* (Washington, D.C., 1910), p. 76.

15. Hawaii Laborers' Association, *Facts about the Strike* (Honolulu, 1920), p. 1.

16. William C. Smith, *Americans in Process: A Study of Our Citizens of Oriental Ancestry* (Ann Arbor, Mich., 1937), p. 52.

17. Ray Stannard Baker, "Human Nature in Hawaii: How the Few Want the Many to Work for Them — Perpetually, and at Low Wages," *American Magazine,* vol. 73 (January 1912), p. 330.

18. Curtis Aller, "The Evolution of Hawaiian Labor Relations: From Benevolent Paternalism to Mature Collective Bargaining," unpublished Ph.D. thesis, Harvard University, 1958, p. 39.

19. Lind, *Hawaii's Japanese,* pp. 161–162.

20. Commission on Wartime Relocation, *Personal Justice Denied,* p. 48.

21. Ibid., pp. 52–53.

22. Ibid., p. 55.

23. Roger Daniels, *Concentration Camps USA: Japanese Americans and World War II* (New York, 1971), pp. 45–46.

24. Commission on Wartime Relocation, *Personal Justice Denied,* pp. 56, 71–72, 80; Lind, *Hawaii's Japanese,* p. 49; Daniels, *Concentration Camps,* p. 62; tenBroek, et al., *Prejudice,* p. 75; Gary Y. Okihiro and Julie Sly, "The Press, Japanese Americans, and the Concentration Camps," *Phylon,* vol. 44, no. 1 (1983), pp. 66–69.

25. tenBroek, et al., *Prejudice,* pp. 79–80.

26. Ibid., p. 80.

27. tenBroek, et al., *Prejudice,* p. 83; Commission on Wartime Relocation, *Personal Justice Denied,* pp. 70–71.

28. Commission on Wartime Relocation, *Personal Justice Denied,* pp. 75, 66, 78.

29. Ibid., pp. 78, 79.

30. Peter Irons, *Justice At War: The Story of the Japanese American Internment Cases* (New York, 1983), p. 20.

31. Commission on Wartime Relocation, *Personal Justice Denied,* p. 85.

32. Ibid., p. 66.

33. Kazuo Ito, *Issei: A History of Japanese Immigrants in North America* (Seattle, 1973), p. 29.

34. Yuji Ichioka, "The Early Japanese Immigrant Quest for Citizenship: The Background of the 1922 Ozawa Case," *Amerasia Journal,* vol. 4, no. 2, 1977, p. 12.

35. Ichioka, "Early Japanese Immigrant Quest for Citizenship," pp. 10, 11, 17; Yamato Ichihashi, *Japanese in the United States* (New York, 1969, p. 298; *Ozawa vs. United States, Decision of the Court,* November 13, 1922, reprinted in appendix, Eliot Mears, *Resident Orientals on the American Pacific Coast* (New York, 1927), pp. 509, 513, 514.

36. Ito, *Issei*, p. 270.

37. "American-Born Japanese in Interstitial Position Say League President," *Japanese American Courier,* April 17, 1928; "Life History of Kazuo Kawai," March 2, 1925, p. 17, Survey of Race Relations, Stanford University, Hoover Institution Library; "Interview with Mr. S. Nitta," January 7, 1925, p. 2, Survey of Race Relations; Yuji Ichioka, "A Study in Dualism: James Yoshinori Sakamoto and the *Japanese American Courier,* 1928–1942," *Amerasia,* vol. 13, no. 2 (1986–1987), p. 57.

38. "Life History of a Japanese Man at Santa Paula, California," December 29, 1924, p. 2, Survey of Race Relations; Ito, *Issei*, p. 497.

39. Report on Vocational Guidance Issue by Kojiro Unoura, in *Japanese American Courier,* September 10, 1938.

40. John Modell, *The Economics and Politics of Racial Accommodation: The Japanese of Los Angeles, 1900–1942* (Urbana, Ill., 1977), pp. 137–138.

41. Aiji Tashiro, "The Rising Son of the Rising Sun," *New Outlook* (September 1934), pp. 36, 40.

42. Ichioka, "Sakamoto and the *Japanese American Courier,*" p. 59.

43. Commission on Wartime Relocation, *Personal Justice Denied*, pp. 111, 121.

44. Congressman Robert Matsui, speech in the House of Representatives on the 442 bill for redress and reparations, September 17, 1987, *Congressional Record* (Washington, D.C., 1987), p. 7584.

45. Monica Sone, *Nisei Daughter* (Boston, 1953), p. 158; Takae Washizu, interview, in Eileen Sunada Sarasohn (ed.), *The Issei: Portrait of a Pioneer* (Palo Alto, Calif., 1983), p. 166.

46. Minoru Yasui, interview, John Tateishi, *And Justice For All: An Oral History of the Japanese American Detention Camps* (New York, 1984), pp. 70–71; Gordon Hirabayashi, "Growing Up American in Washington," the spring 1988 Pettyjohn Distinguished Lecture, Washington State University, March 24, 1988; Gordon Hirabayashi, interview, March 24, 1988.

47. Tom Hayase, in Sarasohn (ed.), *Issei*, p. 166; Commission on Wartime Relocation, *Personal Justice Denied*, p. 132.

48. Sone, *Nisei Daughter*, p. 166; letter by Congressman Norman Mineta's father, quoted in his speech to the House of Representatives, September 17,

1987, *Congressional Record* (Washington, D.C., 1987), p. 7585; Commission on Wartime Relocation, *Personal Justice Denied,* p. 135.

49. Yasui and Tsukamoto, interviews, in Tateishi, *And Justice For All,* pp. 73, 12, 74.

50. Yasui, interview, in Tateishi, *And Justice For All,* p. 76; Sone, *Nisei Daughter,* p. 192.

51. Caroline Aoyagi, "Atonement for the Past . . . Justice for the Future," *Pacific Citizen,* Sept. 18–Oct. 1, 1999.

52. Commission on Wartime Relocation, *Personal Justice Denied,* p. 160.

53. Ibid., pp. 169, 172, 176.

54. Miyo Senzaki, interview, in Tateishi, *And Justice For All,* p. 104.

55. tenBroek, et al., *Prejudice,* p. 150; Commission on Wartime Relocation, *Personal Justice Denied,* pp. 189, 191.

56. Commission on Wartime Relocation, *Personal Justice Denied,* pp. 191–192.

57. Poem by Sunada Toshu, in Constance Hayashi and Keiho Yamanaka, "Footprints: Poetry of the American Relocation Camp Experience," *Amerasia,* vol. 3, no. 2 (1976), p. 116.

58. Commission on Wartime Relocation, *Personal Justice Denied,* p. 195; Sone, *Nisei Daughter,* p. 198.

59. Frank S. Emi, "Draft Resistance at the Heart Mountain Concentration Camp and the Fair Play Committee," paper presented at the Fifth National Conference of the Association for Asian American Studies, Washington State University, March 24–26, 1988, pp. 2–4; Frank S. Emi, interview, March 26, 1986; Kiyoshi Okamoto, "We Should Know," typed speech, February 25, 1944, copy given to author by Frank S. Emi.

60. Commission on Wartime Relocation, *Personal Justice Denied,* p. 195; Emi, "Draft Resistance at the Heart Mountain Concentration Camp," p. 4.

61. James Omura, "Japanese American Journalism During World War II," paper presented at the Fifth National Conference of the Association for Asian American Studies, Washington State University, March 24–26, 1988; Emi, "Draft Resistance at the Heart Mountain Concentration Camp," pp. 6–8; Emi, interview, March 26, 1988; typed statement by the Fair Play Committee for the meeting on March 5, 1944, copy given to the author by Emi.

62. Joseph Kurihara, autobiography, in Japanese Evacuation and Relocation Study, box no. A17.05, pp. 1–52, Bancroft Library, University of California, Berkeley.

63. Crost, *Honor by Fire,* p. 133.

64. Lind, *Hawaii's Japanese,* p. 161.

65. Interview with Hiroshi Kobashigawa, April 15, 1988, by Ben Kobashigawa, transcript in author's possession.

66. Shig Doi, interview, in Tateishi, *And Justice For All,* pp. 165–166; Chester Tanaka, *Go For Broke: A Pictorial History of the Japanese American 100th Infantry Battalion and the 442d Regimental Combat Team* (Richmond, Calif., 1982), p. 100.

67. Shig Doi, interview, in Tateishi, *And Justice For All*, p. 161.
68. Daniel K. Inouye, *Journey to Washington* (Englewood Cliffs, N.J., 1967), p. 85.
69. Ibid., pp. 151–152.
70. Frank Chuman, *The Bamboo People: The Law and Japanese-Americans* (Del Mar, Calif.), pp. 343–344.
71. Shig Doi, interview, in Tateishi, *And Justice For All*, p. 161; Lind, *Hawaii's Japanese*, p. 158.
72. Commission on Wartime Relocation, *Personal Justice Denied*, p. 260.
73. Tanaka, *Go For Broke*, p. 171.
74. Harry S. Truman, *Memoirs of Harry S. Truman: Year of Decisions, 1945* (New York, 1955), p. 417.
75. Lisle A. Rose, *Dubious Victory: The United States and the End of World War II* (Akron, Ohio, 1973), p. 240.
76. Merle Miller, *Plain Speaking: An Oral Biography of Harry S. Truman* (New York, 1986), pp. 242–244.
77. Extract from the Minutes of Meeting held at the White House, June 18, 1945, reprinted in appendix of Martin Sherwin, in *A World Destroyed: Hiroshima and the Origins of the Arms Race* (New York, 1987), p. 342.
78. Joint War Plans Committee, reprinted in Sherwin, *World Destroyed*, appendix, p. 342.
79. Joint War Plans Committee, report of June 15, 1945, in Sherwin, *World Destroyed*, p. 342. Truman was an extremely conscientious reader of reports. According to Assistant Secretary of State Dean Acheson, "Mr. Truman read the documents themselves, and he understood and acted on them." See Miller, *Plain Speaking*, p. 51.
80. Minutes of Meeting at the White House, June 18, 1945, reprinted in Sherwin, *World Destroyed*, appendix, pp. 357, 359, 360–361, 362.
81. William D. Leahy, *I Was There: The Personal Story of the Chief of Staff to Presidents Roosevelt and Truman Based on His Notes and Diaries Made at the Time* (New York, 1950), p. 385.
82. Gar Alperovitz, *Atomic Diplomacy: Hiroshima and Potsdam: The Use of the Atomic Bomb and the American Confrontation with Soviet Power* (New York, 1985), p. 28.
83. Leahy, *I Was There*, pp. 384–385, 259.
84. Ibid., p. 284.
85. Ibid., p. 418.
86. Truman, *Memoirs*, p. 396.
87. Stimson, Memorandum for the President, July 2, 1945, reprinted in Stimson, "The Decision to Use the Atomic Bomb," in *Harper's*, vol. 194, no. 1161 (February 1947), pp. 102–103.
88. Stimson, Diary, July 18, 19, 23, 24, 1945, Stimson Papers, Yale University Archives.
89. Truman, *Memoirs*, p. 391.

90. John Dower, *War Without Mercy: Race and Power in the Pacific War* (New York, 1986), pp. 217, 242–245.

91. John Morton Blum, *V Was for Victory: Politics and American Culture during World War II* (New York, 1976), p. 20.

92. George E. Hopkins, "Bombing and the American Conscience during World War II," *The Historian*, vol. 28, no. 3 (May 1966), p. 470.

93. Edward Said, *Orientalism* (New York, 1979).

94. Studs Terkel, *"The Good War": An Oral History of World War Two* (New York, 1984), pp. 107–108.

95. Ernie Pyle, *Ernie's War: The Best of Ernie Pyle's World War II Dispatches*, edited by David Nichols (New York, 1986), pp. 123, 125, 367.

96. Dower, *War Without Mercy*, p. 36.

97. William F. Halsey and Joseph Bryan, *Admiral Halsey's Story* (New York, 1947), p. 123.

98. William Bradford Huie, *The Hero of Iwo Jima and Other Stories* (New York, 1959), p. 29.

99. Dower, *War Without Mercy*, pp. 34, 161, 37, 85; Blum, *V Was for Victory*, p. 15.

100. Richard Tregaski, *Guadalcanal Diary* (New York, 1942), p. 16.

101. Terkel, *"The Good War,"* p. 64.

102. Tregaski, *Guadalcanal Diary*, p. 15.

103. E. B. Sledge, *With the Old Breed: At Peleliu and Okinawa* (New York, 1981), p. 120.

104. Dower, *War Without Mercy*, p. 66.

105. Craig M. Cameron, *American Samurai: Myth, Imagination, and the Conduct of Battle in the First Marine Division, 1941–1951* (New York, 1994), pp. 98, 127.

106. Dower, *War Without Mercy*, p. 152; Cameron, *American Samurai*, p. 117.

107. Milton A. Hill, "The Lessons of Bataan," *Science Digest*, December 1942, p. 54.

108. James M. Merrill, *A Sailor's Admiral: A Biography of William F. Halsey* (New York, 1976), p. 111.

109. Allen Nevins, "How We Felt About the War," in Jack Goodman (ed.), *While You Were Gone: A Report on Wartime Life in the United States* (New York, 1946), p. 13.

110. Truman to Bess, May 17, 1911, reprinted in Robert H. Ferrell (ed.), *Dear Bess: The Letters from Harry to Bess Truman, 1910–1959* (New York, 1983), p. 34.

111. Miller, *Plain Speaking*, p. 62.

112. Ibid., p. 59.

113. Ibid., pp. 30, 44.

114. Truman, *Memoirs*, p. 295.

115. Truman to Bess, January 6, 1936, reprinted in Ferrell (ed.), *Dear Bess*, p. 385.

116. Truman to Bess, June 22, 1911, reprinted in Ferrell (ed.), *Dear Bess*, p. 39.
117. Margaret Truman, *Harry S. Truman* (New York, 1972), p. 128.
118. Miller, *Plain Speaking*, p. 452.
119. Robert H. Ferrell (ed.), *Off the Record: The Private Papers of Harry S. Truman* (New York, 1980), pp. 53–56.
120. The phrase originated from Dower, *War Without Mercy*.
121. Truman, quoted in Barton J. Bernstein, "The Atomic Bomb and American Foreign Policy: The Route to Hiroshima," reprinted in Bernstein (ed.), *The Atomic Bomb: The Critical Issues* (Boston, 1976), p. 113.
122. *New York Times*, August 7, 1945.
123. Committee for "Children of Hiroshima," *Children of Hiroshima* (Cambridge, Mass., 1980), p. 228.
124. Ibid., pp. 6–7.
125. "Children of Hiroshima" Committee, *Children*, p. 60.
126. Ibid., p. 262.
127. Leahy, *I Was There*, p. 434.
128. Henry A. Wallace, diary, August 10, 1945, reprinted in Michael B. Stoff, Jonathan F. Fanton, and R. Hal Williams (eds.), *The Manhattan Project: A Documentary Introduction to the Atomic Age* (Philadelphia, 1991), p. 245.
129. David McCullough, *Truman* (New York, 1992), p. 460.
130. Paul Boyer, *By the Bomb's Early Light: American Thought and Culture at the Dawn of the Atomic Age* (Chapel Hill, 1994), p. 193.
131. McCullogh, *Truman*, p. 475.
132. Boyer, *Bomb's Light*, p. 193.
133. Robert J. Donovan, *Conflict and Crisis: The Presidency of Harry S. Truman, 1945–1948* (New York, 1977), p. 97.
134. Ferrell (ed.), *Off the Record*, pp. 52–53.
135. Ibid.
136. Leahy, *I Was There*, pp. 441, 385, 434.
137. Ibid., pp. 440, 441.
138. Ibid., pp. 441–442.
139. Rose, *Dubious Victory*, p. 363.
140. Ibid.
141. "Opinion," *Time*, vol. 46, no. 9, August 20, 1945.
142. Boyer, *Bomb's Light*, p. 197.
143. Interview with Alex Romandia's brother, Roberto Haro, July 25, 1998.
144. Walter G. Taylor, *Time*, vol. 46, no. 9, August 27, 1945, p. 2.
145. Hanson W. Baldwin, "The Atomic Weapon," *New York Times*, August 7, 1945.
146. "The Atomic Age," *Life*, vol. 19, no. 8, August 20, 1945, p. 32.
147. *Fortune*, vol. 32, no. 6, December 1945, p. 305.
148. W. E. B. DuBois, *The Souls of Black Folk* (New York, 1961, originally published in 1903), p. v. W. E. B. DuBois, "The Winds of Time: Negro's War Gains and Losses," *Chicago Defender*, September 15, 1945.

149. "El Uso de la Bomba Atomica no Hace Sentido," *La Opinión,* August 7, 1945; "Nuestra Guerra no ha Terminado," *La Opinión,* August 16, 1945; in Celso Castillo, "An Analysis of Mexican and Japanese American Relations during World War II," unpublished paper, 1997, University of California, Berkeley, pp. 12–13.

Chapter 8. Struggling for a World of "No Race Prejudice"

1. Robert Frost, *Complete Poems of Robert Frost, 1949* (New York, 1949), p. 569.
2. Joseph Conrad, *Heart of Darkness* (New York, 1981), p. 118.
3. Isaac Metzker (ed.), *A Bintel Brief: Sixty Years of Letters from the Lower East Side to the "Jewish Daily Forward"* (Garden City, N.Y., 1971), pp. 189–190.
4. Louis I. Dublin and Samuel C. Kohs, *American Jews in World War II: The Story of 550,000 Fighters for Freedom* (n.p., 1947), 2 vols., vol. 2, p. 21.
5. Metzker (ed.), *A Bintel Brief,* p. 174.
6. Dublin and Kohs, *American Jews in World War II,* vol. 2, p. 283.
7. Bernard S. Feinberg, oral history statement, Feinberg Papers, in the Eisenhower Center, University of New Orleans.
8. Fred C. Patheiger, interview with Stephen Ambrose, in the Patheiger Papers, Eisenhower Center, University of New Orleans.
9. Murray Shapiro to his parents, Murray Shapiro Papers, Eisenhower Center, University of New Orleans.
10. Ibid.
11. Ibid.
12. Letter written by Harold Katz, reprinted in Dublin and Kohs, *American Jews in World War II,* vol. 1, pp. 186–187.
13. Sydelle Kramer and Jenny Masur (eds.), *Jewish Grandmothers* (Boston, 1976), p. 64; Abraham Cahan, *The Education of Abraham Cahan* (Philadelphia, 1969), pp. 158, 182.
14. Song, "Purim Gifts," in Mark Slobin, *Tenement Songs: The Popular Music of the Jewish Immigrants* (Urbana, Ill., 1982), p. 155.
15. Sidney Stahl Weinberg, *World of Our Mothers: The Lives of Jewish Immigrant Women* (New York, 1988), p. 83; Irving Howe, *World of Our Fathers: The Journey of the East European Jews to America and the Life They Found and Made* (New York, 1983), p. 121.
16. Howe, *World of Our Fathers,* p. 128; Jewish mother, in Elizabeth Ewen, *Immigrant Women in the Land of Dollars: Life and Culture in the Lower East Side, 1890–1925* (New York, 1985), p. 72; Abrahan Cahan, *The Rise of David Levinsky* (New York, 1960), pp. 172–176.
17. Susan A. Glenn, *Daughters of the Shtetl: Life and Labor in the Immigrant Generation* (Ithaca, N.Y., 1990), p. 90.

18. Ibid., p. 103; Anzia Yezierska, *Children of Loneliness* (New York, 1923), p. 158.

19. Howe, *World of Our Fathers*, pp. 302, 306.

20. *Daily Forward*, in Stephen Steinberg, *The Ethnic Myth: Race, Ethnicity, and Class in America* (New York, 1981), p. 226.

21. Thomas Kessner, *The Golden Door: Italian and Jewish Immigrant Mobility in New York City, 1880–1915* (New York, 1977), p. 98.

22. Steinberg, *Ethnic Myth*, pp. 234, 242.

23. A. Lawrence Lowell, to Professor William E. Hocking, May 19, 1922; A. Lawrence Lowell, to Judge Julian Mack, March 29, 1922, in Steinberg, *Ethnic Myth*, pp. 245, 241; Synnott, *The Half-Opened Door: Discrimination and Admissions at Harvard, Yale, and Princeton, 1900–1970* (Westport, Conn., 1979), pp. 27, 36, 112.

24. John Higham, *Send These to Me: Immigrants in Urban America* (Baltimore, 1984), pp. 169, 145, 135; Howard M. Sachar, *A History of the Jews in America* (New York, 1992), p. 331.

25. Paul Masserman and Max Baker, *The Jews Come to America* (New York, 1932), pp. vi, vii.

26. Haskell Lookstein, *Were We Our Brothers' Keepers? The Public Response of American Jews to the Holocaust, 1938–1944* (New York, 1985), p. 78.

27. Leonard Dinnerstein, *Anti-Semitism in America* (New York, 1994), pp. 108–109.

28. Naomi W. Cohen, *American Jews and the Zionist Idea* (Hoboken, N.J., 1975), pp. 6, 31, 35.

29. Henry L. Feingold, *A Time for Searching: Entering the Mainstream, 1920–1945* (Baltimore, 1992), p. 185.

30. Cohen, *American Jews*, p. 42.

31. Chaim Zhitlowsky, *The Future of Our Youth in This Country and Assimilation* (Pittsburgh: Yiddish Culture Society, 1935), pp. 5, 6, 10, 11, 15.

32. Masserman and Baker, *Jews Come to America*, p. 334; Lucy Dawidowicz, "American Jews and the Holocaust," *New York Times Magazine*, April 18, 1982, p. 48.

33. Aaron Berman, "American Zionism and the Rescue of European Jewry: An Ideological Perspective," *American Jewish History*, vol. 30, March 1981, p. 316.

34. David Brody, "American Jewry, the Refugees and Immigration Restriction (1932–1942)," *Publication of the American Jewish Historical Society*, vol. 45, no. 4 (June 1956), p. 241. Wise saw that Jews had to flee from Germany. In a letter to his daughter, he wrote that they were "finished" and their "only recourse" was to get out of that country. Justine Wise Polier and James Waterman Wise (eds.), *The Personal Letters of Stephen Wise* (Boston, 1956), p. 223.

35. Rafael Medoff, *The Deafening Silence* (New York, 1987), pp. 32–33.

36. Ibid., pp. 34, 53.

37. Ronald Sanders, *Shores of Refuge: A Hundred Years of Jewish Emigration* (New York, 1988), p. 431. On February 24, 1920, Hitler had spelled out this policy for the Nazi party: "None but those of German blood may be citizens of the state. None but those of German blood, whatever their creed, may be members of the nation. No Jew, therefore, may be a member of the nation." In Arthur D. Morse, *While Six Million Died: A Chronicle of American Apathy* (New York, 1968), p. 105.

38. Medoff, *Deafening Silence*, p. 32.

39. Morse, *Six Million Died*, p. 210.

40. Ibid., pp. 203, 205–206.

41. Sanders, *Shores of Refuge*, pp. 448, 449.

42. Saul S. Friedman, *No Haven for the Oppressed: United States Policy Toward Jewish Refugees, 1938–1945* (Detroit, 1973), pp. 86–87.

43. Lookstein, *Were We Our Brothers' Keepers?*, p. 43.

44. Quoted in David S. Wyman, *Paper Walls: America and the Refugee Crisis, 1939–1941* (New York, 1985), p. 67.

45. Medoff, *Deafening Silence*, pp. 59, 69; Wyman, *Paper Walls*, p. 99.

46. Medoff, *Deafening Silence*, pp. 68, 70.

47. Wyman, *Paper Walls*, p. 78.

48. Morse, *Six Million Died*, p. 256.

49. Wyman, *Paper Walls*, p. 97.

50. Friedman, *No Haven for the Opressed*, p. 102.

51. Marie Syrkin, "What American Jews Did During the Holocaust," *Midstream: A Monthly Jewish Review*, vol. 28, no. 8 (October 1982), p. 9.

52. Doris Kearns Goodwin, *No Ordinary Time: Franklin and Eleanor Roosevelt: The Home Front in World War II* (New York, 1994), p. 102.

53. Eleanor Roosevelt, *This I Remember* (New York, 1949), p. 161.

54. Medoff, *Deafening Silence*, p. 58.

55. Lookstein, *Were We Our Brothers' Keepers?*, pp. 84, 86.

56. Arthur Hertzberg, *The Jews in America: Four Centuries of an Uneasy Encounter* (New York, 1989), p. 293.

57. Joseph Berger, "The Voyagers Doomed by America," *New York Times*, March 31, 1999.

58. Lena Friedman, interview with author, November 13, 1998.

59. Lookstein, *Were We Our Brothers' Keepers?*, pp. 46, 65.

60. Medoff, *Deafening Silence*, p. 64.

61. Henry L. Feingold, "'Courage First and Intelligence Second': The American Jewish Secular Elite, Roosevelt, and the Failure to Rescue," in Verne W. Newton (ed.), *FDR and the Holocaust* (New York, 1966), p. 72.

62. Medoff, *Deafening Silence*, p. 74.

63. Zygmunt Bauman, *Modernity and the Holocaust* (Ithaca, N.Y., 1991), pp. 66–72.

64. Stephen Wise, *Challenging Years: The Autobiography of Stephen Wise* (New York, 1949), p. 227.

65. David Wyman, *The Abandonment of the Jews: America and the Holocaust, 1941–1945* (New York, 1984), p. 25.

66. "Nazi Terror Reign Condemned at Meeting," *Los Angeles Times*, August 13, 1942.

67. See Bauman, *Modernity and the Holocaust*.

68. Sanders, *Shores of Refuge*, p. 515.

69. Medoff, *Deafening Silence*, p. 99.

70. Wise to John Haynes Holmes, 1942, in Wise Polier, and Wise (eds.), *Personal Letters of Stephen Wise*, pp. 260–261.

71. Wise, *Challenging Years*, pp. 275–276.

72. *New York Times*, p. 24, December 2, 1942.

73. Morse, *Six Million Died*, pp. 26–27.

74. Feingold, "'Courage First and Intelligence Second,'" p. 76.

75. Wyman, *Abandonment of the Jews*, p. 123.

76. Medoff, *Deafening Silence*, pp. 115, 121.

77. Ibid., pp. 113, 106.

78. *New York Times*, May 4, 1943, p. 17.

79. Monty Noam Penkower, "In Dramatic Dissent: The Bergson Boys," *American Jewish History*, vol. 7 (March 1981), p. 288.

80. Wyman, *Abandonment of the Jews*, p. 91.

81. Friedman, *No Haven for the Oppressed*, p. 124.

82. Wyman, *Abandonment of the Jews*, p. 201.

83. Penkower, "In Dramatic Dissent," p. 296.

84. Dawidowicz, "American Jews," p. 114; Morse, *Six Million Died*, p. 92.

85. Friedman, *No Haven for the Oppressed*, p. 209.

86. *New York Times*, p. 11, January 23, 1944.

87. Medoff, *Deafening Silence*, pp. 143, 144; Wyman, *Abandonment of the Jews*, p. 263.

88. Medoff, *Deafening Silence*, pp. 142, 145.

89. Henry Feingold, "The Roosevelt Administration and the Effort to Save the Jews of Hungary," *Hungarian-Jewish Studies*, vol. 2 (1969), p. 231; Medoff, *Deafening Silence*, p. 145.

90. Martin Gilbert, *Auschwitz and the Allies* (London, 1981), p. 309.

91. Richard H. Levy, "The Bombing of Auschwitz Revisited: A Critical Analysis," in Newton (ed.), *FDR and the Holocaust*, p. 227.

92. Gilbert, *Auschwitz and the Allies*, p. 303.

93. David Wyman, "Why Auschwitz Was Never Bombed," *Commentary*, vol. 65, May 1978, p. 40.

94. Gilbert, *Auschwitz and the Allies*, p. 311.

95. Wyman, *Abandonment of the Jews*, p. 307.

96. Robert H. Abzug, *Inside the Vicious Heart: Americans and the Liberation of Nazi Concentration Camps* (New York, 1985), pp. 29, 30.

97. Tanaka, *Go For Broke*, p. 117.

98. "Reunion," *The New Yorker*, November 11, 1991, p. 33; also report on

Japanese Americans in Jerusalem, reunion between members of the 442nd Regiment and former Dachau inmates, CBS News, May 3, 1992.

99. Brewster Chamberlain and Marcia Feldman, *The Liberation of the Nazi Concentration Camps 1945* (Washington, D.C.: Government Printing Office, 1987), p. 36.

100. Yaffa Eliach and Brana Gurewitsch (eds.), *The Liberators: Eyewitness Accounts of the Liberation of Concentration Camps* (Brooklyn, 1981), p. 13.

101. Ibid., p. 17.

102. Ibid., pp. 37–39.

103. Chamberlain and Feldman, *Liberation of the Nazi Concentration Camps,* p. 98.

104. Lou Potter with William Miles and Nina Rosenblum, *Liberators: Fighting on Two Fronts in World War II* (New York, 1992), pp. 217, 218.

105. Jonathan Kaufman, *Broken Alliance: The Turbulent Times Between Blacks and Jews in America* (New York, 1989), p. 50.

Chapter 9. A Multicultural "Manifest Destiny"

1. James G. Thompson, letter to the editor, *Pittsburgh Courier,* January 31, 1942.

2. Maya Angelou, *Gather Together in My Name* (New York, 1974), pp. 2–3.

3. Maya Angelou, *I Know Why the Caged Bird Sings* (New York, 1971), pp. 224–229.

4. "Mela — Queen of the 12-Inch" (Inland Steel Company), in *Mexican American Harbor Lights,* published by the Señoras of Yesteryear, Indianapolis Humanities Council, Indianapolis, Indiana, 1992, pp. 34–35.

5. Judy Yung, *Unbound Feet: A Social History of Chinese Women in San Francisco* (Berkeley, 1995), pp. 254, 259.

6. D. S. Saund, *Congressman From India* (New York, 1960), pp. 72–75.

7. Brenda L. Moore, *To Serve My Country, To Serve My Race: The Story of the Only African American Wacs Stationed Overseas during World War II* (New York, 1996), pp. 12–13, 171.

8. Walter White, *A Rising Wind* (Garden City, N.Y., 1945), p. 155.

9. Philip McGuire (ed.), *Taps for a Jim Crow Army: Letters from Black Soldiers in World War II* (Lexington, Ky., 1993), pp. 248–251.

10. Commission on Wartime Relocation and Internment of Civilians, *Personal Justice Denied: Report of the Commission on Wartime Relocation and Internment of Civilians* (Washington, D.C., 1982), p. 233.

11. Frank Chuman, *The Bamboo People: The Law and Japanese-Americans* (Del Mar, Calif., 1967), pp. 209–218.

12. Robert Wilson and Bill Hosokawa, *East to America: A History of the Japanese in the United States* (New York, 1980), p. 279.

13. Keiko Nieda, in Lucille and Tomoe Tana (eds.), *Sounds from the Unknown: A Collection of Japanese American Tanka* (Denver, 1963), p. 49.

14. Carey McWilliams, *North from Mexico: The Spanish-Speaking People of the United States* (New York, 1968), p. 261.

15. Sabine R. Ulibárri, *Mayhem Was Our Business: Memorias de un Veterano* (Tempe, 1997), pp. 115, 31.

16. McWilliams, *North from Mexico,* p. 198.

17. Carl Allsup, "A Soldier's Burial," in *Revista Chicano-Requeña,* vol. 4, no. 4 (October 1976), p. 78; Julie Leininger Pycior, *LBJ & Mexican Americans: The Paradox of Power* (Austin, 1997), p. 68.

18. Pycior, *LBJ & Mexican Americans,* p. 70.

19. Santillán, "Midwestern Mexican American Women," p. 98.

20. Richard Santillán, "Rosita the Riveter: Midwest Mexican American Women during World War II," in *Perspectives in Mexican American Studies,* vol. 2, 1989 (Tucson), p. 138.

21. Mario García, "Americans All: The Mexican American Generation and the Politics of Wartime Los Angeles, 1941–45," *Social Science Quarterly,* vol. 65, no. 2 (June 1984), pp. 282–283.

22. Carl T. Rowan, *Dream Makers, Dream Breakers: The World of Thurgood Marshall* (New York, 1993), pp. 102–103.

23. *Brown et al. v. Board of Education of Topeka et al.,* reprinted in Clayborne Carson, et al. (eds.), *The Eyes on the Prize Civil Rights Reader* (New York, 1987), pp. 64–74; "The Atlanta Declaration" of the NAACP, reprinted in Carson, *Eyes on the Prize Reader,* p. 82; Robert Williams, quoted in Carson, *Eyes on the Prize Reader,* p. 36.

24. Fred Powledge, *Free At Last? The Civil Rights Movement and the People Who Made It* (Boston, 1991), p. 74.

25. Harvard Sitkoff, *The Struggle for Black Equality, 1954–1980* (New York, 1981), pp. 41–42, 52; Stephen B. Oates, *Let the Trumpet Sound: The Life of Martin Luther King, Jr.* (New York, 1982), p. 84.

26. King, *Stride Toward Freedom,* pp. 47–48; Oates, *Let the Trumpet Sound,* p. 112.

27. Oates, *Let the Trumpet Sound,* p. 112.

28. Student quoted by James Farmer, in Francis L. Broderick and August Meier, *Negro Protest Thought in the Twentieth Century* (New York, 1965), p. 372; Clayborne Carson, *In Struggle: SNCC and the Black Awakening of the 1960s* (Cambridge, Mass., 1981), p. 64; Oates, *Let the Trumpet Sound,* p. 154.

29. Harvard Sitkoff, *The Struggle for Black Equality,* p. 109; Powledge, *Free At Last?,* pp. 256, 262.

30. Jervis Anderson, *A. Philip Randolph: A Biographical Portrait* (Berkeley, 1986), pp. 328–329.

31. Martin Luther King, Jr., "I Have a Dream," reprinted in Francis L. Broderick and August Meier (eds.), *Negro Protest Thought in the Twentieth Century* (New York, 1965), pp. 400–405.

32. Arthur Hertzberg, *The Jews in America* (New York, 1989), pp. 348–349.

33. Jonathan Kaufman, *Broken Alliance: The Turbulent Times between Blacks and Jews in America* (New York, 1989), p. 83.

34. Lyndon B. Johnson, Commencement Address at Howard University, June 4, 1965, reprinted in Carson, et al. (eds.), *Eyes on the Prize Reader,* pp. 611–613.

35. David Reimers, *Still the Golden Door: The Third World Comes to America* (New York, 1985), pp. 67, 71.

36. Michi Weglyn, *Years of Infamy: The Untold Story of America's Concentration Camps* (New York, 1976).

37. Congressman Robert Matsui, speech in the House of Representatives on bill 442 for redress and reparations, September 17, 1987, *Congressional Record* (Washington, D.C., 1987), p. 7584; Congressman Norman Mineta, interview, March 26, 1988; Warren Furutani, testimony, reprinted in *Amerasia,* vol. 8, no. 2, p. 104.

38. Commission on Wartime Relocation and Internment of Civilians, *Personal Justice Denied,* p. 79; text of Reagan's Remarks, reprinted in *Pacific Citizen,* August 19–26, 1988, p. 5; *San Francisco Chronicle,* August 5 and 11, 1988.

39. Leslie Marmon Silko, *Ceremony* (New York, 1978), pp. 18, 36, 62, 104, 257–258.

40. Stimson, Memorandum of talk with the President, June 6, 1945, reprinted in Stoff, et al. (eds.), *Manhattan,* p. 131.

41. Stimson, diary, May 16, 1945, quoted in Martin Sherwin, *A World Destroyed: Hiroshima and the Origins of the Arms Race* (New York, 1987), p. 197.

42. Henry L. Stimson, "The Decision to Use the Atomic Bomb," *Harper's,* vol. 194, no. 1161 (February 1947), pp. 98, 99, 103, 104.

43. Stimson, Diary, August 10, 1945, Stimson Papers, Yale University Archives.

44. Raul Morín, *Among the Valiant: Mexican-Americans in WW II and Korea* (Alhambra, Calif., 1966), pp. 232–233; Martha Nakagawa, "Supporters Rally for Latino Legend Who Captured 1000 Japanese Soldiers," *Pacific Citizen Weekly,* August 6–12, 1999, pp. 1, 8.

45. David Reyes, "Taking a Stand for a Peaceful Hero," *Los Angeles Times,* August 31, 1998. My thanks to Debbie Rogin for sharing this article.

46. Leon Bass, in Yaffa Eliach and Brana Gurewitsch (eds.), *The Liberators: Eyewitness Accounts of the Liberation of Concentration Camps* (Brooklyn, 1981), pp. 24–25; Lou Potter with William Miles and Nina Rosenblum, *Liberators: Fighting on Two Fronts in World War II* (New York, 1992), p. 219.

47. Belle S. Vankin, "Epitaph to My Son, Michael," in *XIX Corps Scroll,* no. 3 (June 24, 1945), published by the U.S. Army in occupied Germany, copy in the Murray Richard Papers, the Eisenhower Center, University of New Orleans.

48. Herman Melville, *Redburn* (Chicago, 1969; originally published in 1849), p. 169.

49. Francis L. Broderick, *W. E. B. Du Bois: Negro Leader in a Time of Crisis* (Stanford, 1959), p. 196.

50. Langston Hughes, "Lennox Avenue Mural," in Langston Hughes, *The Langston Hughes Reader* (New York, 1958).

51. Thompson, *Pittsburgh Courier,* January 31, 1942; Langston Hughes, "Let America Be America Again," in Langston Hughes and Arna Bontemps (eds.), *The Poetry of the Negro, 1746–1949* (New York, 1951), p. 106.

ACKNOWLEDGMENTS

CAROL TAKAKI JOINED ME on this journey into "a past that is not even past." Through our many discussions and debates, I shared with her my research as well as my reflections. In her critical editing of multiple drafts, she relentlessly pushed me to rewrite again and again in order to make certain my manuscript conveyed clearly and felicitously the history I was struggling so fiercely to piece together. Working together on so many books over the years, Carol and I have always felt a sense of exuberance but also a tinge of sadness when we have brought to an end the creative process of revising a manuscript.

UC Berkeley students participated in this project. José Palafox and Joon Kim assisted in library research; Kent Haldan located the autobiographical statement of Joseph Kurihara in the archives of the Bancroft Library. Benicio Silva translated articles from *La Opinión*, a Spanish-language newspaper published in Los Angeles. Helen Lara Cea helped me gather primary government documents in the National Archives in Washington, D.C.

James W. Zobel, archivist at the MacArthur Memorial Archives, made an extra effort to find and send me copies of primary documents related to General Douglas MacArthur's view on Hiroshima. Judith Ann Schiff of the Yale University Archives saved me a trip to New Haven by informing me that the Henry L. Stimson Papers were on microfilm in the Library of Congress. Karen Carver of the University of Utah Library assisted in making available the transcripts of the Navajo Code Talkers in the Doris Duke Oral History Project. Michael J. Edwards of the Eisenhower Center for American Studies, University of New Orleans, gave his time generously to retrieve oral histories.

The editor of five of my books published by Little, Brown, and Company, Jennifer Josephy, has steadfastly supported my long struggle to write democratic history — history of, for, and also by the people. Our aim has been to give readers a more inclusive and hence more accurate definition of who is an "American" and what it means to be an American. My literary agent, Rick Balkin, has consistently been an incisive and frank critic of my book proposals and drafts of manuscripts. Playwright Debbie Rogin repeatedly voiced concerns that led me to integrate a complex theme more tightly and explicitly into the larger picture. John W. Dower and Gar Alperovitz offered affirming comments that gave me courage to stand by my findings on Truman's decision to drop the atomic bomb. Larry Friedman and I have worked together continuously on our scholarship since we were dissertation students in the 1960s. For this study, his hard-hitting criticisms of my rough drafts drove me to rethink entire chapters.

My thanks to everyone acknowledged. Hopefully, our study of this past will offer guidance to Americans as we enter the "brave new world" of the twenty-first century, when we will all be minorities.

INDEX

Index

Index

Index

ABOUT THE AUTHOR

RONALD TAKAKI is professor of Ethnic Studies at the University of California, Berkeley, where he received his Ph.D. in American history and has been teaching for nearly three decades. The grandson of Japanese immigrant plantation laborers in Hawaii, he has been honored by the Berkeley faculty with a Distinguished Teaching Award, and by the Society of American Historians as a fellow. Takaki taught UCLA's first black-history course in 1967. He has debated Nathan Glazer and Arthur Schlesinger, Jr., on issues of affirmative action and multiculturalism. He has lectured in Japan, Russia, Armenia, and South Africa. Takaki's approach in his scholarship is truly comparative and multicultural. His *Iron Cages: Race and Culture in Nineteenth-Century America* has been critically acclaimed, and his prize-winning *A Different Mirror: A History of Multicultural America* has been hailed by *Publishers Weekly* as "a brilliant revisionist history of America that is likely to become a classic of multicultural studies."